The Pathology of Desire in Daphne du Maurier's Short Stories

The Pathology of Desire in Daphne du Maurier's Short Stories

Setara Pracha

LEXINGTON BOOKS
Lanham • Boulder • New York • London

Published by Lexington Books
An imprint of The Rowman & Littlefield Publishing Group, Inc.
4501 Forbes Boulevard, Suite 200, Lanham, Maryland 20706
www.rowman.com

86-90 Paul Street, London, EC2A 4NE

British Library Cataloguing in Publication Information Available

Library of Congress Cataloging-in-Publication Data

Names: Pracha, Setara, author.
Title: The pathology of desire in Daphne du Maurier's short stories / Setara Pracha.
Description: Lanham : Lexington Books, [2023] | Includes bibliographical references and index. | Summary: "The book addresses critical omissions in du Maurier studies by carefully examining her less well-known shorter fiction. The analysis covers nine stories chosen to illustrate how du Maurier employs the diseased, disabled, and maimed human form as a recurrent symbol for social, political, and domestic misalignment"-- Provided by publisher.
Identifiers: LCCN 2022041054 (print) | LCCN 2022041055 (ebook) | ISBN 9781666907179 (cloth ; alk. paper) | ISBN 9781666907186 (ebook)
Subjects: LCSH: Du Maurier, Daphne, 1907-1989--Criticism and interpretation. | Human body in literature. | Desire in literature. | LCGFT: Literary criticism.
Classification: LCC PR6007.U47 Z79 2023 (print) | LCC PR6007.U47 (ebook) | DDC 823/.912--dc23/eng/20221011
LC record available at https://lccn.loc.gov/2022041054
LC ebook record available at https://lccn.loc.gov/2022041055

Contents

Acknowledgments

With grateful thanks to Christian "Kits" Browning, Daphne du Maurier's literary executor, who generously gave permission to quote from unpublished materials; to Christine Faunch, Angela Mandroli, and the staff at Special Collections, University of Exeter; and to Collin Langley for permission to quote from his unpublished study on du Maurier. To my colleagues at the English Department at the University of Buckingham in gratitude for the tea and support. To my friends for their loving kindness, you know who you are. Lastly to my son Rafael, my last and best project, thank you for your patience.

I

The Corpus

Introduction

Corporeality: The Conceptual Skeleton

The human body is the means by which the human mind interacts with the material world, raising the question of whether this fact renders it, 'the best picture of the human soul,' as Ludwig Wittgenstein argues. This book begins with Peter Stallybrass and Allon White's supposition that '[t]he body is neither a purely natural given nor is it a textual metaphor, it is a privileged operator for the transcoding of other areas. Thinking the body is thinking social topography and vice versa.'[1] This theoretical model interrogates Daphne du Maurier's symbolic and literal representation of parts of the body as a thematic frame for broader discussions of human desire touching on issues of power, culture, and history. Desire may be briefly defined in this work as the impulse by one individual to impose their will on another, often without specifically physical desire for that other; additionally, desire is always mapped onto the desired individual, despite being an attribute of the desiring person. Desire almost necessarily goes unsatisfied in du Maurier's short stories and in the instances where we see a character attain the object of their desire—for instance James Fenton's seeming acquisition of notoriety—this attainment is partial or false (see 'The Alibi'). All humans are susceptible to being scared or attacked, and du Maurier's work takes us readers into that uncomfortable space, reminding us that the apparently safe and secure present may dramatically change in a second. And, that second can take the reader into the depths of phenomenology where the phenomena of lived, subjective experience leads to existential crises that trump the objective and apparently quantifiable.

As is most clear in her short fiction, some of that discomfort is communicated to the reader through a return to the body, our first tangible 'home' and consequently the space in which we are always most vulnerable. This has resonance with many critical approaches but in recent years the emergent field of Body Horror has begun what Xavier Aldana Reyes frames as a 'sustained questioning of the nature of embodiment' commencing from the viewpoint that 'the gothic is [. . .] inherently somatic and corporeal.'[2] There is a clear overlap with works that centralise the somatic but, I would not position du Maurier as a gothic author due to the complexity and variety of her oeuvre. Du Maurier's stories present human bodies that destabilise notions of the anatomically correct form, instead offering transformative states and ambiguous sexualities, including deformity that defies commonly reassuring taxonomic categories. Her fiction raises what Reyes defines as readers' 'awareness of their own bodies, particularly of their vulnerability and shared experience of projected pain through various feelings.'

Du Maurier (1907–1989) was largely inaccurately regarded as a non-canonical author whose writing is merely popular and not terribly good. Critics Avril Horner and Sue Zlosnik note that 'she is still widely regarded as a lightweight middlebrow novelist.'[3] Despite Virago editor Donna Coonan's recent claims of a 'complete reappraisal' of her work it is clear that Virago's centenary reissues of du Maurier's texts have generated a trickle, rather than a deluge, of academic attention and this can be seen at *The Bookseller* website, a publishing industry online magazine. Sarah Shaffi includes comments by Coonan that 'du Maurier's reputation has "flourished" since Virago began publishing her in 2003. "She is no longer seen as merely a writer of historical romances; she is now widely read, increasingly studied and has undergone a complete reappraisal."'[4] However, the critical response has not yet addressed the more experimental short stories that continue to be eclipsed by du Maurier's fame as a novelist. The following chapters offer the first comprehensive mapping of both the published and the unpublished short fiction and illuminate the variety, quality, and scope of texts worthy of greater attention. This research includes a summary and discussion of most of the works and a close critical commentary of eight of the texts. In du Maurier's own words:

> The short story [. . .] still lacks recognition as a work of art.
>
> A novel, to the uninitiated, sometimes wins respect for its length alone. So many thousand words on paper suggest hard work if nothing else, whereas a short story, consisting of a few pages only, is assumed to be dashed off without thought or great concentration, a money-spinner for a magazine.[5]

Du Maurier wrote sixty-eight distinct published stories and there are at least fourteen unpublished stories and sketches in a notebook in the du Maurier archive at the University of Exeter. There may be further unpublished material yet to be discovered, as occurred in 2011 with ' The Doll,' an important but previously disregarded story. To ignore the short stories is to miss the most daring of du Maurier's fiction in which the brevity of the form necessarily condenses the plot until only the most significant details remain. In this exploration du Maurier's cultural critique is revealed through highlighting symbolic embodiment as seen in her short stories: each story in this study centralises part or parts of the body, present or missing. In this achronological examination, stories written over a period of forty years embody the component parts of a dismembered human form that echoes the desires and dreams, trials and traumas, changing values, and technologies of the periods in which they were written. Gretchen E. Henderson's historical study of cultural attitudes towards ' ugliness' explores what happens when we examine parts of the human form individually:

> When treated singly as subjects, limbs and organs transform into literary or historical subjects with agency and identity, calling into question the notion of a person's control over his or her own body. Control is an illusion when the constitutive parts of a body possess identities and wills. Ascribing agency to one part of the human body creates a particular relationship of the part to the whole.[6]

The characters in du Maurier's short fiction are lost, maimed, mute, bereft, diseased, haunted, and trapped. Their bodies are disabled, denied, rejected, dislocated, and destroyed. Contemporary reviewer Nancy Spain highlights the contrast between the novels and the stories in heightened language: '[L] ook what has happened to Daphne Du Maurier, she has joined the *danse macabre. The Apple Tree* has at least three stories that deal with vice, blackmail, corruption, and peculiarly mass murder. [. . .] For it now appears that Miss Du Maurier is as morbidly preoccupied with death as the rest.'[7] Spain misses the point of the stories but her damning summation is accurate in one aspect: the mordant tone. These are plots that trace the framework of human corporeality challenging and critiquing issues including mental health, capital punishment, child abuse, militarism, sadomasochism, and societal fragmentation. The ramifications of social interactions are written across the human physique in stories of energetic ambiguity that disrupt the 'oppositions that strictly delineate [. . .] beauty versus ugliness, native versus foreign, pure versus corrupted, fixed versus broken.'[8] Du Maurier uses the body as a lens to focus on social and societal behaviours. This enables her to convey abstracts in a material world, which in turn manifest the psychological condition of a character, or even of the culture as a whole. These stories demand analysis because they highlight challenging questions reflecting du Maurier's engagement with multiple national and international issues. These include alternatives to life imprisonment, capital punishment, Amnesty International, apartheid, and her resistance to what she saw as the inherent patriarchal oppression within religion, all issues that are manifest in her unpublished correspondence.[9]

However, the traditional stance of the academy has served to associate corporeal transgression with lowbrow art and du Maurier's latent non-canonical categorisation is a direct consequence of this. It is no coincidence that those marginalised and/ or excluded texts from the literary canon are frequently composed by authors whose own bodies do not conform to the 'universal' human archetype (that is, Caucasian, male, middle-aged). The fact is, that the life experience represented by diverse bodies is not on the margins of human life, or outside of the mainstream, or Other. It is common and mundane, habitual, and found everywhere. As Reyes outlines in his definition of the growing field of Body Gothic criticism, 'bodies become a repository of fears that are endemic to the tyranny of power structures lying outside the grasp of the individual.'[10] This is illustrated in du Maurier's careful placement of characters at the mercy of the Church, the state, marriage, geriatric institutions, childcare and medical care, structures purporting to nurture are severely criticised in her fiction, and in the stories no one body type is exempt from the tyrannies of corporeal fate. What Reyes cites as 'the body as a site of fear' is a constant in du Maurier's short fiction, echoing cultural anxieties about wartime experiments and shortages, the implementation of power dynamics and gender, age, and class, through means of visceral illustration that resonates with current work on Body Gothic criticism.[11] As contemporary criticism continues to address the gaps left by twentieth-century critics, Reyes indicates that 'a recuperation of the role and relevance of corporeal transgression might breathe new life into an excessive canon that paradoxically, often ignores the gory and the extreme.'[12] While du Maurier's stories do not tend to be gory, her plots do take the reader well beyond the safe and familiar into the territory Reyes is mapping out, wherein 'corporeal transgression' is defined as "instances of dismemberment, mutilation, mutation, extreme disease or transformative surgery." This is apparent in stories composed by du Maurier that prefigure and yet curiously parallel his definition, as in ' The Apple Tree' (dismemberment), ' The Little Photographer" (mutilation), 'Monte Verita' (extreme disease), and 'The Blue Lenses' (transformative surgery). Once again the author's material is rich for mining examples for another new critical approach.

This corpus of material writes into the tradition of 'blight literature,' in which texts have an implicit moral agenda activated through the presentation of bodies suffering disease, disability, or blemish. Working in a different generic tradition in her study *Difference and Disability in the Medieval Islamic World*, Kristina L. Richardson nevertheless describes how in a period where disease and disability were prevalent, writers of 'blight' literature 'contribute[d] to the diffusion of these themes in religious, literary and historical discourses and in the public consciousness of both native residents [. . .] and visitors.' In du Maurier's work the body of the people is depicted individually and severally, pre, during, and post war, encouraging both particular and general observations. Richardson identifies how '[p]hysical disabilities were visible elements of the Syrian landscape,' in the same manner du Maurier's broken bodies indicate a British psychogeographical terrain traversed by disabled veterans, refugees, service-dodgers and Land Girls.[13] This aspect of du Maurier's work is part of a larger movement within modernism, in which writers and poets attempt the literary treatment of the cultural traumas resulting from two world wars using fragmentation as a tool, and the mythic tradition as a framework.

In recent years Body Gothic has become an emergent field of study, and some of the insights are pertinent to du Maurier's short fiction which reifies the tangible aspects of sentient existence, as well as its limitations. Ian Conrich and Laura Sedgwick state that what tends to be lost in most approaches to the gothic 'is the materiality of the body, and in particular, body parts.' Their study emphasises the cinematic but the work offers some useful insights into approaches to the somatic in literature. One important feature is the way the book's structure echoes the format adopted here with each chapter centralising a particular body. In this manner criticism shows how disparate and singular individual parts are, yet also how dismembered parts are haunted by the unified self. There are fifteen chapters on various body parts from top to bottom (pun intended), repositioning the genre within art history and contemporary culture, from renaissance paintings to the Young British Artists. The coverage focuses mainly on film and screen adaptations including du Maurier and Angela Carter among its authors. They rightly choose multiple approaches to comprehend the Gothic body, including insights by Freud and Bakhtin, Kristeva's theory of the abject, and the Rabelaisian grotesque, as a multiplicity of tools to perform what Conrich and Sedgwick call a 'textual autopsy.' While observing that the body 'consists of components and bits—that can break, be operated upon, sutured and transplanted. They can also be dismembered, penetrated, transformed, and transplanted.'[14] Du Maurier's stories reveal the unstable nature of our physical existence, something humans would rather ignore, and Conrich and Sedgwich's work brings the corporeal into the forefront of criticism. With disturbing accuracy the narratives challenge the reader with the unpalatable fact that '[t]he body changes, ages and mutates, and is constantly poised on a threshold of what it is and what it will become.' While the author should not be condemned to sole identification with gothic writing and the emergence of the Body Gothic approach, it is undeniable that, 'within Gothic the boundaries of the body are being creatively disturbed and redefined.'[15] The body is at once a tangible substance and a liminal space, a paradox wherein constructions of realty can be existentially questioned and examined to expose the effects of self-deceit and reveal the effect on disrupted internal narratives.[16]

Du Maurier's writing exhibits a modernist tendency to incorporate mythological themes, a practice for which 'high modernist' writers are renowned. Critics often pair du Maurier with Agatha Christie, however, this examination demonstrates that it is more useful to consider her work alongside poet Hilda Doolittle (H.D. 1886–1961), Katherine Mansfield (1888–1923), Rebecca West (1892–1983), and Elizabeth Bowen (1899–1973). All deal in darker themes such as the 'corruption and emptiness of the adult world' and trace how the 'contradictory yearnings of human relations are followed to their often-violent end.'[17] There is documentary evidence that Mansfield's writing inspired du Maurier from when she first read *Bliss and Other Stories* at the age of 16. In an unpublished letter Du Maurier describes Mansfield's stories as 'wonderful, and wonderfully written' to her governess Maud Waddell (19 June 1928).[18] Although *Bliss and Other Stories* [1920] is not mentioned by title, du Maurier's comment on 'The Dill Pickle' as one of several Mansfield stories that she had read suggests that she had read the entire collection. There are multiple references in her unpublished letters on unwittingly having had Mansfield as a neighbour in Hampstead, the parallels in their lives, and du Maurier's chagrin at her perceived inability to match Mansfield's writing style. Her letters indicate du Maurier's fascination with Mansfield and her writing, foregrounding the writer as a primary literary influence. Du Maurier gleefully informs confidante and reading guide Maud Waddell that 'K. M. used to live at Hampstead,' was 'terribly interested in the du Maurier children" and that Mansfield 'longed to know us.' The young writer has clearly chosen her mentor: 'I'm sure I should never have started writing stories if I hadn't had her example before me,' concluding that 'she honestly is quite my favourite writer.'[19] Like Mansfield, the self-labelled 'little colonial,' who commented 'And I am the little colonial walking in the London garden patch—allowed to look, perhaps, but not to linger,'[20] du Maurier came from the privileged classes but her writing continually mocks the bourgeoisie, and as she pointedly comments to fellow author Leo Walmesley in 1958: 'you don't want to get the high-brow reader, you want to get the ordinary man and woman who live ordinary little lives.'[21]

Women writers of the period were often critically marginalised by a largely masculine modernist elite, but the mythological framework referenced in their work is increasingly recognised as being within the modernist mode. H.D.'s poetry focuses on Helen of Troy and the Trojan priestess Cassandra, rewriting mythic themes to incorporate the voices of hitherto silenced characters and thus empower them, examples include 'Helen,' 'Cassandra,' 'Demeter,' 'Circe,' and 'Ariadne.'[22] This scrutiny of du Maurier's short stories reveals how the gender of characters is sometimes subject to an authorial switch, to generate new perspectives on myths recorded by Ovid and Homer. References within the texts explicitly or implicitly include the myths of Pygmalion, Daphne and Apollo, the blinding of Tiresias, centaurs, Odysseus's journey into the Underworld, Hephaistos and Aphrodite, and the Eumenides (Furies).[23] Other stories with mythic themes include, but are not limited to, 'Not After Midnight,' (Silenus and Dionysus) from *Not After Midnight* (1971), 'The Chamois' (Diana and Actaeon), 'A Border-line Case' (Cinyras and Myhrra), and 'Ganymede' (Zeus and Ganymede) from *The Breaking Point* [1959].

This practice re-forms venerable stories into a new mode that addresses cultural and political change; one that challenges intellectual and emotional stasis by creating a written response to conflict. The immediacy and drama of the works focuses attention on experience as it is lived through the body and as with the writing of Rebecca West, du Maurier's fiction often questions the 'moral isolation of those protected by wealth.'[24] Gender and disability are foregrounded as are marginalised groups such as children and patients, and alternative sexual practices from fetishism to celibacy. Du Maurier's implementation of modernist literary devices ties in with Dominic Head's substantive list which includes paradox and ambiguity, a dependence upon symbolism, the fragmented, dehumanised self and episodes that suggest a full-length life. Head's summary includes a dialogic style, reiteration through patterning, foregrounding of technique, the ambivalent portrayal of character and internal rather than external action. All of these modes are characteristics of du Maurier's short stories.[25]

Du Maurier was keenly politically aware and her move to Gollancz Publishers in 1934 confirmed her as a subtle observer and commentator on her times.[26] Victor Gollancz (1893–1967) was a British publisher, humanitarian activist, and Christian Socialist, best known for supporting left-wing causes, for predicting the Nazi extermination of the Jews, and for founding the Left Book Club (1936), an important vehicle for social and political change. He was du Maurier's main publisher from 1934 when he published her memoir of her father, *Gerald: A Portrait* [1934]. Gollancz sent du Maurier a constant stream of the latest books, as she wrote to Maud Waddell in 1943, 'I sometimes wonder if my Left Book Club monthly books would interest you. They are not light, but they give one to think.'[27] Another significant influence on her writing was Sheila Hodges, her editor at Gollancz from 1943 to 1981, who described du Maurier as 'a very careful craftsman' who nonetheless had 'never been able to spell or paragraph.'[28] This claim is supported by evidence from du Maurier's unpublished correspondence.[29]

This book comprises three sections. Section I 'The Corpus' is a brief examination of the current field of du Maurier studies in a chapter outlining the major collections published within the author's lifetime. These consist of *The Apple Tree* [1952]; *Early Stories* [1955]; *The Breaking Point* [1959]; *Not After Midnight* [1971]; and *The Rendezvous and Other Stories* [1980]. The 'Anatomy of the Short Story Collections' part highlights the lack of concrete data on editorial changes made to the short stories by du Maurier's publisher Victor Gollancz and long-term editor Sheila Hodges, both of whom were strong influences on the author. This makes reading the collections as an integrated whole problematic and supports a non-linear approach as the best segue into a comprehensive analysis of the narratives. The optimum analysis is the text-by-text reading delivered here. Section I indicates the gap in criticism that this book addresses and establishes the core argument of a corporeal conceptual framework. It sets up the central argument, which is developed in section II 'The Dismembered Self,' presenting the eight chapters of close reading as evidence for the hypothesis of corporeality as the unifying aspect of the narratives and repositions Daphne du Maurier as a short story writer of note. Section III, 'The Pathology of Desire' is a chapter summarising the research entitled 'Reconstructive Surgery' that suggests directions for future study. An appendix, 'The Bare Bones: The Stories, Dates of Publication, Page Counts, Locations, and Themes' concludes by offering fans and researchers hitherto uncollected data on du Maurier's published and unpublished short story material.

The first chapter in section II focuses on 'Split Second' a story that symbolises the 'head' of this corpus of short fiction. The rationale for this story choice is the dislocated mind and body of the protagonist that occupy two distinct temporal spaces within the narrative—the past where dramatic events occurred, and the alienating present. Henderson writes about *Les gueules cassées,* who were the soldiers most dramatically afflicted by facial wounds after World War I. Regarding the photographs of patients their 'brokenness was appropriated to upset a singular focus, it contributed to an aesthetic that removed bodies from their contexts, offering an uncomfortable unity beyond the wounds of war. [. . .] the presence of the broken faces and other bodily deconstructions worked into a collective post-war aesthetic that permeated art, literature, advertising, and other aspects of culture.'[30] 'Split Second' foregrounds the brain as the receptacle of memory and identity, showing that when it malfunctions, we are lost in space and time. The character of Mrs Ellis is physically healthy but, minus familiar referents, she is an unwelcome revenant, perhaps an escapee from an asylum or the casualty of a road traffic accident. Either way, her dislocated experience catalogues post-war society and is a reminder of trauma, individual or national, that is subject to deliberate cultural amnesia. Dominic Head positions the short story as a vital part of capturing the 'episodic nature of twentieth century experience,'[31] and 'Split Second' shows that somatic symbols are useful tools that illustrate the 'ultimate elements of social classification itself.'[32] This chapter analyses how the fragmented and dehumanised state of one psyche leads to bodily disorientation, a condition that du Maurier employs to particularise the condition of a people, a city, and a nation acclimatising to post-war realities. Du Maurier is critical of the war and portrays victims of warfare in several stories, yet she was married to a central figure in the command. Lt-Gen. Frederick Browning was the leader of airborne troops in operation 'Market Garden': laying a carpet of airborne troops across the waterways of the lower Rhine culminating in a bridgehead force north of Arnhem. 'Market Garden' later came to be seen by many as a military disaster and Browning suffered considerable criticism for the part he played as outlined by Stephen Badsey in his book, *Arnhem 1944: Operation 'Market Garden.'* The fragmentation of Mrs Ellis as a person centers on damage to her head and this is the primary cause of her social disintegration as her body suffers what her mind cannotendure, a fact of which du Maurier was well aware from her marriage to a hero recovering from service in not one but two world wars.

Chapter 3 develops the evidence for du Maurier's use of corporeality in an interrogation of the conflation of sight and perception in 'The Blue Lenses.' The narrative explores how physical changes in sensory impressions (sight, sound, touch, smell) are used to destroy the illusion of equitable power relations. 'The Blue Lenses' reviews the linking of visual acuity with accurate interpretation, questioning the Judeo-Christian tradition of blindness as a spiritual or moral condition, and the wisdom of choosing not to see ugly realities. Marda West's new eye lenses reveal animal heads that indicate the previously hidden immorality of their human bearers. The reader only gets to 'see' through Marda's eyes and then only within the lexical framework of the text. The gap between seeing and understanding as sited within the human female body can be regarded as part of du Maurier's broader debate regarding corruption and control. As cultural commentator Elizabeth Grosz argues:

> That may help explain the enormous investment in definitions of the female body in struggles between patriarchs and feminists: what is at stake is the activity and agency, the mobility and social space, accorded to women. Far from being an inert, passive, noncultural and ahistorical term, the body may

> be seen as the crucial term, the site of contestation, in a series of economic, political, sexual, and intellectual struggles.[33]

The hybridised bodies in this story reveal hidden motivations and thus serve as vehicles of truth. This analysis shows that 'The Blue Lenses' erodes notions of strict categories of human and animal. Using mythic and psychoanalytic cues, this reading examines the acceptance or rejection of the animal aspects of humanity, exploring the use of the hybridised body to show our sensitivity to, and vulnerability within, the world. This text is included in this study for two reasons: in part because it engages with du Maurier's work with mythic and animal material, and in part because it reveals the phenomenologically significant grounding of perception of the body. For a contrasting treatment of the same theme, see 'Don't Look Now' in *Not After Midnight* [1971], in which the male protagonist, John, ignores his premonitions with fatal consequences.

Chapter 4 focuses on 'The Lordly Ones,' a story contrasting the distressed, silenced, human form with healthy, but marginalized equine bodies. 'The Lordly Ones' challenges the assumption that animal is lesser category than human, questioning the hierarchy of values that reserves the deepest and most sophisticated emotions for the category of 'human.' This echoes Jeffrey A. Weinstock's comparative study of human, animal, and cyborg, in his essay on freakishness and the somatic, illustrated in du Maurier's plot which considers morality and mortality in parallel.[34] In this text the oppressed and rejected central character, the child Ben, moves from being unable to speak to making the positive choice to remain silent, thereby rejecting the family and world that deny his humanity. In this story Ben's muteness places him outside of his own family and outside the broader human tribe as a whole. Without the facility of speech he is treated like a beast and, consequently, he prefers to be with animals—in this case, horses. This gives prime importance to the body as a socialising force and as a symbol for social disorders: the lack of rights, importance, and respect. This chapter investigates how the role of Ben is culturally metonymic: an exemplar for Britain, a country struggling to articulate the fallout from militaristic aggression. The story reveals the human dependence on speech as a means of identity, and the devastating scenario Elaine Scarry outlines in which pain obliterates expression: '[p]hysical pain—to invoke [. . .] its single most familiar attribute—is language-destroying.'[35] Once again the somatic illustrates the demarcations of lived experience and du Maurier invokes the corporeal to question human desire and dependency.

The correlations between the body and landscape are most insistently presented in 'Monte Verità,' in which physical demands on individual characters range from mountaineering to celibacy and leprosy; the story forms the focus of the next chapter. Leprosy is a physical condition which disables and deforms and du Maurier's somatically challenged characters feature in a tradition in which anthologies of stories serve to 'reconfigure bodily aesthetics' and 're-member' the damaged human form. 'Monte Verità' celebrates an escape into a sexually feminized landscape of mountains and crevasses, where the character of Anna abandons her husband Victor to join an all-female retreat. Anna joins a community that exalts the androgynous body, and the plot privileges freedom for women and spiritual communion over marital union and biological reproduction. In a negation of the body, its needs, and its functions, 'Monte Verità' locates the struggle for self-actualization and effort to overcome desire in the body and, as Anna's body becomes more distressed, the idea that it is the site of Anna's self is made increasingly clear to the reader. Du Maurier suggests that the desire for freedom from conventional roles is attainable only at the expense of physical beauty and health.

The following chapter assesses corporeality in 'The Apple Tree,' a story of psychological violence where the wife's body is manifested by a tree on which her husband projects unwanted memories of her. The story confirms du Maurier's somatic emphasis as the central symbol of the tree echoes the life stages of human biology, including maturation, fecundity, sterility, and death. Marriage and mortality are entwined in 'The Apple Tree' where the widower finally hacks the tree down, severing the limbs and trunk in a ghastly semblance of a ritualised sacrifice parodying a murder. Du Maurier's reworking of mythical and biblical themes challenges the traditional dismissal of the female body to the natural realm and instead positions the male character as instinctual and irrational. In this narrative, thwarting female desire for respect, care, and protection precipitates violence, and bodies from the past remain psychologically present and vengeful. Again, the body is the nexus where desire and destruction conjoin and du Maurier highlights the human capacity for ignoring the essential biological condition of humanity.

Another text of climactic violence resulting from frustrated desire can be found in the following chapter, which is a critique of 'The Alibi.' The story is one of the most overtly modernist of the short stories because of its motifs of dislocation, corporeal and otherwise. Returning to the setting of post-war London (see chapter 1), 'The Alibi' chronicles James Fenton's sterile marriage, his sexual self-denial, and his quest to become the self-appointed executioner of post-war society's flotsam. Delaying his enactment of the murders Fenton instead paints the semblance of his intended victims, Anna and her son Johnnie, yet denies the corporeal reality of the woman and her child. Here, du Maurier uses somatic symbols to satirise art and artistic pretensions, centring on Fenton's portrayal of the human form. He sexually rejects Anna, who subsequently gasses herself and her infant son. 'The Alibi' is considered in terms of a modernist emphasis on fragmentation and the dehumanised individual, isolated in a cultural and emotional wasteland. This example illustrates how the bodies in the text are rejected and broken, the physical and emotional needs of the characters are ignored, and dismemberment operates on a multitude of levels: personal, marital, familial, and societal. This complex text necessitates close reading to more fully realise the various ways in which the body is symbolically used to convey du Maurier's cultural critique.

Chapter 8 assesses the inclusion of the trope of impairment in 'The Little Photographer' in a textual reading that establishes links with the myth of Aphrodite and Hephaestus and interprets the material against social, ethical, and theoretical approaches to the disabled body. This analysis offers an evaluation of du Maurier's theorisation of the abject, in a story that displays how 'the grotesque body [. . .] keeps opening and messing up categories, [and] strict definitions of ugly and related terms do not succeed in establishing stereotypes.'[36] M. Paul, the eponymous 'little photographer' is a congenital cripple whose body is literally thrown away over a cliff by his lover, yet, he survives genetically as a 'seed of difference' in the Marquise's womb. The hint that M. Paul's lover is pregnant indicates that in biological terms the categories of "othered" and not "othered" are not mutually exclusive, thus implying the dangerous theory that as the body is permeable so are class, economics, and society.

'The Doll' is the subject of chapter 9, which draws on the discourses concerning objectophilia, trans-humanism, and sadomasochism. In the story a musician, Rebecca, rejects a living male body for a sexual relationship with an automaton. The frame narrative takes the form of an abandoned journal rescued by a doctor and reluctantly published. Dr Strongman implies that the narrator of the story has drowned himself, a seemingly rational rejection of his own body as useless compared to the manufactured Julio, the perfect doll/ man. The human body is replaced by a superior and preferable copy and the story anticipates late twentieth-century anxieties over the increasingly mechanised nature of human existence. Du Maurier also considers male angst over female independence using the body of Julio as the site of the struggle for power and autonomy. In this final chapter of close reading the human form is entirely fabricated, desired and beloved by one character and violently loathed by another. 'The Doll' typifies human ambivalence regarding physicality and is an apposite text to conclude this demonstration of the overarching corporeal concept.

Du Maurier's short stories frequently include disabled and freakish characters acting as catalysts for controversies. They evoke 'romance' in the true medieval sense of a 'marvellous story' but they are also implicated in what Rosemarie Garland Thomson sees as the move from 'a narrative of the marvellous to a narrative of the deviant.'[37] However, David T. Mitchell and Sharon L. Snyder posit that '[n]early every culture views disability as a problem in need of a solution,'[38] and they cite 'narrative prosthesis' as a positive stance refuting Thomson's view that in the evolution of literature: 'wonder becomes error': the awesome becomes the awful. This research does not examine du Maurier's development as a writer, except to comment on recurring themes within her writing. The focus addresses the gap in critical reception of these significant works, and explores corporeality as a continually central force in du Maurier's work. The theme of corporeality is used by du Maurier to illustrate and pathologize desire and it is a persistent presence in stories outside the scope of this study, many of which are referenced in the commentaries, examples include 'Ganymede' and 'The Pool' [1959], 'Don't Look Now,' 'Not After Midnight,' and 'The Breakthrough' [1971]. References to du Maurier's unpublished correspondence will contextualise and support the textual interpretations as they are extratextual statements of her beliefs and philosophy, both of which underpin her writing.

NOTES

1. Peter Stallybrass and Allon White, *The Politics and Poetics of Transgression* (New York: Cornell University Press, 1986), p. 192.
2. Xavier Aldana Reyes, *Body Gothic: Corporeal Transgression in Contemporary Literature and Horror Film* (Cardiff: University of Wales Press, 2014) p. 2, p. 18, p. 2.
3. Avril Horner and Sue Zlosnik entry for du Maurier in the *Encyclopaedia of Women's Writing 1900–1950* ed. by Faye Hammill, Esme Miskimmin, Ashlie Sponenberg (London: Palgrave, 2006). p. 76–77.
4. Sourced at: <http://www.thebookseller.com/news/virago-plans-new-du-maurier-editions> [accessed 26 January 2016].
5. Du Maurier, 'Preface,' Phyllis Bottome, *Best Stories of Phyllis Bottome* (London: Faber and Faber, 1963), p. 10–11.
6. Gretchen E. Henderson, *Ugliness: A Cultural History* (London: Reaktion Books, 2015), p. 91.
7. Nancy Spain, 'How The Witch Cult is Growing!' (review of *The Apple Tree*) in *The Daily Express* 7 August 1952. Sourced at *The Daily Express* Online Archive. <http://www.ukpressonline.co.uk/ukpressonline/?sf=express> [accessed 5 February 2016].
8. Henderson, p. 105.

9. Du Maurier letter to Victor Gollancz. MSS.157/3/1/DM/12, courtesy of Modern Records Centre, University of Warwick.

10. Reyes, p. 1–27, p. 13.

11. Reyes, p. 166.

12. Reyes, p. 171, p. 11.

13. Kristina L. Richardson, *Difference and Disability in the Medieval Islamic World* (Edinburgh: Edinburgh University Press, 2012), p. 123, p.104, p.130.

14. Ian Conrich and Laura Sedgwick, *Gothic Dissections in Film and Literature: The Body in Parts* (London: Palgrave Gothic, 2017) p. 1, p. 8, p. 1.

15. Conrich and Sedgwick, p. 262, p. 261, p. 1.

16. Gina Wisker, 'Undermining the Everyday: Daphne Du Maurier's Gothic Horror,' *Revue LISA/LISA e-journal*, vol. 19, no. 52 | 2021, 22.11.2021, URL http://journals.openedition.org/lisa/13590 ; DOI : https://doi.org/10.4000/lisa.13590 [Accessed 22 June 2022].

17. Leigh Wilson, entry on Elizabeth Bowen, *Encyclopaedia of Women's Writing 1900–1950,* p. 22–23.

18. Permission to quote from Daphne du Maurier's unpublished letters is kindly granted by her son and literary executor, Christopher Kits Browning. Du Maurier letter to her governess Maud Waddell, 4 February 1924. EUL MS 207/6/4/1, courtesy of Special Collections, University of Exeter.

19. Du Maurier letter to Maud Waddell, 19 June 1928, p. 2–4. EUL MS 207/6/4/1, courtesy of Special Collections.

20. Katherine Mansfield quoted in Emmanouil Aretoulakis, 'Colonialism and the Need for Impurity: Katherine Mansfield, The Garden Party, and Postcolonial Feeling," in *Katherine Mansfield and the (Post)colonial,* ed. by Janet Wilson, Gerri Kimber, and Delia da Sousa Correa (Edinburgh: Edinburgh University Press, 2013), p. 45–62 (p. 45).

21. Du Maurier letter to Leo Walmesley 29 April 1958. EUL MS 207/6/4/1, courtesy of Special Collections.

22. Hilda Doolittle (H.D.) *H.D. Collected Poems 1912–1944,* ed. by Louis L. Martz (New York: New Directions Books, 1986).

23. M. C. Howatson, *The Oxford Companion to Classical Literature*, 2nd ed. (Oxford: Oxford University Press, 1989).

24. Rebecca West entry in *The Cambridge Guide to English Literature* ed. by Michael Stapleton and Nicolas Barker (Cambridge: Cambridge University Press, 1983), p. 945.

25. Dominic Head, *The Modernist Short Story*, chapter 1, 'The Short Story: Theories and Definitions,' pp. 1–36.

26. Sheila Hodges, *Gollancz: The Story of a Publishing House 1928–1978* (London: Gollancz, 1978) and Ruth Dudley Edwards, *Victor Gollancz: A Biography* (London: Gollancz, 1987).

27. Du Maurier letter to Maud Waddell, 24 March 1943. EUL MS 207/6/4/1, courtesy of Special Collections.

28. Hodges 'Editing Daphne du Maurier' in *The Daphne du Maurier Companion,* ed. by Helen Taylor (London: Virago, 2007), p. 25–43 (p. 34).

29. Hodges, *Gollancz*, chapter 5 'The Mid-Thirties,' p. 96.
30. Henderson, p. 104.
31. Head, p. 1.
32. Stallybrass and White, p. 26.
33. Elizabeth Grosz, *Volatile Bodies: Towards a Corporeal Feminism* (Bloomington and Indianapolis: Indiana University Press, 1994), p. 19.
34. 'Freaks in Space: "Extraterrestrialism" and "Deep-Space Multiculturalism"' in *Freakery: Cultural Spectacles of the Extraordinary Body*, ed. by Rosemarie Garland Thomson (New York: New York University Press, 1996). p. 327–37 (p. 335).
35. Elaine Scarry, *The Body in Pain* (Oxford: Oxford University Press, 1985), p. 18.
36. Scarry, *On Beauty and Being Just* (London: Duckworth, 2006), p. 73.
37. Rosemarie Garland Thomson, 'Introduction: From Wonder to Error: A Genealogy of Freak Discourse in Modernity' in *Freakery,* pp. 1–19 (p. 3).
38. David T. Mitchell and Sharon L. Snyder (eds.) *Narrative Prosthesis: Disability and the Dependencies of Discourse* (Ann Arbor: University of Michigan Press, 2002), p. 47.

Chapter One

'The critics will never forgive you for writing *Rebecca*'

Repositioning Daphne du Maurier and an Anatomy of the Short Story Collections

The 2013 entry in the *Encyclopaedia of the British Short Story* includes the comment that, '[p]robably because of its popular appeal, du Maurier's work has not been the subject of much scholarly criticism.'[1] This reinforces the insufficiently examined assumption that the popular success of an author's work and its claims to merit scholarly attention are somehow antithetical. Du Maurier was well aware of the paradox, even warning her publisher to edit out any mention of her success in promotional material: 'I wrote [to] Victor to beg him not to advertise me as Best-Selling, because nowadays it puts people off, and has almost become something to be ashamed of (though god knows why, inverted snobbery), but I'm sure he won't take any notice.'[2]

The limiting label of 'writer of romances' has dogged du Maurier's reputation for much of the twentieth century. Rebecca, the eponymous heroine of her best-known work, haunts her creator's reputation, just as she haunts the nameless second Mrs de Winter in the novel.[3] A contemporary review in *The Times* defined *Rebecca* as a 'lowbrow story with a middlebrow finish,'[4] and Sir Arthur Quiller-Couch commented that the critics would never forgive Daphne du Maurier for writing the book, knowingly observing that the royalties would exacerbate the disapproval of the literati. In an interview in 2014 her son, Kits Browning said 'he measured his mother's success not by reputation or critical acclaim but by the pleasure her works continue to give fans. *Rebecca*, published two years after *Jamaica Inn* in 1938, still sells 4,000 copies a month.'[5] These comments indicate that a thorough critical reappraisal of her shorter fiction is long overdue. Like Thomas Hardy's Wessex, Cornwall is du Maurier country for critics and fans who commonly first encounter her as a novelist. The psychogeography of her short stories frames moments of authentic, and unattractive, human behaviour. The short stories are bolder than the novels, unified by an identification and analysis of the insistent corporeality that saturates her stories.[6]

This chapter outlines the context for considering the critical fate of the short stories, which are often omitted from academic scrutiny or if included, only partially addressed. Despite increasing critical attention paid to the short story form, it is common for writers of novels to be considered primarily as such and thus their stories are often regarded as experimental works, sketches, ancillary works, or juvenilia. The Brontës are one example with their tales of the mythical land of 'Gondal.' This is pertinent as Du Maurier was fascinated by the family of writers to the extent of writing a biography of Branwell Brontë; friend and fellow author Oriel Malet explains how she uses 'Gondal' and 'gondalling' as shorthand code for '[t]o make believe, to pretend.'[7] For du Maurier the story form offers a freedom and brevity that encourages transgressions in theme, style, and form, illustrating how 'writers [take] advantage of the avant-garde reputation of the short-story form to explore illicit desire and "other" sexualities.'[8] This chapter also gives a sense of the variety, length and thematic concerns of the short story collections, briefly explored story by story in order of publication within a collection. There is additional discussion of literary and biographical influences and a move towards repositioning du Maurier among women writers. This serves as a basis for the more detailed analysis of individual texts in the eight chapters of commentary which follow.

Recent feminist criticism has edged du Maurier towards the label of the 'female gothic,' a mode in which 'cultural anxieties' are written out and the supernatural becomes manifest in the real world, placing her in a tradition that includes Mary Shelley among others.[9] Lucy Armitt includes Daphne du Maurier in her study of the 'fantastic' in women's fiction, positing that 'boundaries, borders, and thresholds are always key concepts for any reading of the fantastic, linking together concepts of nation and otherworldly, bodies and the grotesque, housing and haunting' and the interrelations of men and women.[10] Armitt cites du Maurier as a 'mid-century ancestor to the female gothic with a key intertextual influence upon those strategies of ghosts and ghosting which connect women with women during the contemporary period.'[11] The plots are not supernatural so much as psychological, but they do present interior 'hauntings' and revenants, and thus centralise the human body as the site of unnatural occurrences and illicit desires.

Du Maurier was born on May 13, 1907, the middle daughter of bohemian theatrical parents in the last years of the Edwardian era, and she died in 1989. The family inheritance of artistic creativity can be traced back through her own fictional, and factual, biographies of her father Gerald du Maurier and other antecedents. Although known as a novelist Daphne du Maurier's corpus includes several biographical works which blur the boundaries of the purely factual and the imaginatively realised, these include: *Gerald* (London: Gollancz, 1934), *The Du Mauriers* (London: Gollancz, 1937), *The Parasites* (London: Gollancz, 1949), *Mary Anne* (London: Gollancz, 1954), *The Glassblowers* (London: Gollancz, 1963). In *Gerald* (1934), she wanted to catch 'the essence' of her father and, according to contemporary reviews, was successful. *The Times* review called the biography 'a remarkable book.'[12] *The Parasites* (1949), is her fictional account of a less-than-idealised theatrical family, and *Mary Anne* is an account of her great-great-grandmother Mary Anne Clarke—the mistress of the Duke of York. Whether writing biography, fiction, or a blend of both, du Maurier's writing is unified by a focus on psychological politics, referencing Freudian and Jungian theory, as it maps out national and cultural trauma on individual bodies.

Richard Kelly's book *Daphne du Maurier* (1987) reveals that du Maurier's short stories came before she 'embarked upon her career as a novelist,' but this is contradicted by the subsequent comment that she 'continued writing short stories for the next five decades.' Kelly's early study compares du Maurier's literary reception to Mary Shelley's critical trajectory.[13] Du Maurier is a writer, not a novelist, and her preference for the short story form is evidenced by her use of the form throughout her career. Du Maurier herself comments: 'they are rather horrific short stories, I brew about it. [They] are different. Something wells up inside you, not your own life, but some sort of facet of it–and then the nagging old thing comes again.'[14] The reissue of the stories by Virago Modern Classics for the centenary in 2007, and du Maurier's recent inclusion in text-books on the short story form, indicate changing perceptions within academic circles of this popular, but critically underrated, author.

In parallel with Kelly's dismissal of the shorter fiction, Margaret Forster's biography positions the early stories as a type of therapy, through which du Maurier expresses her angst over her parents' marital challenges. By the time of the publication of the initial stories in magazines and journals, however, she had eleven stories written and was trying to find a publisher for a collection. This was more than therapy, and although du Maurier stated that for her writing was 'like a purge,' she regarded writers as a 'kind of medium, who can think him or herself into almost any character' and often 'the plot of a story came to her complete.'[15] The first short stories were completed in the late 1920s, however, and they are crafted with more skill than this comment suggests.[16] Forster's biography skims over du Maurier's literary influences lightly despite the author's personal correspondence, which indicates Robert Browning, Guy de Maupassant, and Katherine Mansfield as sources of inspiration.

Even the earliest stories are a vehicle for protest at sanctimony and corruption: figures of authority such as doctors, husbands, and clergy are treated unsparingly, and their duplicity mars the bodies of those in their power. ‘And Now to God the Father’ is a satire on religious hypocrisy, which is one symptom of a broader corruption du Maurier returns to in other stories. Its publication in *The Bystander* magazine (1929) was aided by the editor, her maternal uncle Willy Beaumont. ‘The Doll’ (1928), has a characteristic du Maurier plot that explores the mind-space of two psychopaths and outlines their interactions with precision. What Forster cites as the depressing themes of a further five early stories may reflect emotional fault lines within the du Maurier family, but they also plot the author’s lifelong interest in the power dynamics of intimate relationships. Like Katherine Mansfield, her inspiration, du Maurier is a precise observer of the human animal and likewise unafraid to detail the ‘dreary, hopeless, pathetic’ aspects of other people’s lives.[17] Commenting on her story ‘Panic,’ du Maurier explains to fellow author Oriel Malet,: ‘I don’t notice a woman’s dress but I do notice the beady glint in her eye to the man opposite. I suppose it wouldn’t do if we all noticed the same things! [. . .] I’m working away at the short stories at the moment.’[18] ‘Panic’ was first published in *The Saturday Review* 5 January 1931, and although published in 1955 in *Early Stories*, ‘Frustration,’ ‘Piccadilly,’ ‘Tame Cat,’ ‘Mazie,’ ‘Nothing Hurts For Long’ and ‘The Weekend,’ were all first published in journals and magazines between 1927 and 1930. Her letter suggests that a mature du Maurier viewed her early writing more positively than Forster’s model of catharsis suggests: ‘[w]hat fun to get suddenly inspired, so that you couldn’t stop, like K. M. [Katherine Mansfield], I used to feel like that when I was about twenty-two and wrote one short story after another.’[19]

The responsibilities of marriage and motherhood resulted in du Maurier briefly becoming ‘writing tired’ but the change in status and responsibility also provided additional plot material and a growing impetus to financially support her growing family. ‘The Happy Valley’ was published in *The Illustrated London News*, 1932, in the same year as Daphne du Maurier’s marriage to Tommy ‘Boy’ Browning; by May 1933 she was seven months pregnant with her first child. She wrote to Leo Walmesley: ‘I don’t think it was entirely meeting Tommy and getting married last year that prevented me from doing any work—I was honestly “writing tired.”’[20] Her decision to live and write in Fowey was made possible by a succession of ‘helps’ with children and chores, a secluded garden hut in which to write, and above all an independence of spirit exemplified in her personal dictum of ‘be your own mistress always.’[21] This freedom to write resulted in sixteen novels, biographies, travel books, and five story collections, which are *The Apple Tree*

[1952], *Early Stories* [1955], *The Breaking Point* [1959], *Not After Midnight* [1971], and *The Rendezvous and Other Stories* [1980]. Other collections such as *Classics of the Macabre* (London: Guild, 1987) are reissues of stories from earlier collections.

Critical introductions to the Virago republications suggest the difficulty in finding a label for du Maurier that sticks. 'Are We Allowed to Enjoy Daphne du Maurier?' is the plaintive title of Slavoj Žižek's proposed introductory essay to *The Birds and Other Stories.*[22] Although I disagree with Žižek's insistence on a psychoanalytic reading, his comments highlight the need for greater attention to her short fiction. As Žižek suggests, her short stories not only catalogue the changing mores of the twentieth century, in intriguing ways, they prefigure them. He posits that:

> There is one term that encapsulates everything that renders this space—and du Maurier's writing itself—so problematic for contemporary feminism: feminine masochism. What du Maurier stages again and again in a shamelessly direct way is the different figure of 'feminine masochism,' of a woman enjoying her own ruin, finding a tortured satisfaction in her subjection and humiliation [. . .] The central four stories present four versions of why sexual relationships fail.

Žižek is clear about the best way to read the stories and his argument relies on their order within the collection. They must be read: '[I]n the same way that Claude Levi-Strauss interpreted myths: instead of directly searching for a hidden meaning within each of them, they should be interpreted through each other, read side-by-side—the moment one does it, one perceives they form a precise structure.' However, while noting that Žižek offers a useful thematic reading of the collection his analysis is flawed, as the order in which he addresses the stories is not the same as the first edition [1952]. This approach is useful, but undermined because the stories were reordered by the editors at Virago without reference to du Maurier's wishes and Žižek is responding to the subsequent order. In the 2004 Virago edition 'The Birds' and 'Monte Verità' swap positions and the first story becomes titular. This title and format follows the Penguin edition of 1963, *The Birds and other Stories* (London: Penguin, 1963). Also worthy of comment is that this essay was originally intended as an introduction to the Virago Modern Classics 2004 republication of *The Birds and Other Stories* but was rejected by Virago 'for being too theoretical and disrespectful of du Maurier' despite Žižek's repositioning her as a writer flanked by the influence of Romanticism on one side, and Freudian psychoanalysis on the other. This provides a segue into du Maurier's sophisticated treatment of narrative and literary devices and, as is frequently seen in her writing (and in five of these six stories), there is a first-person male narrator whose statements, actions, and motives the reader is invited to judge.

The author's fascination with the inner life is revealed in her comment to her publisher Gollancz, 'You know how a first-person narrative helps me to identify.'[23]

There has indubitably been increased interest in Daphne du Maurier since her centenary in 2007. Much to her chagrin in her lifetime she was generally regarded as a 'romance writer,' yet the longevity and popularity of *Jamaica Inn* (1936), and *Rebecca* (1938), raise intriguing issues surrounding high/low culture and why popularity can be the academic death knell for a writer. Avril Horner and Sue Zlosnik argue that she is regarded within the academy as 'a storyteller who can spin a good yarn' which they rightly claim has eclipsed for too long her 'versatility and skill as a writer.'[24] Sheila Hodges, du Maurier's longtime editor at Gollancz, describes her writing practice:

> Some of the short stories she described as being symbolic of situations in her own life. As she pointed out, each of them 'requires its own mood, and in a way they are trickier than going flat out on a novel.' They are extremely varied in situation and treatment, and it is remarkable how her style changes to fit the subject matter. Like her novels, many are written in the first person, and no doubt it was the compulsion to identify with her characters that gave her a chameleon like skill in adapting her style to suit their way of thinking and talking, and in endowing the tales with such an authentic ring.[25]

This serves as evidence that du Maurier did not regard her stories as experimental sketches for novels. The publication of her story 'The Breakthrough' in *Not After Midnight* (1971) is determinedly framed by Forster somehow as a 'rehearsal for the novel' published later, called *The House on the Strand* [1969]. This is echoed by other critics such as Ronald Bryden who sees du Maurier as a writer who 'gratifies one's most secret social ambitions. Each novel is a country-house weekend in fancy dress [. . .] you are instructed while made at home and equal.'[26] Reductive accounts of her achievement as a novelist are irreconcilable with the mythic violence, transgression and retribution that characterises the short stories and the emphasis on one is made at the expense of the other. More recently du Maurier has been re-designated as a writer who reframes 'some of the most intractable problems of twentieth century history.'[27] Consistently regarded as a novelist, she has 'recently been reassessed as having more in common with her avant-garde contemporaries than previously thought.'[28] Du Maurier challenges heterosexual marriage as the principal social unit, often mockingly illustrating the dangers of romance for both men and women. Thus she defies the label of romance novelist applied so determinedly by many critics.

Daphne du Maurier's life (1907–1989) spans enormous change and this is reflected in her writing. Living through and responding to two world wars and changes in monarchy, she was writing during the spread of psychoanalysis, the onset of the permissive society, and a shift to the rejection of marriage as the only sanctioned form of relationship and the commercialisation of romance as a marketing tool. As Robert McKee comments, 'The enthusiasm for romance that opened this century has turned at its close to deep malaise that brings with it a dark, sceptical attitude toward love.'[29] Her earliest stories were written during the suffragist struggle for political enfranchisement and unsurprisingly a recurring central theme is the desire for autonomous power, over the body and the self. Clearly, some writers are immediately regarded as novelists while others become critically regarded for a variety of genres James Joyce and Virginia Woolf are two pertinent examples. James Joyce has the reputation of being the twentieth century's greatest novelist despite the fact that he is the author of only two novels. Yet, recent editions of du Maurier's work indicate her as the author of either novels or non-fiction, completely erasing her work as a short story writer.[30] Her shorter fiction focuses on 'forbidden passions,' rejecting sentimentality for themes of physical and psychological escape, violence—sexual and otherwise—fantasy, and incest.[31] Her delight in the short story form evokes the comment made by Henry James: 'by doing short things I can do so many, touch on so many subjects, break out in so many places, handle so many of the threads of life.'[32] Thus, genre can be an unnecessarily limiting factor in examining the full range of a mature writer's art.

Du Maurier wrote sixty-eight published, and at least fourteen unpublished, stories and consistently returned to the form throughout her writing career. Some of these stories, composed when she was just twenty, were published in journals and magazines and have been resurrected in recent collections by Virago Press. In this study I will be referencing the stories within the following republications: *The Birds and Other Stories* (London: Virago, 2004), *The Rendezvous and Other Stories* (London: Virago, 2005), *The Breaking Point: Short Stories* (London: Virago, 2009), and *The Doll: Short Stories* (London: Virago, 2011), except where a discussion of the original edition requires specific references. In addition to the sixty-eight stories that appear in published collections there are eleven sketches in the wartime propaganda booklet *Come Wind, Come Weather* (1940) and a few solo publications such as *Happy Christmas* (1942). There are also seventeen unpublished stories and outlines of unwritten stories in a black notebook in the du Maurier archive which have not been substantively discussed before in any critical forum.

Five major short story collections were published during du Maurier's lifetime. These are: *The Apple Tree* (1952, published under the title of *Kiss*

Me Again, Stranger in the USA); *Early Stories* (1955); *The Breaking Point* (1959); *Not After Midnight* (1971, published under the title of *Don't Look Now* in the USA); and *The Rendezvous and Other Stories* (1980). All the collections were published by Gollancz except for *Early Stories,* which was published by Todd, and this section summarises both those stories selected for analysis, and those outside the scope of this study. The paucity of criticism on the short stories renders the summary a necessary and useful inclusion, and highlights them as a rich vein for future analysis. Three of the stories in this study are selected from *The Apple Tree,* three from *The Breaking Point*, one from *The Rendezvous and Other Stories* and one from *The Doll Short Stories*. The earliest story is 'The Doll' written in 1928 and the rest were written after World War Two. Although this is not a developmental to chronological study the texts considered do span thirty years of du Maurier's writing, demonstrating that she was a continual practitioner of the short story form for the whole of her writing life. The short stories remain largely unexplored and, perhaps due to their brevity, they illustrate the daring aspects of du Maurier's craft more clearly than her novels: they are multivalent, dialogic, tricksterish artworks. Du Maurier's comments on their genesis indicate that the stories are carefully crafted works of fiction, and their subtlety and complexity reward close reading. As their author explains in her 'Note to the Reader': 'Often a story would well up in my mind but would take a long time to mature. At last—and perhaps after some months—I would be ready to sit down in front of the typewriter and turn it into words.'[33]

Much of what has been celebrated about Angela Carter (1940–1992) in short story criticism can also be seen in du Maurier's stories written decades earlier. Du Maurier is a literary ancestor to Carter, Margaret Atwood (1939–) and Jeanette Winterson (1959–), authors famed for defying convention in style and structure. Du Maurier's *The Apple Tree* (1952), contains six stories with female characters who are forebears of Carter's 'female vampires, girls transformed into beasts and women unafraid of violence,' a description straight from a summary of Carter's *The Bloody Chamber* (1979). And, prefiguring Carter again, du Maurier's plots demonstrate 'the strategies women need to adopt to free themselves from passivity and a heterosexuality that is always on male terms.'[34] The writing of Carter, Atwood, and Winterston delves into, combines, and reworks genres from the fairy tale to historiography, but du Maurier got there first.

Throughout her career du Maurier's stories parallel Mansfield's interest in the tyrannies of domestic life and simultaneously foreshadow Carter's reworking of the fairy-tale form to frame the politics of the personal. There is not space to cover all the stories in this book, but this analysis can illustrate the breadth of their 'cryptic and many-sided' characters and plots.[35]

The concerns with incarceration and escape, whether physical, economic or psychological, are directly tied to du Maurier's corporeal symbolism, in which '[t]he body is mapped and charted' into 'zones and hierarchies,' each of which represents a feature of human existence. Isobel Armstrong's summation neatly outlines the corporeal framework for studying du Maurier's stories. 'This is to accept the ethos of bodies, that they are acted upon, formed by the outside world as well as psychic needs: indeed, psychic needs are a response to the pressure of the material. Second, bodies are acted upon in history and culture.[36] Using Armstrong's comments as a starting point we will see how Maurier uses the historically contingent nature of the human body as a means to map out the issues in her stories.

THE APPLE TREE (LONDON: GOLLANCZ, 1952)

In 2004 Virago Press republished *The Apple Tree* as *The Birds & Other Stories*, exploiting Alfred Hitchcock's film adaptation of the titular story to enrol a new generation of du Maurier fans. The collection was first published in August 1952 subtitled 'A short novel and some stories' with 'Monte Verità' in the initial position as the novella. Virago's 2004 republication follows the format of the Penguin edition of 1963, the year Hitchcock's film was released, repositioning 'The Birds' as the titular story in the primary position and relegating 'Monte Verità' to second place. 'The Birds,' a dystopian tale of inexplicable avian violence, is the best known of her stories and a suitable introduction to a writer of range and versatility. Farmworker Nat Hocken's cottage is the site of avian attacks that are compounded by his terrifying isolation.[37] Friend Oriel Malet explains how, 'Daphne had been steadily at work upon a collection of macabre short stories called *The Apple Tree* [. . .] some of these had been written during my visit and over others she was still brooding. I remember the afternoon we were walking over a field, while a crowd of seagulls wheeled and cried above us. "I've often thought how nanny it would be if all the birds in the world were to gang up together and attack us," she said suddenly, "They could you know."' (The du Mauriers often used code words and 'nanny' is 'anything frightening or threatening'). The story was composed in the winter of 1951. Du Maurier wrote that the germ of an idea came when she walked on the Cornish cliffs and watched the farmer ploughing, 'his tractor followed by flocks of gulls screaming and crying. As they dived for worms and insects I thought: "Supposing they stop being interested in worms?"'[38] The absence of any information, local or central, exacerbates Nat's fear and his increasingly desperate measures for self-protection. This open-ended narrative provides no motive for the aggressive birds, no haven for Nat and his family, and the dialogic ending typifies the discomfort that readers familiar with du Maurier's short stories will recognise.

The Apple Tree (1952) republication begins with the novella 'Monte Verità,' and the story sets the tone for a collection of stories marked by illicit desire with violent consequences. The mention of a 'short novel' on the cover indicates the publisher's aim of capitalising on du Maurier's reputation as a novelist and the author of *Rebecca.* It is a dramatic story in the tradition of an adventure by R. L. Stevenson, in which the quest for spiritual peace is successful for those who ascend the Mountain of Truth, and ends in frustration for those who fail. The adventure is risky and 'no one who is called to Monte Verità returns' (68).[39] The plot is quintessentially 'du Maurian' in that conventional gender behaviour is reversed—an adventurous woman rejects convention in search of fulfilment in a remote community, and it is her husband who waits a lifetime for her return.

The Christian symbolism of the Holy Grail quest is juxtaposed with pagan imagery of the moon, Greek mythology, and a virginity cult where young girls are 'called' away from the world to devote their lives to . . . what? The mystery is unsolved and for the anxious narrator 'Monte Verità' is the 'uncanny' on a mountainous scale. The male narrator wants to save Anna and seems to arrive at the perfect time, yet she has saved herself, moving from spiritual exile in the world to a communal and platonic union on the mountain. The mysticism of this story suggests the haunting of Protestant rationalism with the Catholic revenant of 'smells, bells, and rituals' arising from a spiritual need that Protestantism does not satisfy.

From 'Monte Verità,' where beautiful Anna's path to freedom involves embracing a marriage she will not sustain, to 'The Apple Tree' where widowed Buzz's freedom heralds neurosis, psychic imprisonment, and death. In 'The Apple Tree' Buzz sees himself as a victim and his relation of events enrols the reader in his version of himself. However, du Maurier builds an elaborate critique of the man through hints about his lack of war service, the benevolent lens through which he presents his motivations, and his actual position as a wistful outsider from social groups. This analysis shows that du Maurier is not only writing from an ideologically feminist standpoint, but is working as a serious feminist thinker and propagandist. She propagates a challenging model and critique of gender relations through implicit consideration of character in her stories, offering a template into which a reader must generate their own text. As Roland Barthes states, 'The work is held in the hand, the text in language.'[40] Because this critique is not made explicit or expounded upon, but must instead be created by the reader, her ideas are more effectively propagated: an illustrative rather than a didactic method in line with postmodernist criticism. And this point is made by Graham Allen in his work on intertextuality, a key feature in the craft of these short stories.[41]

The fourth story in the collection is 'The Little Photographer.' The story centralises power relations using photographic replication as a portal to describe the oscillation between emotional distance and intimacy. The text explores the dangers of desiring an image above a person, and continues an early theme from stories like 'The Doll' that play with the Barthian and Sadeian roles of object and subject. Du Maurier's iteration of separate body parts is an echo of traditions in the embodiment of specific attributes, and indicates an 'aesthetics of suspicion' towards both beauty and ugliness, both of which are united in this story.[42] Her photographer is artistically creative and physically handicapped, an adept, lame artisan with skilful hands; his subject is the Marquise, who is anatomically perfect. In the photographic act the Marquise is caught as an image, not a person, but she subsequently resurrects herself to personhood through the murder of her photographic 'captor.' Her lack of morality is an interior monstrosity disguised by exterior beauty, a feature that supports Roger Scruton's summation of the medium of photography as 'inherently pornographic.'[43] In this text '[h]uman deformity raise[s] a constellation of questions about embodiment, incorporation, personhood, and the afterlife.'[44] Du Maurier is interested in the representation of the human form in diverse media and how this can be used to enact both artifice and authenticity. The novels and biographies parallel this theme, which stretches across the collections from the earliest narratives to the final stories. 'The Little Photographer' reworks the myth of Hephaistus and Aphrodite and the romance plots of fairy tales such as 'Ashputtel,' 'Snowdrop' and 'Rosebud.'[45] The narrative focus on deceit and sexual violence employs physical difference as the signifier for personal and social chaos. Yet, if, as Michel de Montaigne asserts 'nothing is contrary to nature,' then du Maurier's gallery of grotesques shows that it is natural for humans to be deformed, incomplete, immoral.[46]

In 'Kiss Me Again, Stranger' du Maurier foregrounds how ordinary lives are dramatically altered by war and indicates unease at the increasing pace of social change.[47] A cinema usherette lures RAF men with the promise of a 'bit of love-making' before she stabs them to death 'right in the guts' (230). In this story 'real life' turns out to be more dramatic and violent than any screen representation. As Žižek opines, the stories act intertextually *within* the collections as well as dialogically in a wider context, thus this story continues the theme of 'The Little Photographer' by foregrounding the unreliability of another medium of reproduction which privileges human facsimiles—film.

The final story in the collection is a ten-page inversion of the Oedipal myth climaxing in the murder of a son by his jealous father. The first-person witness to events narrates them in a realist style that is all the more shocking. The twist is that the family drama involves swans though the discourse is that of the human domestic arena: '[t]hey were free to be together again, and there was no longer a third to divide them' (242). This unifies the themes of this collection; the human/animal dialectic of 'The Birds' and 'The Old Man'; the homicidal plot of 'The Little Photographer' and 'Kiss Me Again, Stranger'; and the freedom quests of 'The Apple Tree' and 'Monte Verità.' The concluding image is one of beauty and transcendence though the cost of this freedom is murder: 'I watched the two swans fly out to sea right into the face of the setting sun, and I tell you it was one of the most beautiful sights I ever saw in my life: the two swans flying there, alone, in winter' (242). In the Virago edition, the yearly cycle is mirrored by the story order which begins and ends in winter with the topic of avian violence. *The Apple Tree* is a collection written by a mature and developed prose fiction writer that shows du Maurier did not use the short story as a vehicle to experiment before writing the novel. She continually wrote short stories as legitimate works of artistry in their own right. This collection of six stories introduces themes of familial and domestic violence, physical and mental disability, transgression and freedom, that were hinted at in du Maurier's early stories, most of which were published in the next collection under discussion.

EARLY STORIES (LONDON: TODD, 1955)

This collection contains du Maurier's initial forays into fiction which were written specifically for publication in journals and magazines. Collin Langley's research indicates that the earliest and arguably most entertaining 'shorts' were written between 1926 and1932 when du Maurier was between nineteen and twenty-five.[48] The first edition is a bright yellow cheaply bound paperback priced 2s 6d with illustrations of the dramatic events in the stories. These are black-and-white woodcuts which include images of a drowning girl in 'And Now to God the Father' (p. 56), a leering man in 'Tame Cat' (p. 108), and a limp female arm hanging out of a bed in 'Panic' (p. 6). There are no details as to the identity of the artist. The back cover describes the edition as an 'experiment in low-price publishing' at a fifth of the usual price of 10s. 6d. The book was made and printed in Holland for Valency Press. Two stories were published under the aegis of her maternal uncle, Willie Beaumont, a literary agent, and the editor of *The Bystander.* These are 'And Now to God the Father' (15 May 1929) and 'A Difference in Temperament' (26 June 1929).[49]

How the stories are approached by contemporary readers is surely influenced by du Maurier's lingering reputation as a romantic novelist. However, readers expecting conventional boy-meets-girl scenarios encounter a blend of vices including greed, lust, envy, selfishness, and wrath. These mordant narratives are not 'love-stor[ies] combined with wild adventure' but rather different forms and stages exhibiting love as the cause of self-delusion and ensuing disaster. This theme spreads its corruption throughout the collection. Du Maurier destabilises the reader by her presentation of an ugly, 'morally unstable universe,' which is closer to the one we live in than the one we wish to inhabit.

The eighteen stories can be grouped into five major themes of courtship, marriage, the church, the theatre, and freedom. The keynote story, 'Panic' relocates the plot of 'Little Red Riding Hood' into Montparnasse in Paris and the story culminates in sexual violence and death as in the original tale. Clearly there are Mansfieldian echoes in du Maurier's stories,[50] and one illustration is a comparison between what is arguably the grimmest narrative in this collection, 'Panic,' and Mansfield's 'Je Ne Pas Parle Francais' (1918).[51] As in Mansfield's story it is clear from the first paragraph that this anti-romance will have no happy-ever-after:

> The hotel was one of those *narrow, obscure* streets that lead from the Boulevard du Montparnasse. It was a *grey, drab* house, that *shrank away* from between two buildings, as if *ashamed*, as if conscious of its own squalor. The very sign appeared *unwilling to attract attention* as it swung high above the door, in faded gold letters, 'Hotel'; and then lower down, *humble and mean*, the word 'Confort.' (76, italics mine)

The lexical choices establish a transit of attributes between the girl and her surroundings which can be seen in other du Maurier stories. Forming isologues in this manner is a sophisticated trope and a favourite device, whereby figures share a domain without the sharing being made definite by the indicators of either metaphor or simile.[52] Once in Paris the lover realizes he has mistaken his prey for an experienced woman and the interlude appears as cheap and as sordid as the hotel and its denizens. The only heat generated is that of the sweltering summer temperatures until the girl suddenly dies postcoitally and the lover flees leaving his wallet behind by mistake. The macabre humour invites readers to smirk at the misfortunes of those who deserve no pity. And so we do, uncomfortably.

Destabilising reader expectations is du Maurier's speciality and the romance plot of mutual care and protection is a fertile field for this device, and it recurs in 'La Sainte-Vierge,' 'Nothing Hurts for Long,' and 'Weekend.' In the first story Marie, a Breton housewife, is deceived by her adulterous husband, then deceived by her faith in what she mistakenly perceives as a sacred visitation. This dramatic moonlit vision is actually her husband's adulterous coupling, which Marie perceives as a holy promise that her husband will return safely from the sea. Du Maurier boldly outlines scenarios that illustrate 'how close to humour must disgust and horror always be . . . in a bedroom farce it is disgust at what might happen—disgust mingled with furtive excitement—that makes the audience scream.'[53]

'Adieu Sagesse,' which translates as either 'farewell wisdom' or 'goodbye caution,' concerns Old Ferguson's escapes to sea from a stifling marriage in a seaside town resplendent in its smug superiority. The name is spelled 'Furgerson' in *Early Stories* [1955], but becomes 'Ferguson' in *The Rendezvous and Other Stories* (London: Virago, 2005). The backbiting at the yacht club is done by a drunken, retired vicar, and an ex-army major, who denounce dull local banker 'Old Ferguson' as a satyr indulging in Bacchanalian orgies. These 'friends' quaff his whisky and revel in malicious gossip regarding what he does on board '*Adieu Sagesse*,' his—as yet un-sailed—boat in the harbour. Attacks on pretentiousness characterise these stories which deflate and punish the hypocritical and dull. 'Adieu Sagesse' commences a collection marked by icy cynicism, where only fools have faith and their disillusion is lightened only by the acerbic humour of the author.

Inexplicably, du Maurier has not yet been celebrated for the variety of humour in her fiction. This takes many forms including ridicule, satire, farce, slapstick, tragicomedy and 'humour black, blue, provocative, anticipatory and anecdotal.' Stories such as 'Angels and Archangels' and 'And Now to God the Father' display du Maurier's irreverence regarding conventional authority and stultifying orthodoxies enabling her to 'vent [. . .] her long held views on religious hypocrisy.'[54] The Reverend James Holloway, Vicar of St Swithin's, Upper Chesham Street, is a man who 'never talks about religion' and who 'was careful never to speak about God, or anything embarrassing.' This recalls Alexander Pope's 'soft Dean,' who 'never mentions Hell to ears polite.'[55] A man whose 'exquisitely furnished' Georgian house 'adjoined' the church in much the same way that he adjoins the Church, namely, that he is not a part of the moral and spiritual substance, but rather adjacent in location, morals, and ethics. His 'broadmindedness' manifests itself as a tendency to gamble and womanise. Just as this high-minded critique begins to feel gauche it is leavened by sceptical humour.

The reverend is the epitome of a hypocritical, excessively worldly, Christian 'shepherd,' more interested in bedding society women than guiding his parishioners through life's travails.[56] Despite attending church with her grandmother, the young Daphne determined that: 'If God demanded such self-abasement from one who only brought happiness to those about her, then I wanted no part of HIM,' a bold stance declared in a short section entitled 'This I believe.'[57] 'And Now to God the Father,' du Maurier's first published story (1929), begins her lifelong writerly challenge to authority figures who exhibit vanity and hypocrisy. The anti-paternal titular riposte signposts Lacan's lexical signifier the 'Name-of-the-Father,' upon which concept the author lays her depiction of systemic corruption played out somatically.[58] Young, pregnant and destitute, Mary Williams drowns herself because faith is gone, faith in her young lover and faith in God as represented by the Reverend. In this story, as in others, corruption is played out on the body—in this case that of a vulnerable girl. The abuse of spiritual power is a theme du Maurier returns to and fiercely satirises in a significantly longer, later story called 'The Way of the Cross.'

Du Maurier's anti-establishment views seem unlikely at first, given her upbringing in a seemingly conventional Edwardian household of governesses and servants. However, it is precisely this background that provided the insight to craft these stories attacking the bourgeois middle classes from within. The darkness of the plots satirising religion and courtship is only equalled by those foregrounding marriage in which the protagonists are mercilessly mocked. 'Frustration' immediately follows 'Adieu Sagesse,' which portrays an escape from a stale marriage, and the narrative foregrounds sexual desire frustrated and fettered by the constraints of reality. In 'Frustration' a honeymoon couple are beset by series of unfortunate circumstances that delay their sexual union indefinitely.

Again, du Maurier presents the trappings of a heterosexual romantic plot devoid of romance. 'The bridegroom tripped over his feet, fumbled with the ring, forgot his lines, and looked at the bride as though she were a piece of chocolate and he a Pekinese' (69). The honeymoon descends into farce as the penniless newlyweds, forced to camp on Berkhamstead Common in a tent which collapses in the pouring rain, suffer a stolen car and a lost wedding ring. With increasing difficulty they romanticise the situation: 'Isn't this the most romantic thing that's ever happened?' (70)[59] In the denouement they find employment, but discover their jobs preclude time together. The lack of time equates to a lack of physical intimacy, and there will be no consummation. Du Maurier ends the story with a biting play on words: 'He stared at her as one who has heard sentence of death' (75).

'The Lover' and 'Leading Lady' follow each other in *Early Stories* and they are both examples of sexual manipulation for worldly gain. The dialogue is influenced by du Maurier's theatrical background, and the outmanoeuvring of the gullible is laced with acid humour. As with the depictions of the clergy these are the insights of one who has witnessed the charade. The 'Leading Lady' cozens the big producer with flattery, telling him 'you're an absolute genius,' while she thinks 'The fatuity of this man!' (141–43, all further references to 'Leading Lady' and 'The Lover' are from the Virago 2005 edition). The worryingly good minor actor is manoeuvred with maternal vulnerability into worshipping her until the 'light of a fanatic is in his eyes' (162). The free indirect mode succinctly portrays an experienced female bored by a younger man. 'If he went on much longer she felt she would scream. It was incredible that anyone should talk so much. What a fool he was! She turned her rising yawn into a smile. 'You know, you remind me of myself,' she told him.' (149) Du Maurier's titles are often witty and ambiguous and the Machiavellian Mary Fabian leads while unwitting men blunder in her wake, never realising they have been played by a professional actress, on-stage and off.

Du Maurier's playfulness is usually missed because of an emphasis on the macabre elements of her fiction, but in this briefer form the humour is easier to appreciate. 'The Lover' is the obverse story to 'Leading Lady' centralising a male whose romantic expertise procures free lunches, cars, and useful introductions. Du Maurier's stories are often ironic mis-titles, hence, 'The Lover' could be retitled 'The Cad' or 'The Player.' Examples in this collection include 'Nothing Hurts for Long,' 'Fairy Tale,' and 'The Lover.' Du Maurier shares this trait with Katherine Mansfield, whose writing she admired. In this sense Mansfield's misnamed short story 'Bliss' could be accurately retitled 'Ignorance.' Again, devious charm delivers results and after the first two pages of dialogue between a clingy woman and her indifferent 'Lover' the description of women as 'damn silly' seems an accurate statement (179). The familiar refrain of 'Let's do it—Let's fall in love' is playing in the background while the Lover thinks: '[w]hat an effort it was, this continual lying. If one told the truth for one moment there was the devil to pay. Women were a cope—a decided cope. Still, difficult to live without them—one way and another' (178). The humour bites when his latest conquest decides to abandon her wealthy husband and run away with him, declaring: 'We love each other. I don't care about losing my money; we could live in a garret, in a tent.' Du Maurier's keen eye for human behaviour delivers consummate artistry.

> He forced a laugh. "Aren't you wonderful!" Surely she would not dream of losing her head to such an appalling extent! Women had no sense of proportion at all.
>
> "Just think, you and I starving in a garret," she went on, dreamily.
>
> "Yes, but it would be the action of a cad," he said quickly. "I should never forgive myself. How could I be so brutal to drag you away from all your comforts and luxury! It would be criminal." He struck his fist upon the table. Rather dramatic, this. He almost believed it himself (179).

This story shows the influence of family friends Noel Coward and Gertrude Lawrence, and the dialogue is reminiscent of Coward's play *Private Lives,* staged at the Phoenix Theatre in London in 1930 starring both Coward and Lawrence. The theme of dysfunctional courtship is continued in 'Piccadilly' and 'Mazie' which follow the same character, a maid who turns thief for love in 'Piccadilly,' then reappears as a prostitute in 'Mazie.' 'Piccadilly' uses a frame to position the reader as an interviewing journalist. 'You funny little fellow with your notebook and your inky fingers. I'll tell you a story. Maybe it's true and maybe it isn't. You want to pry into the humble lives of people like myself'— a telling accusation for author and reader (79). The fragility and danger of truth, faith, and ideals are reiterated Cassandra-like by the dubious heroine: '[w]e're like that, every one of us. Believing in legends, believing in symbols, believing in signs—the only thing we don't believe in are fairies' (79). This is an ironic intertextual comment by du Maurier considering her family's intimate friendship with 'Uncle Jim,' James Barrie author of *Peter Pan* [1911 under the title *Peter and Wendy*], and the need for children in theatre audiences to believe in fairies for Tinkerbell to survive the poison she imbibes. Du Maurier starred in the play many times in the du Maurier nursery for an audience including Barrie. In addition, Maupassant's influence on du Maurier's writing is apparent in the subject matter that centralises the economics of prostitution and the choices available to ordinary people. The plots of Maupassant's 'The Graveyard Sisterhood' and 'Madame Tellier's Establishment' both focus on the oldest profession.[60]

'The Supreme Artist' returns to the relationship between artifice and truth: truth as it appears to the individual and the lack of desire—or ability—to see ourselves as we are. After a performance an ageing actor is confronted with drama in his dressing-room with the unexpected visit of an old girlfriend. He does not recognise the weather-beaten, thick-ankled woman, but drawing on his professional skills, pretends to be 'overwhelmed with joy and astonishment' (57–64). Despite a thirty-year gap since their last meeting he slyly claims: 'of course I knew you the moment you came into the room' and through the free indirect mode the reader is privy to the contrast between his thoughts and verbal parries. The game is nearly up when he allows his overly creative imagination to run free: '"Then, because I loved you so much, I'd want to strangle you, and . . . " He stopped short, dazzled by his own imagination, and a little hurt at the astonished expression on her face.' This is another echo of Robert Browning, this time 'Porphyria's Lover' is referenced, wherein the impassioned protagonist strangles his lover with her golden hair. Du Maurier was a fan of Browning's dramatic monologues and the motif is used again in 'The Doll,' and 'The Little Photographer,' and is a central motif in the novel *My Cousin Rachel* [1951]. What is humourous is that his depiction of overemotional youth is surprisingly accurate: 'I had forgotten all that' his visitor responds, adding prosaic details of ham sandwiches that 'spoil everything' for the actor (60–61). His melodramatic declaration of (invented) feelings culminates with, '"Don't you know success has not brought one grain of happiness to me, that always in the depths of my heart I've known you were the only thing that mattered?" He blew his nose noisily, and poured himself out another drink. His eyes were red and his hands trembled with emotion.' (120) However, the audience for his 'supreme artistry' may be perpetrating precisely the same fraud upon him while he is misdirected by his own elaborate illusion. This exact exposition of the male ego is utterly convincing and the story neatly ends where it began—with the actor's vanity. His casual snatch of song, 'Why are you so mean to me?' breaks off into a querulous demand to a young actress: '[t]ell me,' he said suddenly, 'that woman — did she seem really old to you, really old?' (64) The visitor takes the actor's illusion of agelessness away and her final comment is: 'Now you're just acting.' This song is cited as being sung by Daphne's father Gerald du Maurier, a commensurate actor and faithless husband and the connection serves to back up Forster's argument that for du Maurier the stories are, on one level, a form of catharsis.[61]

The mockery in these stories is a continuing echo of Katherine Mansfield's work which also resonates with 'Tame Cat' (91–105).[62] In this story the happiness of a schoolgirl's homecoming and her exposure to the facts of adult behaviour resembles the inner journey and revelations of Bertha Young, the central character in Mansfield's 'Bliss.' The nubile girl, who has outgrown the pet name 'Baby,' upsets a household predicated upon the attentions paid by 'Uncle' John. As her girlhood ends and her womanhood begins she swiftly finds that her mother dislikes rivals. In this marketplace youth and beauty trump money and experience and the mother knows it: 'You work quickly for a child of your age, don't you? You might at least have the decency to go somewhere else, and not use my house' (102). Margaret Forster sees these early stories as catharsis for du Maurier's adolescent confusion over the 'stable' of girlfriends her father Gerald, indulged in. Her mother Muriel tolerated his habit of infidelity which apparently varied according to the libido of the character he was playing at any given time. The character's gender is changed but the girlish cynicism comes directly from the author's first-hand experience of *paternal* promiscuity. 'Baby's' fall is hard and the disillusionment bitter, but while the more experienced writer Katherine Mansfield shows us Bertha Young ineffectually asking 'What will happen now?,' du Maurier allows her character to voice her thoughts.[63] 'So being grown-up was this: a sordid tissue of intimate relationships, complicated and vile. No loveliness, no romance. She would have to live like this in her turn, be false, wear the same mask as her mother.' (104) According to Forster, if du Maurier had not read Katherine Mansfield's short stories she might never have thought about writing at all.

This collection of early works illustrates du Maurier's cynical humour regarding the illusions people live by and the ramifications when disillusionment follows. Pretension and falsehood are held up to ridicule and it is the human body that serves as the nexus for a dissection of a diseased society.

THE BREAKING POINT AND OTHER STORIES (LONDON: GOLLANCZ, 1959)

An obsession with faith and disillusion, reality and perception, is a thematic strain running through the early stories to *The Breaking Point* [1959], where du Maurier shows that socially and culturally 'both discourse and the body are unstable, equally capable of transformation.'[64] Of the eight stories three focus on violent death, two on violent abuse, and the rest deal with the loss of selfhood. Although the plots appear diverse, ranging from the onset of menses in a young girl to a revolutionary uprising, the theme of chaos and disillusion visited upon the body is constant. 'Deborah, her cheek on her hand, stared at the empty sky. The heaviness of knowledge lay upon her. A strange deep sorrow. "It won't come back. I've lost the key." The secret world, like ripples on the pool so soon to be filled in and fenced, was out of her reach, forever.' (38)

The locus of the narratives is the risks of self-deception in a world where those with illusions are prey for clear-eyed, worldly predators. *The Breaking Point* was published between *The Scapegoat* [1957], a novel of family relations and psychological stress, and du Maurier's scholarly biographical study *The Infernal World of Branwell Brontë* [1960], both texts that explore the destructive capabilities of the family unit. It was during this period that du Maurier's husband suffered a breakdown from which he never fully recovered, and she finally faced his infidelity. Considered together the stories are a remapping of emotional territory in the light of unwelcome revelations, and they offer no solutions to the intractability of human relations. Du Maurier's correspondence with journalist and fellow MRA colleague Peter Howard illustrates her concerns: 'Yes, I agree about the country being in peril. [. . .] The attack on the monarchy is only one of the signs [. . .] The rot that has been setting in, in the daily press for the past year is part of it. [. . .] But the present weapon in the hands of the enemy is to confuse ordinary men and women about standards of life, and about values, and to spread a desire for self -preservation.'[65]

On the first page James Fenton declares 'I can't go on' (1). His bald statement is the 'breaking point' that characterises all the stories in a collection where sight deceives ('The Blue Lenses'), and language is unintelligible ('The Lordly Ones'). In two stories the natural states of puberty and physical attraction are the catalyst for brutal events ('The Pool' and 'Ganymede'), and in others technological developments threaten unspecified dangers ('The Archduchess' and 'The Menace'). Du Maurier commented that 'the basic themes of a few of them had lain dormant for years [. . .] I think the only allegory was the archduchess story, and I dare say this could have been made into a proper story, even a novel, about an imaginary country, but then it would have become Ruritanian.' Her correspondence with fellow author Phyllis Bottome shows that the 'breaking points' in each story are as much global as individual. 'I intended it as a kind of cry at the way the world is going, and the archduchess can represent anything, from the Catholic Church to Poetry – depending upon one's taste!' 'The Alibi' and 'The Chamois' concern the hunt for prey and in both texts the prey is human. 'Stephen was after chamois. I was after Man. Both were symbolic of something abhorrent to our natures, and so held fascination and great fear. We wanted to destroy the thing that shamed us most' (48). Du Maurier confessed the complexity of the themes in a letter to de Phyllis Bottome:

> The Chamois is far too difficult for even me who wrote it to try and explain. It's something to do with trying to destroy what you most fear in yourself, and the very hunting of it turns it into a monster. But religion is mixed up in it. Hence the goatherd Jesus, upon whom the narrator projected her own inhibitions, yet he saved Stephen. No, I can't explain. Yes, I read Death in Venice, but strangely enough a year or more after [. . .] I had been myself to Venice, seen Ganymede, and thought out the story, when in company with rather a dilettante old friend of mine.[66]

The old friend is retired diplomat Ronald Armstrong, du Maurier's correspondent and travelling companion. His nickname, 'Pen Friend,' identifies him in her correspondence and he was one of the human 'pegs' on which several characters were based, including the protagonists in 'Ganymede' and 'Not After Midnight.' Du Maurier comments that friend and actress Gertrude Lawrence was the 'peg' for the character of Rachel in *My Cousin Rachel* and revealed that friend and lover Christopher Puxley was the peg for the misogynistic character Buzz in 'The Apple Tree.'[67]

NOT AFTER MIDNIGHT (LONDON: GOLLANCZ, 1971)

Many of the stories were serialised in magazines to promote the publication of a new collection, as in for example, 'Don't Look Now' in *Ladies Home Journal* (December, 1970). The jacket of *Not After Midnight* advertises five 'long' stories with none less than forty pages, indicating a gradual lengthening from the early works which average ten to twentypages. This correlates with the increasingly complex and oblique later stories. In the style of other collections published by Gollancz the titular story is placed second and so 'Don't Look Now' is the first narrative. This story returns to the theme of false and true visions that began with 'The Blue Lenses' (1959) and the setting recasts romantic Venice as a sinister labyrinth of echoes and darkness where lead character John's rational bias is a handicap. The unmarried sisters are a reminder of the spinster generation resulting from the decimation of a generation of males in two world wars, and the murderous dwarf symbolises the ugliness of John's constant motivation from fear rather than faith. It is his run from help towards danger that costs him his life.

The title story is another imperative warning, 'Not After Midnight,' and again the protagonist's curiosity leads him to ignore peril and drink from the Greek rhyton jug that infects him with the curse of Dionysus—drunkenness. The classics schoolmaster is one of du Maurier's neurotic middle-aged narrators whose dreams featuring ivy-wreathed boys relate the events to the plot of 'Ganymede' where repressed desires result in violent death (1959). Having imbibed the forbidden liquid the narrator discerns the 'demon shadow emerging from a jug' (94) and realizes too late that now he personifies the satyr with a swollen face, hooves, and a horse's tail. The reader is left uncertain as to whether or not he can prevent himself frombecoming a 'drunken sot' (105). The next story, 'A Border-line Case,' is another Greek tragedy in that the characters are the unwitting agents in incest between father and daughter which becomes apparent through the medium of photography and the theatre. Authenticity and artifice are the lodestone of du Maurier's craft and this story marks simulacra as 'duplicitous: at one and the same time fake and truth-telling.'[68]

The religious theme is one of the great traditions of English literature from Milton to Blake, Wollstonecraft to Eliot, and 'The Way of the Cross' continues the debate using slapstick and satire to illustrate the shortcomings of humanity even within the temple of faith. This story celebrates ironic humour, not by illuminating the modern period's move towards science over faith but by exploring our relationship with religion and other aspects of everyday life: social position, economics, and sex. Du Maurier's 'Last Supper' narrative is sincere and mischievous with betrayals and forewarnings of violence and dissension, and human touches of frailty and discomfort. It is sensitively represented despite the tone of disapproval.

The theme of 'The Breakthrough' parallels that of du Maurier's novel *The House on the Strand* in a plot that questions the ethics of scientific experiment. The narrator is an electronics expert sent to Saxmere, a former radarstation in a remote coastal location, where brooding, grey towers are a fitting spot for the experiments conducted within. Saxmere evokes nightmare scenarios of recent Nazi experimentation at death camps. The station is staffed by zealots dedicated to the 'Charon' hypothesis and is described as 'a deserted Dachau' (248). The constant mythological references (Cerberus, Styx, Jove, Ganymede) heighten the tension of a plot that presents scientific overreaching in the form of a Greek tragedy. The 'experiments of a dubious nature' are aimed at discovering 'the answer at last to the intolerable futility of death' (254–59), but the results include no evidence of the afterlife and the disgraced scientists vow to continue their research elsewhere. This collection has recently been republished in Virago's series of classic authors under the title *Don't Look Now and Other Stories* in a 'beautiful hardback designer' format. Virago's investment in this edition shows the increasing attention being paid by publishers towards du Maurier's short stories. The advertising reads: 'Daphne Du Maurier's *Don't Look Now and Other Stories* showcases her unique blend of empathy and spine-tingling suspense.[69] Virago's title change suggests that the titular story may be better known due to Nicolas Roeg's film version (1973), which du Maurier thought 'good' but 'pretty grim.'[70]

THE RENDEZVOUS AND OTHER STORIES (LONDON: GOLLANCZ, 1980)

The Rendezvous and Other Stories (1980) comprises ten narratives written before 1947 when du Maurier was between thirty and forty years old. The ten stories in question appear in *Early Stories* (London: Todd, 1955). These are: 'Panic,' 'La Sainte Vierge,' 'The Supreme Artist,' 'Adieu Sagesse,' 'Angels and Archangels,' 'Indiscretion,' 'Fairy Tale,' 'The Closing Door,' 'The Lover,' 'Leading Lady.' The four new stories are 'No Motive,' 'Escort,' The Rendezvous,' and 'Split Second.' 'No Motive,' 'Split Second,' and 'Escort' were all written during the Second World War and unsurprisingly all foreground the threat of annihilation. This relates to another publication, du Maurier, *Come Wind, Come Weather* (London: William Heinemann, 1940). This is the MRA sponsored booklet of fictionalised 'true stories' designed to raise the general public's morale and foregrounds du Maurier's fears during the war. The departure from her usual style is noted by the author in her correspondence of the period. 'Here is an advance copy of my 'Moodle' booklet. You will find it rather different from "my usual." But some of it may interest you, all the same, and actually every story is true.'[71] 'No Motive' concerns the initially inexplicable suicide of a happy wife, which is caused by the random appearance of the illegitimate child she had as a teenager. Her father, a vicar, discarded his daughter when he discovered the fact of her pregnancy, and the trauma left the woman an amnesiac. Unable to face the shame she kills herself and her unborn child, a device returned to in a later story 'The Alibi' (1959). From an early age du Maurier had strong views on sex, illegitimate children and hypocrisy: 'People don't see anything wrong with one married woman having ten children—but if one poor unmarried mut has one! Oh, isn't it all unwholesome?'[72]

The eponymous 'Escort' relates to the voyage of *Ravenswing*, a tramp steamer bearing cargo from Scandinavia to Hull in the early days of the Second World War. The narrator is William Blunt (by name and nature) first officer, who assumes command when the captain is struck ill. A U-boat is spotted and Blunt makes for a fog bank to avoid being torpedoed. In the fog *Ravenswing* nearly collides with a sailing ship and a jolly-boat arrives bearing an English lieutenant. Blunt visits the ship and realises it is a man o'war with a crew in antique uniforms. The 'one-eyed captain' offers to escort *Ravenswing*. Blunt accepts, and the escort vanishes with the dawn. 'Split Second' presents another amnesiac, Mrs Ellis, whose confusion may be the result of bereavement or physical damage from a road accident. Her eventual fate is unknown as the story ends inconclusively, and this ambiguity is a feature of the later stories which are invariably open-ended narratives open to multiple interpretations.

'The Rendezvous' addresses intellectual vanity and the waning of literary fame. The middle-aged male ego is a thematic staple of du Maurier's stories, but this time her mocking depiction of Robert Scrivener the writer has a personal edge. Her correspondence indicates her unease: 'It's a form of inferiority complex, perhaps, but I am sure my status is so low in the modern younger critic's eye, that if they see anything written by me thy will automatically think it is going to be bad — a hot headed old romance full of purple passages!'[73] What she referred to as her 'No. 2 self' demanded escape through writing and she too feared writer's block.[74] Scrivener's punctured conceit is the result of rejection by a disinterested younger woman and the realisation that the academic plaudits he prizes are worthless. His epiphany is couched in lines redolent with du Maurier's irritation at reviews that constantly positioned her as a hack writer. 'Only then, [. . .] did he realise that what he had been seeing, what had moved him so much, was the adaptation of that best-selling novel he had always despised, that unworthy potboiler written a year or so ago by the fellow-writer whose wedding he had attended [. . .] His cup was full.' (128). The biblical reference is a classic du Maurier touch and is from Psalm 73.10: 'Therefore his people return hither: and waters of a full cup are wrung out to them.'

THE DOLL: SHORT STORIES (LONDON: VIRAGO, 2011)

This final collection was published by Virago in 2011 after the discovery of the provocative title story in a book of editorial rejections: *The Editor Regrets* (1937).[75] The five additions to the earliest published narratives are briefly summarised here and they are: 'The Doll,' 'East Wind,' 'The Happy Valley,' 'And His Letters Grew Colder,' and 'The Limpet.' 'East Wind' concerns the 'stolid' inhabitants of St Hilda's (3), a remote island where a change in wind direction becalms a ship whose undisciplined crew disrupt the monotonous lives of the St Hildeans.[76] 'Their desires had never been lit but lay imprisoned within their souls. They lived blindly, happily, like children, content to grip in the dark and never to search for the something that lay beyond their darkness' (2). When the east wind blows the island people change, '[t]he island was a new place now, broken of peace, swayed by suggestion and filled with strange desires' (8).

St Hilda of Whitby, or Streanaeshalch is mentioned in Bede: 'Thus this handmaid of Christ, the Abbess Hilda, whom all that knew her called Mother, for her singular piety and grace, was not only an example of good life, to those that lived in her monastery, but afforded occasion of amendment and salvation to many who lived at a distance, to whom the blessed fame was brought of her industry and virtue.' This strikes an odd note in a tale of primal violence in an idyllic location. The resulting drunken madness leads Harbourmaster Guthrie to take an axe to his adulterous wife in a brutal homicide. Du Maurier described the story as 'sordid [. . .] brutal and essentially primitive' and the plot echoes 'The Birds' in locating the source of violence in the natural world.[77] To be 'unmindful of desire' is presented positively in this story as is to be 'ignorant of distress,' yet, du Maurier balances this by indicating that not to suffer is not to be alive and not to evolve (4). The sensuousness of the descriptions where Jane, Guthrie's wife, wants to feel the fierceness of the wind are Brontëan in feel and tone. 'It would strike upon her breast and sweep the hair from her face, she would smell the salt tang of the spray as it stung her lip and her eyes. The longing came upon her to laugh with the wind, to cry with the sea, to open wide her arms and be possessed . . . ' (5). The yearning for freedom and escape for these childlike people in their prelapsarian Eden and the ensuing brutality shows how a 'somatic symptom becomes a dramatization of impalpable psychic pain.'[78] 'East Wind' is only one of many examples where the short stories portray a variety of locations, remote and urban. This challenges du Maurier's primary association with Cornish locations as typified in *Rebecca* [1938], *Jamaica Inn* [1936], *The House on the Strand* [1969]. As well as providing evidence that 'Du Maurier Country' is a misnomer, this also raises the issue of the limitations of readings that focus only on her novels.

The dangers of uncurbed sexual desire are continued in 'The Doll.' Du Maurier was aware of the provocative nature of her subject matter: 'I like the idea, though it's pretty extravagant and mad. I hope the important bits will come out all right.' The ground-breaking nature of the topic challenged du Maurier: 'It's so difficult when I think it over, it sounds weak and hopeless. But it will be a wonderful kick to finish it, probably tomorrow. More power with a story than a poem, because there's real sitting-down work to it.'[79] Her youthful lack of confidence was unwarranted as this late arrival is one of her most provocative stories, modernist in the destabilising inclusion of alternative voices (Dr Strongman), and postmodernist in form with its framing letter, ellipses, and fragmentation. Other works in the tradition of the story of Pygmalion from Ovid include E. T. A. Hoffmann's 'The Sandman' in *Tales from Hoffmann* [1817], Vernon Lee's 'The Doll' in *Hauntings and Other Fantastic Tales* [1896] and Angela Carter's 'The Loves of Lady Purple' in *Wayward Girls, Wicked Women* (1986). Though the subject of automata and dolls has a rich literary history, the presentation of a male doll as partner, sexual and otherwise, appears to have no parallel and is challengingly new.

An unnamed narrator encounters Rebecca, an immigrant violinist, at a party where her playing entrances him. Infatuated with her, he seeks to further the acquaintance and they become lovers. His discovery of a life size sex doll that she keeps at home fills him with jealous rage, and the story ends with a visit to her Bloomsbury garret which he finds deserted. The unlikely meeting, and attraction, of two psychopaths is the combination of humour and danger that characterises the shorter works. With this story du Maurier is contributing to the debate on female sexuality in the 1920s, continuing the tradition of daring subject matter in New Women's writing of the fin de siècle. In 'The Doll' du Maurier foregrounds female desire a decade before the publication of *Rebecca*, and unlike the novel, here the heroine escapes punishment to enjoy her sexual transgression to the full.

'The Happy Valley' is the second story in the collection where emotional, psychological and literal geography combine to forewarn the protagonist of their doom. The name is also part of the Manderley estate in *Rebecca,* and this story of a wife haunted by visions of her own ghost introduces the theme of psychological invasion and dominance by another character.[80] The recurrent yearning for a place of safety characterises du Maurier's stories and this plot, which centralises the home the protagonist enjoys only briefly, suggests not only the author's own struggles to keep her own home of Menabilly but also the twentieth century's endemic displacement of people in two world wars. The title may be a reference to Samuel Johnson's character of Prince Rasselas, whose journey towards self-knowledge takes him away from the ignorant safety of seclusion in the Happy Valley, into the wider world where disillusionment and suffering teach him that what he left behind was worth keeping.

There are lighter works in this collection, but it is comedy in the du Maurier style. 'And His Letters Grew Colder' is a story in the epistolary form; letters are sent between a married woman 'Mrs AB' and her brother's friend, 'XYZ,' who has recently arrived in the UK from his plantation in China. This new acquaintance soon develops into a romantic liaison and under the practised confidence of XYZ, rapidly passes through the stages of attraction, consummation, detachment, and finally alienation and rejection. En route, XYZ's passion includes romantic cliché such as jealousy, worshipful adoration, pleading, and helplessness in the face of strong attraction. The latter is not his responsibility, of course. As he says: 'You are perfectly free. When you laugh like that I want to strangle you –and then I want to love you' (166–67). The strangling of women by male lovers is a recurrent motif in both stories and novels by du Maurier. One instance in this collection occurs during the scene of initial attraction in 'The Doll,' another in 'The Alibi,' from the collection *The Breaking Point* (1959), and in *My Cousin Rachel* [1951]. The ascending and descending formality of the appellations presents much of the acid humour in this sorry but predictable tale, and the increasing intimacy of the pair is framed by the distanced reader who only has initials for identification. Thus, Mrs AB, becomes Mrs B, the more informal first A, and in turn: My Dear, My darling, Beloved, Sweet, Angel, My beloved Sweet, My own, Sweetheart, and the final rejection by telephone message to the resurrected formality of Mrs B, 'Mr XYZ. sailed for China today' (177). The letter code transmits the secrecy of an extra-marital affair and du Maurier invites us to mock the pathetic aspects of humanity even as we squirm in unwilling recognition. The theme of the dangers of self-deception is constant throughout her short fiction.

'The Limpet' is a dramatic monologue that starts with an emphatic clue to Dilly Sawbones' personality: 'No one can call me an insensitive woman' (179). The story title refers to the tenacious, gastropod that attaches itself with its sucker-like mouth, a symbol for Dilly's capacity to permanently attach herself to others; a succubus of joy. Du Maurier would have seen limpets on her walks around Fowey as they are commonly found on Cornwall's rocky shores. In old English *lempedu*, from medieval Latin *lampreda* 'limpet, lamprey,' is an eel-like vertebrate of the family *Petromyzonidae,* having a round sucking mouth for clinging to and feeding off the blood of other animals. A darkly comic subtext to this exposition on human nature. The opening defensive statement calls Dilly's character into question and raises the reader's suspicions about the accuracy of her worldview. 'Why am I so unlucky and so unhappy?' she pleads, as the ghosts of her past coalesce around her (207). Having lived a life of what she sees as self-sacrifice Dilly suddenly recognises that 'they want to be rid of me. They can't bear to be shadows. They'd like to get out of my memory and my life' (207). This truncated bildungsroman has a protagonist who brings doubt, disaster, and death, to anyone unfortunate to become proximate. Her dominating behaviour spreads anxiety and personally illustrates the dangers of 'toxic' people whose notion of 'duty' harms others (180). Dilly's passive-aggressive character parallels Alice Pemberton in Rebecca West's story 'The Salt of the Earth,' a woman whose well-meaning interference destroys the lives of those around her.[81] In despair Alice's husband Jimmy cries: 'That's the worst of you Alice. You find what people live by and you kill it.' Whereas Dilly's husband retreats into alcoholism, Alice's husband is slowly poisoning her, as her behaviour slowly poisons others.

It is clear why critics concerned with the gothic mode will increasingly turn to du Maurier's fiction, as it circles around the concerns of the human body besieged by age, disease, technology and all the rest that flesh is heir to. As Catherine Spooner convincingly argues, 'Contemporary Gothic's preoccupation with freaks, scars, diseased flesh, monstrous birth and, above all, blood is an attempt to reinstate the physicality of the flesh in an increasingly decorporealised information society.'[82] Gina Wisker's recent work reminds us that although Alison Light helped recover du Maurier from populist obscurity, she positioned her as an author providing a stable basis for readers of her works. It is when considering how brutally the human form is handled textually that we can see this for the misunderstanding that it clearly is, du Maurier is the mistress of unease, whose intent is to destabilise and disturb.[83] Wisker's work takes us into the existential and phenomenological arena, where the writer compels the reader to witness, and sometimes suffer, the delusions characters are subject to. To read her short stories in particular is to become disoriented as things, places and people become unrecognisable. In du Maurier's writing the body is more than physical, more than simply a vehicle through which to experience being in the world. Her exploration of the extremes of physicality as a means to interrogate human behaviour includes the overlapping categories of grotesques, monsters, robots and facsimiles, symbolic 'figures of liminality and in-between-ness.'[84] These beings are excluded from the family, the community, the nation, and are used as a 'code or a pattern or a presence that unsettles what has been constructed to be received as natural, as human.' The stories examine the position of 'the monster, the Other who does not fit the construction of Selfsame.' They enable the blurring of the 'manifold boundaries (temporal, geographic, bodily, technological) that constitute "culture" boundaries which J. J. Cohen states 'become imbricated in the construction of the monster—a category that is itself a kind of limit case, an extreme version of marginalisation.' Like Mary Shelley, du Maurier deconstructs the human form and scatters the pieces among her short stories, knowing the reader must reassemble the parts. Just as '[t]he monster commands 'remember me": restore my fragmented body, piece me back together, allow the past its eternal return,' du Maurier's short stories insist upon readerly participation to achieve their full effect.[85] This thesis introduces this trope with a view to analysing du Maurier's stories as a corpus with interconnecting themes set against the backdrop of twentieth-century social politics, and encouraging analysis along such lines where there is not adequate space for fuller exploration.

NOTES

1. Leah Larson entry on du Maurier in *Encyclopaedia of the British Short Story*, 2nd edn, ed. by Andrew Maunder (New York: Infobase Learning, 2013). Ebook.

2. Oriel Malet, *Daphne du Maurier: Letters from Menabilly* (London: Weidenfeld & Nicolson, 1993). Du Maurier letter to Oriel Malet, 18 March 1957, p. 88.

3. Du Maurier, *Rebecca* (London: Gollancz, 1938).

4. R. D. Charques, review of Rebecca, *Times Literary Supplement*, 6 August 1938. Sourced at <http://www.the-tls.co.uk/articles/public/then-and-now-1938-2/> [accessed 25 April 2016].

5. Padraic Flanagan, interview with Kits Browning, *The Telegraph*, 14 April 2014. 'Daphne du Maurier "overlooked" by literary critics,' her son says.' <http://www.telegraph.co.uk/culture/books/10766444/Daphne-du-Maurier-overlooked-by-literary-critics-her-son-says.html> [accessed 29.6.22].

6. A. L. Rowse, *Friends and Contemporaries* (London; Methuen, 1989), p. 281–86.

7. Malet. 'Glossary,' p. x, p. 87.

8. Emma Liggins, Andrew Maunder, Ruth Robbins, *The British Short Story* (London: Palgrave Macmillan, 2011), p. 61.

9. Andrew Smith, *Gothic Literature* (Edinburgh: Edinburgh University Press, 2007), p. 140.

10. Lucie Armitt, *Contemporary Women's Fiction and the Fantastic* (London: Palgrave, 2000), p. 1.

11. Armitt, p. 5.

12. Forster, *Daphne du Maurier* (London: Chatto and Windus, 1993), p. 112–16.

13. Richard Kelly, *Daphne du Maurier* (Boston, USA: Twayne, 1987), p. 25.

14. 'Daphne du Maurier,' *Modern Writers,* BBC2, 31 August 1971. TV interview by Wilfred De'ath, BBC Times Life Production. Sourced at <http://www.bbc.co.uk/archive/writers/12222.shtml> [accessed 29.6.22].

15. Malet, p. 71–86.

16. Forster, p. 32.

17. Letter from du Maurier to Maud Whaddell, 4 February 1924. EUL MS 207/6/4/1, courtesy of Special Collections.

18. Letter from du Maurier to Maud Whaddell, 4 February 1931.MS 207/6/4/1, courtesy of Special Collections.

19. Malet, p. 87.

20. Du Maurier letter to Leo Walmesley, 26 May 1933. EUL MS 207/6/4/1, courtesy of Special Collections.

21. Du Maurier letter to Maud Whaddell 25 May 1943. Courtesy of Special Collections.

22. Slavoj Žižek, 'Are We Allowed to Enjoy Daphne du Maurier?' Sourced at <http://www.lacan.com/zizdaphmaur.htm> [accessed 29.6.22.]

23. Hodges, *Gollancz: The Story of a Publishing House 1928–1978.* No further details provided. p. 96.

24. Avril Horner and Sue Zlosnik, *Daphne du Maurier: Writing, Identity and the Gothic Imagination* (London: Macmillan, 1998), p. 172.

25. Du Maurier letter to Victor Gollancz, 22 January 1952, quoted in Sheila Hodges 'Editing Daphne du Maurier' in *Women's History Review*, 1, no. 2 (2002), p. 301. MS 206/11, courtesy of Special Collections.

26. Bryden, p. 154.

27. Horner and Zlosnik, p. 172.

28. Catherine Spooner and Emma McEvoy (eds), chapter 6, 'Gothic in the Twentieth Century' in *The Routledge Companion to Gothic* (London: Routledge, 2007), pp. 38–48.

29. Robert McKee, *Story* (York: Methuen, 1998), p. 96.

30. Du Maurier, *The House on the Strand* (London: Virago 2003) and *Julius* (London: Virago, 2004), see section entitled 'By the same author.'

31. Du Maurier, Introduction, *Myself When Young,* p. vi.

32. Henry James quoted in Valerie Shaw, *The Short Story: A Critical Introduction* (London: Longman, 1983), p. 10.

33. Du Maurier, *Classics of the Macabre* (London: Guild Publishing, 1987), p. 11.

34. Liggins, Maunder, Robbins, p. 239.

35. Auerbach, *Haunted Heiress* p. 48.

36. Isobel Armstrong *The Radical Aesthetic* (Massachusetts: Blackwell, 2000), pp. 27–28, p. 218.

37. Malet, p. 20, p. x.

38. Du Maurier, 'Note to the Reader,' *Classics of the Macabre* (London: Guild, 1987), p. 12.

39. Du Maurier, *The Birds and Other Stories* (London: Virago, 2004). All page references are to this edition unless otherwise stated.

40. 'Roland Barthes, 'Theory of the Text' in *Untying The Text: A Post-Structuralist Reader*, ed. by Robert Young and Kegan Paul (London: Routledge, 1981), pp. 31–47 (p. 32–39).

41. Allen. 'Origins,' *Intertextuality* (London; Routledge, 2000) p. 8–58.

42. Henderson, p. 9.

43. Roger Scruton, 'Surface and Surfeit,' *An Intelligent Person's Guide to Modern Culture* (London: Continuum, 1998), p. 101.

44. Stephen Pender 'No Monsters at the resurrection: Inside some conjoined Twins' in J. J. Cohen, *Monster Theory: Reading Culture* (London: University of Minnesota Press, 1996), p. 143–67(p. 162).

45. Brothers Grimm, *Grimm's Fairy Tales* [1812] (London: Penguin, 1966).

46. Michel de Montaigne, chapter 11 'Of Cripples' in *Les Essais de Michel de Montaigne* [1580], quoted in *Monster Theory: Reading Culture,* ed. by J. J. Cohen (Minneapolis: University of Minnesota Press, 1996) p. 173.

47. Du Maurier, *The Birds and Other Stories* (London: Virago, 2004), p. 208. All further references are to this edition unless otherwise stated.

48. Collin Langley, 'But the Laughter Lingers...Daphne du Maurier – A Sense of Humour Celebrated,' EUL MS 363 Add. 2, courtesy of Special Collections.

49. Forster, p. 66–67.

50. Liggins, Maunder, Robbins, p. 204, p. 208, p. 204.

51. Katherine Mansfield, *Selected Stories* (London: Norton, 2006), p. 63–94.

52. Don Paterson, *Reading Shakespeare's Sonnets: A New Commentary* (London: Faber, 2012) p. 184.

53. Du Maurier, *The Scapegoat* (London: Virago, 2004). p. 56.

54. Langley, p. 6, p. 13.

55. Alexander Pope, 'Moral Essays Epistle IV' in *The Complete Poetical Works,* ed. by Henry W. Boynton. (New York: Houghton, Mifflin & Co., 1903), LL 149–50.

56. Du Maurier, *Not After Midnight* (London: Gollancz, 1971), p. 173–240.

57. Du Maurier, *The Rebecca Notebook and Other Memories* (London: Gollancz, 1981), p. 108–19.

58. Madan Sarup, *An Introductory Guide to Post-Structuralism and Postmodernism* (London: Harvester Wheatsheaf, 1998), p. 28.

59. Du Maurier, *The Doll: Short Stories* (London: Virago, 2011). For continuity all further references will be to this edition, which contains some of the narratives published in *Early Stories*. The rest of the stories discussed in this section can be found in *The Rendezvous and Other Stories* (London, Virago, 2005), references to the Virago editions are supplied in corresponding endnotes.

60. Guy de Maupassant, *Selected Short Stories* (London: Penguin, 1971). p. 77–122.

61. Du Maurier, *Gerald: A Portrait* (London: Penguin, 1970), p. 206.

62. Du Maurier, *The Doll: Short Stories* (London: Virago, 2011).

63. Mansfield, 'Bliss,' *Bliss and Other Stories* (London: Penguin, 1920), p. 110.

64. Armstrong, p. 215.

65. Du Maurier letter, 17 October 1957. EUL MS Add 5, p. 3, courtesy of Special Collections.

66. Du Maurier letter to Phyllis Bottome, 6 June 1959. BL MSS 78861, courtesy of the British Library.

67. Forster, p. 257.

68. Horner and Zlosnik, 'Glimpses of the Dark Side' in Taylor, pp. 242–48 (p. 246).

69. Sourced at <virago.co.uk> [accessed 31 October 2021].

70. Du Maurier letter to Alec Guinness 8 October 1973. BL MS 890015/ 2/7/12, courtesy of the British Library, p. 3.

71. Du Maurier letter to Maud Waddell, 3 August 1942, EUL MS 207/6/4/1, courtesy of Special Collections.

72. Du Maurier letter to Maud Waddell, 2 March 1925. EUL MS 207/6/4/1, courtesy of Special Collections.

73. Du Maurier letter to Leo Walmesley 29 April 1958. EUL MS 206, courtesy of Special Collections.

74. Forster. pp. 415–16.

75. *The Editor Regrets,* ed. by George Joseph (London: Michael Joseph, 1937).

76. *Bede's Ecclesiastical History of England, A Revised Translation* by A. M. Sellar (London: George Bell and Sons, 1907) chapter XXXIII, p. 271. Sourced at <http://www.gutenberg.org/files/38326/38326-h/38326-h.html#toc231> [accessed 29 January 2021].

77. Du Maurier, *Myself When Young*, p. 150.

78. Mara Sidoli, *When the Body Speaks*, ed. by Phyllis Blakemore (London: Routledge, 2000), p. 97.

79. Du Maurier, *Myself When Young,* p. 127.

80. Samuel Johnson, *The History of Rasselas, Prince of Abissinia*, ed. by Thomas Keymer (Oxford: Oxford University Press, 2009).

81. Rebecca West, *The Harsh Voice* [1935] (London: Virago, 1982), p. 133–85, p. 172.

82. Catherine Spooner quoted in Reyes, p. 168.

83. Wisker, section 2.

84. Michael Uebel, 'Unthinking the Monster: Twelfth-century Responses to Saracen Alterity' in Cohen, pp. 265–91 (p. 266).

85. Cohen, 'Preface: In a Time of Monsters,' p. ix.

II

'The Dismembered Self'

Chapter Two

'Split Second' [head] (1980)

Du Maurier is a more political writer than her current reputation suggests, and the brutalities of twentieth-century struggles for power are a persistent subtext in her stories. The surface details disguise plots that carry urgent warnings of the broader ramifications of war. As literary theorist Charles E. May argues, '[i]n the short story the hard material outlines of the external world are inevitably transformed into the objectifications of psychic distress.'[1] The inner life is one arena where this is played out, whereby some memories and truths are too ugly to face, and thus for her characters, 'forgetting' is often an active process. According to *Black's Medical Dictionary* painful memories may be repressed out of consciousness, and buried in the 'unconscious mind,' may be the source of anxiety and neurotic behaviour. The story entitled 'Split Second' symbolises the 'head' and 'brain' of the corpus of short fiction examined in this research, inviting the reader into a space where psychic distress is enacted.

To date there is little or no accessible information on how decisions were made regarding the order of the stories within the collections. In this case du Maurier originally intended 'Split Second' to form part of *The Apple Tree* collection [1952] but instead listened to her publisher, Victor Gollancz, who found the story 'poor' so she dropped it despite feeling 'a tinge sorry.'[2] Further evidence of Gollancz's influence over du Maurier can be sourced in Edwards, who cites du Maurier's literary agent, Spencer Curtis Brown, as 'driven to distraction by Victor's ability to persuade Daphne du Maurier that he was in the right—and Brown in the wrong—on almost every issue.'[3] Evidently this story was important to the author, dealing as it does with loss and literally being lost, and questions of whether people, places and even the self can ever be found post-trauma. In 'Split Second' the effects of violence and dislocation are visited upon one woman, but the physical and mental disorientation experienced by Mrs. Ellis symbolises the broader after-effects of warfare on civilians. The character may be operating under a couple of possible physical conditions. *Blacks Medical Dictionary* indicates brain fever as 'a state of prostration following some severe mental strain,' and concussion as 'a bruising of part of the brain as the result of a blow on the head.'[4] The denotation even includes a wry comment on the literary potential of such conditions. 'Cases vary in severity from mere giddiness to complete loss of consciousness lasting for weeks and include those curious instances of lost memory for facts or even for personal identity which have been much used by novelists.' The story was finally published by Gollancz in 1971 when it appeared in *The Rendezvous and Other Stories*, and it is clear today that the prescient theme of the degenerating mental health of an ageing, vulnerable person is more pertinent than ever.

The plot is set in the period immediately after the Second World War, an era characterised by the slow recovery from the ascent and overthrow of fascism. After 1945 the British began the process of reintegrating war veterans into a society haunted by revenants of the missing and lost. As reports from concentration camps gradually emerged with varying degrees of public acceptance, the broken minds and bodies of disabled veterans and civilians were a reminder of what society would prefer to forget. Richard Dimbleby's report from the Bergen-Belsen camp was first broadcast by BBC Radio on 19 April 1945, two weeks before the end of the war. Dimbleby accompanied the British 11th Armoured Division when they entered the camp on 15 April and compiled a report whose shocking contents delayed the broadcast for several days. Dimbleby only reports corroborated facts and during the report he breaks down as he describes the 'nightmare' of 'bony emaciated faces' of the dying prisoners. An estimated seventy thousand people died at Belsen, which was the only concentration camp to be liberated by the British.[5]

Written in the context of this type of gradually disseminated information, the subtext of 'Split Second' addresses how individuals did, or did not, gather the threads of their lives after the disruption of the Second World War. Du Maurier's political sensitivity is shown in the exchange of letters between her and her publisher, the campaigner and activist Victor Gollancz, in which she writes:

> Imagine, as you must have done a thousand times, what would have happened if the Nazis had indeed conquered Europe? [. . . I]f I was still writing, I would be doing some governmental work, some sort of new Britain propaganda. [. . .] I can imagine the totalitarian mind having considered all invalids of conquered countries as being useless mouths to feed, so into a gas chamber right away.[6]

The correspondence between Gollancz and du Maurier positions him as a vital influence on her political and ethical stances. He was an indefatigable campaigner, writing against capital punishment and the nuclear arms race. His biographer Ruth Edwards describes the way 'Victor applied himself to *The Devil's Repertoire or Nuclear Bombing and the Life of Man* and finished it in six weeks. It was a forty-thousand-word religious justification for unilateral nuclear disarmament, addressed to all countries, with the emphasis on discussion of ethical and spiritual responsibility and a few details about the effects of radiation thrown in.'[7] In her correspondence du Maurier anticipates that 'the next few years will see tremendous social changes,' before adding 'and a damn good thing too.' She goes on: 'But it seems so bloody stupid to be spending everything on weapons to kill our fellow creatures when an earthquake in Turkey does it for nothing.'[8] In the light of her preoccupation with the national and international post-war climate, 'Split Second' represents the body as the locus of security both individually and collectively, but portrays the loss of mental integrity as irredeemable. The narrative pattern is circular, and the protagonist is continually attempting her return to a home that is impossible to access in reality; as Per Winther highlights, in short narratives 'any aspect of the beginning, through verbal or situational echo, is one form of antithesis.'[9] Mrs. Ellis's home, as symbolised by her human anatomy or actual domestic house, is employed by du Maurier in Jan Gretlund's terms as a 'mediator between the past and the present, and the interior and exterior landscapes' of 1930s and 1950s Britain.[10] Her virtual home is real to her but the physical place no longer exists in real time. Du Maurier's curiosity regarding Carl Jung's theory of the collective unconscious spills over into this story where time appears to be 'all-dimensional—yesterday, today, tomorrow running concurrently in ceaseless repetition.' The quotation comes from *The House on the Strand* [1969] (42), another du Maurier text focussing on temporality. To read this story is to enter a repetitive cycle which encircles an unknown truth. Is Mrs. Ellis lost in time, or space, or trapped in unending trauma?

A corporeal reading of the text encompasses issues of consciousness, memory, and temporality as processed by the brain and experienced by the subject. Memory is the foundation of identity and in this text it turns out to be false before fading altogether: lost without home and family, without context, the protagonist is adrift in time and space. The disjunction between interior and exterior realities leads to anxiety, fear, and violence as the focalizer literally becomes someone else. Du Maurier presents the reader with unpalatable truths about mental health, showing how our existence within the world is dependent on the reliability of our internal reality. Reading 'Split Second' is disorientating due to its lack of stable referents, offering a reading experience that parallels that of the protagonist whose increasing rootlessness signifies the fragmented dehumanised self in a post-war wasteland. As with many of du Maurier's works, the plot exemplifies Dominic Head's observation that in artistic terms, disorder and contradiction can be productive.[11] As humans experience physical damage or degeneration through the ageing process, bodily we feel the shock as our faculties fail us. Whether this is a sudden or a gradual process, as it happens at some point our interactions will make no sense to other people and they will make no sense to us—like Mrs. Ellis, we too will be lost in space and time. Her bodily dislocation is the corollary for being mentally lost, and this is, perhaps, our greatest fear.

It depicts twenty-four hours in the life of a middle-class widow who loses, or regains, her memory. The twenty-year delay in publication is notable as the story belongs in the group of stories whose corporeal theme most resonates with Britain's post-war atmosphere.

The woman who calls herself Mrs. Ellis is first encountered in the drawing-room of her home surrounded by familiar possessions and people. By the end of the story she is located in a room of strangers, intent on either rejecting or incarcerating her. Mrs. Ellis is an 'Everywoman' figure living a mundane but pleasant life until it is cruelly shattered by an unknown force that hits her like the sudden blow to the head it is hinted she may have experienced. Her 'methodical and tidy' existence in 1930s Hampstead foregrounds the comfortingly English distaff domains of linen cupboards and larders, drawing-rooms and tea-rooms. Du Maurier painstakingly represents the smallness of Mrs. Ellis's existence in the familiar objects that reflect her status as wife and mother: 'all the things she had gathered about her during ten years of marriage, which meant herself, her home' (226).[12] Home and family are the core of her life, even as they form the core of this narrative in which all is dislocated: physical self, relatives, security, selfhood. The first eight pages are a lengthy description of mise-en-scène before the narrative arc takes the reader outwards into the locale, the nation, and finally through the convolutions of Mrs. Ellis's psychological space (226).

The story presents domestic and cognitive order before disintegrating into geographical and psychological chaos: the protagonist, in 'clearing mood,' tidies her desk in her cosy and bright home in 1932. In modernist style du Maurier ignores traditional starting points to begin the narrative in medias res inviting the feeling that we know this woman well before introducing contradictory elements which remain unresolved, for example, whether or not she is involved in a road traffic accident. The first sentence is a straightforward statement of character: 'Mrs. Ellis was methodical and tidy' (220).

Safe and secure, she clears her desk and complacently considers her life of middle-class rituals as dictated by the hour. Modernist influence is evident in a focus on the human relationship with temporal and synchronic time—there are four references to time in the first paragraph alone (a feature later echoed in her novel *The House on The Strand* [1969] with its focus on scientific time travel). 'Today,' we learn, is the first day of the month and the 'bright, clean 1'on her calendar's new page, inspires Mrs. Ellis to keep the 'hours ahead of her somehow [. . .] untarnished like the date; she must let nothing slide' (220). Self-control, firm authority over servants, and an ordered environment peg Mrs. Ellis as a lower middle-class woman with a refined sensitivity to status, manners and appearance. This pre-war life was lived by women of a certain class and economic bracket, fictionalised in novels such as E. M. Delafield's *The Diary of a Provincial Lady* (1930), in which 'placid, conformist, ordinariness' is celebrated.[13] Like Delafield's unnamed narrator, Mrs. Ellis is the epitome of respectable matronhood as she spends her mornings: 'shopping in the town, her basket over her arm. The tradesmen knew her, treated her well. Morning coffee at eleven, at the Cosy Cafe opposite the bookshop [. . .] a brisk walk in the afternoons, [. . .] and in the evenings she read or sewed.' (222) This is the pattern of a newly widowed woman for whom time is obscure and February a 'leaden' month (223).

The first pages of 'Split Second' detail Mrs. Ellis's attitude towards her late husband Wilfred, her daughter Susan, and her servant, Grace Jackson. Wilfred is described as irritable, fractious, and melancholy, a man with 'a difficult nature' which luckily Susan has not inherited as, according to her mother, she has a 'gift for enjoyment' (225). The implication here is that this is unlike her moody father.The positioning of Wilfred's portrait reflects his marginalised status in the family group as it is put away 'in that dark corner behind the bookshelf,' a distancing pattern repeated in Susan's being sent away to boarding-school thirty miles away, and in her consequent reluctance to return. Mrs. Ellis tries to ignore her desire to have her daughter living at home—her customary pattern when confronted with difficulty. 'Life, if she thought deeply about it, which she did not, because to think deeply made her feel uncomfortable, was built around Susan. Susan was nine years old and her only child' (222). Mrs. Ellis's cerebral activity is the focus of the plot but with deliberate irony she is presented as a character whose thought processes are limited. She is portrayed initially as the organised mistress of her home and affairs, skilled in housekeeping and parenting, before swiftly fragmenting into a querulous crone of impaired mental capacity. She is like Thomas Hardy's character Tess who views the 'numbers of tomorrows just all in a line [. . .] as they stand further away

[. . .] fierce and cruel,' feeling an 'ache of modernism' that she cannot fully articulate.[14] Then this character is plucked out of her own time and context and reappears exactly two decades later. Suffering psychic pain from the disjunction between mind and body in 1952 Mrs. Ellis is a revenant in the present, an unwelcome reminder of the past, an 'odd boundary creature,'[15] for whom 'the absence of pain is the presence of world: the presence of pain is the absence of world.'[16]

Mrs. Ellis and Delafield's provincial lady both live narrow and heavily structured lives, struggle with 'the servant problem,' and aspire but fail to exercise power within their homes.[17] The servant Mrs. Ellis grandly refers to as her 'cook-general' smokes, calls the drawing-room the lounge, and has a casual attitude towards her mistress, who places responsibility for any chaos firmly on her maid-of-all-work (241). Mrs. Ellis's initial satisfaction with her home gradually changes with the recognition that, 'the district *is* losing class,' and her prescient fear that, 'I shall have lodging-houses for neighbours soon' (27). The toilet brush, later glimpsed hanging on a neighbour's wall, triggers dismay over the declining respectability of the neighbourhood, while mention of her library book and single string of *cultured* pearls reveal her sensitivity to class markers; a sensitivity that will be chronically out of place in a post-war Britain bereft of the certainties of the 1930s. Du Maurier constantly holds a mirror up to less-than-flattering human traits, and Mrs. Ellis's evident snobbery *is* funny, even as it describes the cruellest and most inevitable aspects of loss. Her anxiety over control and appearances starts the dramatic twenty-four hour mental decline during which this middle-class widow becomes an itinerant bag lady. While her body remains healthy and mobile her psychological state is impaired and thus she is herself corporeally dislocated.

Each detail in the story prefigures the way Mrs. Ellis will soon lose everything. The wave of 'intense melancholy' she experiences just before her walk, and the twice-experienced sight and sound of the swerving laundry van (significantly the only event of the day repeated in both timelines), are clues to future events, which Mrs. Ellis ignores. (226) This failure to read the signs is a form of illiteracy that seasoned du Maurier renders perforce experience as dramatic irony. It is a recurring theme from du Maurier's early stories such as 'The Happy Valley' [1932], to later ones such as 'Don't Look Now' [1971], in which characters ignore dreams and visions with fatal consequences.

The crux of the plot is Mrs. Ellis's apparently innocent 'walk' from her home, around the Heath and back, which usually takes an hour but this time jolts her twenty years into the future. At the start of her habitual stroll the lexical choices foreshadow the impending trauma: 'It was not an inviting afternoon,' a 'muggy, murky sky' looms over '[s]olitary men in mackintoshes' and old women, by the 'sombre' and 'shrouded' fairground (228). As Mrs. Ellis crosses the road she is mentally choosing a new red bicycle for her daughter Susan and it is at this point that the laundry van brakes and swerves and she thinks '[o]ne of these days there will be an accident.' Suddenly, time slips ahead two decades, and, although the change gradually becomes apparent to the reader, it is not confirmed until the final pages where another calendar indicates that an uncanny temporal (or psychological) anomaly has occurred. Two narrative shapes—circular and linear—are demonstrated by the repetitive pattern of Mrs. Ellis's walk as it occurs *before* and *during* the story, an example of the modernist trait of repetition with difference in the plot.

The reader metaphorically 'follows' Mrs. Ellis as she returns from her walk to a different world: a daymare in which she vainly tries to make sense of the defamiliarized spaces and (to her), brutalised people. The worst has happened and the petty class distinctions of 1932 pale beside the realities of 1952: a world of bomb craters and social upheaval. Buildings are replaced, familiar authority figures are missing, the telephone book lacks an entry for Ellis, her home is a lodging-house and, perhaps most significantly of all, people are not out at work in the daytime. The economic realities are lightly touched upon here and elided by the amusing, and continuous, snobberies of the protagonist. There is mordant humour in the contrast between Mrs. Ellis's horror at the declining moral standards of 1932, and the realities of 1952, in which minor domestic failures are insignificant in the face of unemployment, rationing and the greyness of post-war austerity. No maid answers the front door of seventeen Elmhurst Crescent, people are rude to Mrs. Ellis and to each other, and officials (the police and the psychiatric nurse) provide no refuge from 'the most terrible disorder' (232). 'There was a sound of a window opening below and a man thrust his head out of the window. He was in his shirt sleeves. "What are you bawling your head off about?" he said.' (230) This 'lout' is a typical denizen of the post-war period in Elmshurst Crescent.

Bewildered, Mrs. Ellis wonders 'What would people think?,' unaware that in 1950s Britain the '[h]igh crisis' she predicted earlier in the story has come and gone, and with it any pre-war certainties (231). A series of disrupted, damaged and restructured locations increase her anxiety and transmit it to the reader, who, like the protagonist, becomes increasingly desperate to source stable referents in a narrative that consistently denies them. Graham Allen uses Julia Kristeva's work to show that in the short story form 'ideas are not presented as finished, consumable products, but are presented in such a way as to encourage readers themselves to step into the production of meaning.'[18] It is easy to miss the deeper resonances of this text but considering it against other of her short stories rewards the critic with another strand in du Maurier's post-war critique. She makes the London of 'Split Second' the locus of paralysis as Dublin was for James Joyce in *Dubliners*, who stated 'I chose Dublin for the scene because that city seemed to me the centre of paralysis.'[19] Mrs. Ellis's trials correlate with the lived experiences of people enduring changes wrought by the War, and the open-ended plot exemplifies disorder. 'She sat back in her chair exhausted. No nightmare, she told herself, could ever have the horror, the frustrated hopelessness, of her present plight. Little incident piled on little incident. [. . .] And all the while those thieves, those devils, breaking up her home, getting away with her precious things, her belongings . . .' (247).

The careful detailing of domestic items continues in du Maurier's concretisation of geographical locations: seventeen Elmhurst Road, Charlton Court, Parkwell Gardens and Moreton Hill—the Asylum. This last underlines the sober aspects of the mental health theme, yet, it is leavened with du Maurier's characteristic humour which surfaces at the darkest narrative moments, such as when the protagonist returns from her walk to find her home tenanted and almost unrecognisable. The dramatic irony is unmissable as Mrs. Ellis dryly observes: 'It did not do to antagonise lunatics.' (237) There is much future research to be done on du Maurier's macabre humour and the short fiction is rich in this aspect of her work.

The text however, encourages subtler readings, one of which is that the woman may be an inmate in a local asylum. Mrs. Ellis's 'walk' could be her escape from Moreton Hill Asylum, the potential site of a permanent incarceration that protects her from the confusing reality of 1952; a place where she can dwell in a fictitious world already twenty years out of date. In this reading the authorities support the lie and the headmistress keeps Susan permanently at school, protected from the knowledge that her mother is incapable of stable mental function. There is evidence for this reading in Mrs. Ellis's resistance to being taken to the police station, her attitude towards Sister Henderson, and her knowledgeable references to the asylum and its routines. She expresses satisfaction when the Sister has to look for her, and has detailed, resentful, opinions about the routines of asylum staff: 'Not much running about for her at Moreton Hill. Cups of tea at all hours, and sweet biscuits, while the patients are given bread and water.' (271) The reader is invited to wonder exactly how the character has such detailed insider knowledge of an institution she has apparently never visited.

Tension heightens in the narrative as inner and outer temporalities clash, and the protagonist doggedly clings to her version of reality while violently resisting all evidence to the contrary. She is intercepted at the location she considers to be her home, now confusingly converted into bed-sits occupied by strangers, by a policeman intent on helping a dotty old woman.

> 'I am not going with you,' she said swiftly.
> 'Now, Mrs. Ellis,' said the Constable, 'don't give any trouble. You shall have a cup of tea down at the station, and no one is going to hurt you.'
> He seized her arm. She tried to shake it off. The young policeman moved closer.
> 'Help,' she shouted, 'help . . . help . . . ' (243)

The identity of the character the reader identifies as Mrs. Ellis becomes increasingly uncertain as she fails to confirm it with the other characters. No one recognises her, she is not listed in the telephone directory, her doctor does not answer when called, and the addresses of her friends are bomb-sites. During the interview at the police station she is tantalisingly glimpsed through the eyes of a brother looking for his missing sister: 'this isn't Ada. Ada isn't so stout, and this woman's teeth seem to be her own. Ada wore dentures. Never seen this woman before' (255). Even as we enjoy the humour of discomfiture at this unflattering comment, we recognise that Mrs. Ellis's amnesiac condition mirrors a society in recovery from a seismic cultural and economic shock. The inclusion of a family seeking a lost relative is pertinent in this representation of a shaken world where much was destroyed, and lost, and never recovered.

At the end of the war soldiers returned to a country (and a populace) profoundly altered from the one they left, and if they found society unrecognisable, they too were radically different from the men who left for war. Mrs. Ellis's confusion is interpreted as lunacy by other characters: '"Balmy" said the man from the basement, "you can see the straw in her hair"' (241). This may be a typographical error from the slang term 'barmy' meaning crazy, though the first edition has the same spelling. The calm tranquillity of fine weather foregrounded in denotations of 'balmy' is an ironic contrast to the 'barmy' temper of Mrs. Ellis at this point and is another 'split' between presentation and internal reality. However, like a shell-shocked soldier she may not remember what happened to her because it is less painful to forget. 'I am not hysterical' is her unconvincing refrain as her life disintegrates around her: 'She had now lost all restraint. She could hear her voice, usually low and quiet, rising to a hysterical pitch' (240–41). Du Maurier specialises in showing the human condition under stress and hysteria is an appropriate reaction for a person in Mrs. Ellis's situation. Later Susan, the woman who turns out not to be her daughter, accurately observes that, '[s]o many people are bats these days, one extra doesn't make much difference' (271). A chiasmic structure is already evident in Mrs. Ellis's perception that the 'lunatics have escaped from an asylum' (235), unaware that she is herself considered to be one of them. This is an intelligent and accurate assessment in a post-war world where everything is inaccurate, even the date: 'She took a last glance around the room, and she saw with a shrug of her shoulder that even Mrs Drew's calendar had a printing error. It said 1952 instead of 1932. How careless . . . .' (272).

The 'split second' of the title has myriad applications in an overview of the text. It could be the moment in which the laundry van swerves, in which the reader is faced with slippage between the time period in which the protagonist is living (1932), and the era lived in by the rest of the characters (1952). 'Sequential and non-sequential time move through a montage of images where clock and calendar time, the astronomical and the geological, contrast with time as a function of the human mind.' Mary Roehberger's work on modernist writer Katherine Mansfield has parallels in du Maurier's short stories where the 'passing of time and motion in a present moment [. . .] simultaneously suggest[s] past and future' (Roehberger 2004, 10–11). Du Maurier's portrayal of a life located—and then removed from—a specific time period exposes the frightening impermanence of the referents that order our realities, and without which, we are lost.

Mrs. Ellis is escorted by a psychiatric nurse to the home of Susan Ellis—speculatively thought to be her adult daughter—who is now Mrs Drew and the mother of a small boy. Mrs Drew works from home while looking after her infant son, and has 'no help' (i.e. servants): her messy house is as distasteful to Mrs. Ellis as her slovenly behaviour. This is commented upon in Mrs. Ellis's thoughts, composed with bitter irony: '"Badly brought up," thought Mrs. Ellis, "and such rough, casual manners. But poor girl, if she had no mother . . . "' (272). During the visit conversation provides tantalising clues that solve nothing, and no one is identified. Three quarters of the way through the narrative, Susan relates how her pretty and 'very kind' mother was killed in a street accident when she was nine years old and away at boarding school. The split second of the road accident seems to have resulted in temporal stasis for (this) Mrs. Ellis, but the bereavement develops resilience in Susan, whose unsentimental adult summation of her plight is simultaneously on theme and devastatingly honest: 'I was pretty tough [. . .] *I don't remember much about it*' (270 italics mine). Again, the *leitmotif* of remembering is present, combined with the issue of personal control over what one *chooses* to recall.

The text denies Mrs. Ellis, and the reader, the satisfaction of certainty of any kind by mirroring the fragmentation of structures, landscape, and the social fabric. Any chance of definitive identification is clouded by Sister Henderson, who asks the wrong questions: 'if you will just say whether this person is Grace Jackson or not.' (268) Asked to make an identification Mrs Drew predictably fails to do so, since Grace was 'stouter, darker, older too' (269). Paradoxically, Mrs. Ellis does inwardly identify her 'daughter' through her strong physical resemblance to her sister-in-law: 'That same thin nose and rather peeved expression. [. . .] The resemblance, though, was really quite extraordinary. [. . .] Her voice was so like Dorothy's. [. . .] The same note of complaint.' (270) The dramatic irony is sustained throughout, as Mrs. Ellis's investment in her version of reality determines her adherence to it in the face of all evidence to the contrary. In this instance the human mind is portrayed as tough enough to withstand fact in preference of a prettier fiction. In characteristic modernist fashion the denouement does not resolve whether or not Mrs Drew is Mrs. Ellis's daughter, although significantly the reader knows that her maiden name was Susan Ellis.

Mental instability and personality fragmentation are common features of the short stories, which use them as tropes to instigate disruption. 'Split Second' also foregrounds age as a significant factor—Mrs. Ellis is not physically described but she is thirty-five years old in 1932 and her putative daughter, Susan, was born in 1921. In 1952 Mrs. Ellis would be fifty-five years old. There are several references to her youthful appearance which suggest that she has not materially aged, a physical impossibility unless the story has a supernatural element for which there is no other evidence. In '1952' the doctor jovially compliments Mrs. Ellis that she 'does not look any older' than thirty-five (which she is not), commenting '[y]ou certainly don't look more.' The officer disregards her confusion over the purposeof ration books (a feature of daily life in Britain until 1954), while the doctor condescendingly asks his new patient, 'How are you feeling today? [. . .] A little more like your true self?' (254). The moments of levity sustain a narrative with a darker purpose, to remind us that we too are trapped in context, and without it we too are lost.

Du Maurier singles out authority figures for ridicule in these stories, like the clergy doctors are mocked and examples include medical malpractice in 'The Blue Lenses' and Dr Strongman in 'The Doll.' Mrs. Ellis's reaction to those enforcing (an often nonsensical) order becomes more violent before culminating in a direct threat to Sister Henderson, who is attempting to force her return to a controlled environment. '"I don't want to go," said Mrs. Ellis calmly, "and you have no right to make me go. [. . .] If you come near me, I shall stab you"' (271). Du Maurier's choice of knife as a weapon in the hands of a violent female links to the character of the usherette in 'Kiss Me Again, Stranger,' and the inclusion of female violence is another recurring theme.

One of the major social developments that altered life in general, and women's lives in particular, was a dramatic reduction in domestic service after the First and the Second World War: and Mrs. Ellis's servant Grace Jackson is destined to become a vanished species.[20] Many middle-class women had previously not had to run a household, cook, or raise their children, and lacking the skills necessary for a wife in post-war society, they struggled and foundered. Mrs. Ellis's early struggles shadow those of her daughter Mrs Drew two decades later. There are literary parallels with the character of Mrs Ramsey in *To The Lighthouse* [1927] which include time shifts, women's roles, and hauntings, and Laura Marshall in *One Fine Day* [1947], a novel that traces twenty-four hours of unequal domestic battling with a 'tyrant of a house.' Du Maurier's writing was predicated upon leisure afforded through the domestic work of other women but this story shows that she was not unaware of their efforts.

This is one of several stories that explores cultural anxieties in a symbolically remodelled landscape, other examples are 'Kiss Me Again, Stranger,' 'The Alibi,' and 'The Breakthough.' Here, the reader is compelled to identify with the confusion of Mrs. Ellis in her unsuccessful search for family and home. The failure of familial relationships to deliver the promised story of affection and intimacy runs through du Maurier's shorter fiction, demonstrated here in the sundered lives of a mother and daughter, neither of whom are happy in marriage, motherhood, or domesticity. For those who favour biographical readings, there is plenty of material to connect both Daphne and her mother's lives to her anti-romantic plots. These link to what Beauman calls the 'rise of modern feminism': she posits that '[b]ecause the hidden past is often domestic, and very often female, interest in these two aspects shares the same approach, the egalitarian one.'[21] Du Maurier's political awareness of gender is highlighted by Beauman when she directs readers of *Rebecca* to the usefulness of reading newspapers of the period. '[P]eople were reading Rebecca at the time of the 'phoney war'; any good historian should read it in tandem with contemporary newspapers.' Beauman describes the power of the novel as located in the reader *being* Maxim de Winter's nameless second wife; in 'Split Second' an unknown middle-aged woman speaks to a generation finding its way through a brutalised post-war world through identification with her dislocation. The power lies in the choice of an ordinary woman on a mundane walk in an average location divested of everything that confirms her identity, position, context. Although not a polemicist, du Maurier anticipates the drive of the feminist movement to end female reliance on marriage and maternity for fulfilment.

Mrs. Ellis's disorientation acts metonymically for symptoms of general uncertainty and exhaustion in post-war British society, something David Kynaston calls a 'widespread sense of disenchantment.'[22] Like Mrs. Ellis whose presence haunts 1952, even as she is haunted by 1932, the Second

World War itself is a ghostly revenant in du Maurier's stories. This evokes Woolf's summation of the Great War by which she felt both haunted and inspired: 'we breakfast upon a richer feast of horror than served our ancestors for a twelve month.'[23] The story raises questions regarding the consequences of traumatic change, what happens when that trauma is revisited, and the complexities of post-war cultural amnesia. Here, the 'anti-nostalgic equation of memory with terror' echoes the widely shared wartime trauma in a story describing the ordeals of one character. Sceats and Cunningham use this phrase with reference to the trend whereby the haunted house is replaced with the psychiatric ward and the hospital, and the external objects used in earlier plots are replaced with introspective haunting.[24]

The close of the story does not resolve the identity of the woman or the events of her life. As the character is not identified as being Mrs. Ellis, the mother of Susan, nor as Mrs. Ellis, a patient at the asylum, who is she and where is her home? The ending leaves the woman successfully evading the police and the nurse before wandering off into London, heading northwards in search of truth. 'Mrs. Ellis let herself out of the house and slipped away . . . She turned northward, like an animal scenting direction, because northward was her home.' (273) Mrs. Ellis literally and metaphorically walks out of her time and into the future of the story and post-war Britain, and the denouement sees her walking away out of the narrative and into the unknown—a stranger to herself, and others. 'No one looked at her; no one bothered with her; they were all intent upon their business, either going from home or returning, and it seemed to Mrs. Ellis, as she toiled up the hill towards Hampstead, that for the first time in her life she was friendless and alone.' (273) Her plight parallels that of many people trying to find their way back to normal life, not realising that there can be no return, only forward motion after irreparable change.

The act of flânerie traditionally involved a gentleman taking a stroll through the city, an action that became emblematic of modernism and modern subjectivity as shaped by urban experience. Although the practice was most associated with Paris in the late nineteenth and early twentieth centuries, Du Maurier switches the gender and the purpose of flânerie so that the saunter becomes a brisk walk while the female flâneuse makes plans for a future that disappears.[25] Initially Mrs. Ellis's constitutional walk is part of her day as a lady of leisure, but by the denouement she is a wanderer and a detached observer of city life in the original sense of the word. As an instance of a case of amnesia Mrs. Ellis is literally, a person 'out of time,' in a story which ends as it began, with a woman going for a walk.

'Split Second' thus exemplifies 'modernism's engagement with discourses of fragmentation (such as psychoanalysis and degeneracy)' foregrounding du

Maurier's key device of using the mundane to illustrate the extraordinary.[26] In a reversal of Virginia Woolf's comment that a novel should start with 'an old lady in the corner' du Maurier *ends* her story with an old woman wandering away to unknown places. 'I believe that all novels begin with an old lady in the corner opposite [. . .] Mrs Brown is eternal, Mrs Brown is human nature, Mrs Brown changes only on the surface.'[27] By the end of 'Split Second' a prosperous matron has speedily become a friendless, nameless vagrant, whose experience of time places her outside the story of her family, her community, and her nation. There are hints of the plot in an earlier story draft located in the archives at the University of Exeter. 'The Old Woman' is the last of the unpublished stories in the black lined notebook write-in pencil and dated 1926 on the flyleaf. The plot of this early text shows du Maurier's interest in characters on the margins of life, like Mrs. Ellis, the unwanted older mother abandons her home and wanders alone into the night, destination unknown. 'La mere stepped out into the night, closing the door softly behind her, and set her face towards the long white road that led into the darkness. Later, when the moon rose, casting queer shadows through the trees, she was walking, always walking. There are so many roads leading to nowhere . . . .'[28] This madwoman's search for certainty and her defiance of authority is framed in the modernist style of 'the encompassing of time and motion in a present moment while simultaneously suggesting past and future.'[29] The passing of twenty years alters Mrs. Ellis's experience of herself as 'the body we experience is always mediated by constructs, associations, images of a cultural nature.'[30] Du Maurier's disrupted chronology is mapped out on the female body as crone, reminding us that 'age, like gender is a social category that affects our status and our everyday interactions with others.'[31] This resonates with her contemporary Samuel Beckett's choice of outsider protagonists: '"I knew that woman in Ireland," Beckett said, "I knew who she was—not 'she' specifically, one single woman, but there were so many of those old crones, stumbling down the lanes, in the ditches, besides the hedgerows."'[32] Not being known, not knowing ourselves, and being lost are our greatest fears and they coalesce around the ageing human body that most of us will experience. The influence of Katherine Mansfield can be discerned in the choice of older female protagonists. See 'Miss Brill' and 'The Life of Ma Parker' in *Selected Stories* [1920]. 'Split Second' focuses on the passage of chronological, biological, and psychological time as experienced by the individual and the collective, summed up in Woolf's well-known statement: 'on or about December 1910 human character changed [. . .] All human relations have shifted—those between masters and servants, husbands and wives, parents and children. And when human relations change there is at the same time a change in religion, conduct, politics, and literature.'[33] Yet, du

Maurier's story presents a challenge to the apparent inevitability of Woolf's model of social equality and positive change, which goes on to celebrate a newfound community of cultural interests between the lady of the pre-war house, and her cook. Mrs. Ellis is damaged but her genteel snobbery remains devastatingly real.

The repercussions of the Second World War resonate well into the twenty-first century, and this story, written soon after the end of the war, begins the process of articulating a national trauma at the personal level. Hints in du Maurier's literary autobiography, *Myself When Young* [1977], date the composition of the story to some point during the 10 years between 1937 and 1947, a period covering the Second World War and du Maurier's thirties (du Maurier 2005). At this time she was raising her young family in Cornwall while her husband Lieutenant General Frederick Browning was away fighting, and mention of details such as the bombed-out flats in the story potentially tilt the composition date to the years after the Blitz, thus, post-1942. Minette Walters' introduction to the 2005 edition of *The Rendezvous and Other Stories* describes the plot as only relating 'tangentially to the war,' in which: 'a pleasant but not overly bright woman who can only function in a structured environment, comes home from an hour long walk to find her house inhabited by strangers.' (xi) Walters' simplistic and reductive summary ignores du Maurier's characteristic trait of writing broader topical themes into the apparently quotidian.

Du Maurier terrorises her readers even as she romances them, and her shorter fiction epitomises Roehberger's comment that 'a good short story is never, upon consideration, what [it] first appear[s] to be.'[34] The public's disenchantment with a peace of endless rationing, petty officialdom and austerity, resulted in what Kynaston calls 'a certain sense of malaise, a feeling that society which had broadly speaking held together during the war, was no longer working so well, was even starting to come apart.'[35] Mrs. Ellis's 'coming apart' is enacted through implied head trauma which then affects her mind, illustrating Grosz's argument that, '[t]he mind is the idea of the body to the exact degree that the body is an extension of the mind.'[36] 'Split Second' depicts the domestic and social changes between life in the inter-war period and life post Second World War, using the thought processes of an ordinary woman whose confusion is like a slow death. Servants, security, and civility are all things of the past as the London of 1932, and of 1952, are considered in parallel, to question what was lost, and what was gained. Du Maurier writes out trauma on the body and brain of Mrs. Ellis showing that 'the body is not opposed to culture, a resistant throwback to a natural past; it is itself a cultural, *the* cultural, product.'[37] The experiences of Mrs. Ellis are an illustration of Grosz's reminder that the body is the *only* way we have of engaging with the world. Reyes' work on Body Gothic extends this idea in describing how 'these oppressed bodies connote a sense of helplessness that stems from a frustrating confrontation with the realisation that transcendence of the physical world may be only an illusion. Body gothic relies, partly, on the horror of a secular present and thus paints the body as a vulnerable bag of flesh and bones without any meaning beyond that which is socially constructed.'[38] This is why ageing is so terrifying to those living in the West, because existing medical and social care structures are failing to treat individuals as humans with emotions as well as bodies and the elderly are at the mercy of these institutions. 'Split Second' invites the reader to experience for a brief while the reality of an ageing woman, lost and confused, scared and unsupported by professionals or family. Mrs. Ellis is potentially those of us living in the twenty-first century western hemisphere, where the elderly are commonly abandoned in hospitals and care homes to await their death.

This chapter has introduced du Maurier's use of the body as the symbolic site of contestation for the individual, the community, and the nation. An ordinary woman has an extraordinary experience that unifies issues of class, maternity, family, economics, through the dismemberment of her mind and body. As a person, Mrs. Ellis is 'divided into parts or sections,' her physical and mental integrity is destroyed, and like her the nation is 'divided and partitioned.' The *OED* denotes the resonant verb 'dismember' as: 'To divide into parts or sections, so as to destroy integrity; to cut up, cut to pieces, mangle, mutilate: in recent use chiefly, To divide and partition (a country or empire).'[39] The separation of the physical human self is a mirror for multiple issues and a site of contestation which the author returns to again and again, as is clear in the way du Maurier blends politics and gender by foregrounding the head, the location for the human mind.

In discussing William Blake's radical representation of the partitioned body Isobel Armstrong notes that '[t]he zone of the sublime is the head from which both Burke and Kant explicitly excluded women.' Armstrong further describes how '[t]he head is separated from the heart, the region of pathos, that new affective area of imaginative empathy [. . .].' This narrative move towards the grotesque mind and body and away from the Sublime serves as another refutation of du Maurier's label as inheritor of the Romantic tradition. Here the reader is compelled to navigate the world with only what registers within a female mind. Powerless and commonplace, Mrs. Ellis is the antithesis of the sublime. Armstrong's work nevertheless establishes the corporeal as vital in understanding society and culture through the materiality of flesh. She elaborates: 'bodies are matter as well as mattering, matter as well as morphology. Though they may be imagined as form, not strictly correlative with anatomical structures, it is an extraordinarily idealist reading of bodies that abstracts them from their nature as substance. It is not to adopt a literal reading of the body to say that it is subject to material experience.[40]

'Split Second' represents the head and brain of the corporeality theme as the locus for frustrated desires and introduces the impaired human form as a trope that runs through this examination of the short stories. Like a person under a curse, the body of Mrs. Ellis wanders the world in search of her wits. With her mind in one decade and her body in another, the story recalls Grosz's argument of the 'disavowal of the body,' and the 'corresponding elevation of the mind as a disembodied term.'[41] Like many writing after the First World War du Maurier is crafting texts for a shell-shocked generation of readers, living in a world very different to the one into which they were born. In 1942 a government report compiled by Sir William Beveridge, British economist and social reformer, described the five 'Giant Evils' of 'Want, Disease, Squalor, Ignorance, Idleness' prevalent in Britain in the inter-war period. World War Two interrupted plans for the implementation of reforms which were not resumed until the late 1940s (Taking Liberties–Star Items–Beveridge Report).[42] It is against this backdrop that du Maurier's stories must be examined, the first story in the corpus begins the process of outlining the unifying theme of embodiment and disembodiment that will be fully explicated in the following chapters.

This line of enquiry continues in the commentary on 'The Blue Lenses,' where the conflation between sight and understanding is interrogated in an unusual way, incorporating both theriomorphic hybrids and blindness in the tradition of ancient myths. Following on from the physical and mental dislocation and disorientation of 'Split Second,' 'The Blue Lenses' draws the reader into a world of sensory impressions, where hearing and touch provide vital information in the absence of sight. Gretchen Henderson asserts that touch is vital because it, 'permeates all the other senses, since skin represents the border between exterior and interior realms. [. . .] Seeing, hearing, smelling and eating extend feeling and tactility.'[43]

As 'Split Second' depicts distorted thought, so the next story illustrates warped, or accurate, sight, pinpointing the moral choice between confronting new truths, or pretending nothing has changed. In 'The Blue Lenses' animal-headed humans embody personality traits in a narrative that charts the dangers of distorted perception. Also written shortly after World War Two, 'The Blue Lenses' is a response to the brutality of Nazism, and questions the morality of remaining wilfully blind to evident abuses of power, whether personal or public. In her study of the political physiology of dominance Donna J. Haraway outlines a 'domination based on differences seen as natural, given, and therefore moral.'[44] This model operates as both a definition of fascism, and a justification for the continuance of a hierarchy that places animals at the bottom, a template in which we see the structures of dominance and abuses of power illustrated by du Maurier in 'The Blue Lenses.'

NOTES

1. Charles E. May, *The New Short Story Theories* (Ohio: Ohio University Press, 1994), p. 18.
2. Forster, p. 259.
3. Edwards, p. 338.
4. C. W. H. Havard (ed.) *Black's Medical Dictionary,* 35th edn (London: A & C Black, 1987).
5. Sourced at <Richard Dimbleby describes Belsen–BBC Archive> [accessed 29.6.22].
6. Du Maurier letter to Victor Gollancz, 19 October 1958. MSS.157/3/I/DM/1–43, courtesy of The Modern Records Centre, University of Warwick (pp. 2–3).
7. Ruth Dudley Edwards, *Victor Gollancz: A Biography* (London: Gollancz, 1987), p. 76.
8. Du Maurier letter to Leo Walmesley, 19 April 1939, p. 3. EUL MS 207/6/4/1 courtesy of Special Collections.
9. Winther, p. 58.
10. Gretlund, p. 148.
11. Head, p. 25.
12. Du Maurier, *The Rendezvous and Other Stories* (London: Virago, 2005) p.226. All further references are to this edition.
13. Nicola Beauman, *A Very Great Profession: The Woman's Novel 1914–39* (London: Virago, 1989). 'Introduction,' p. vii–xvii.
14. Thomas Hardy, *Tess of the D'Urbevilles,* chapter 19, 'Phase the Third: The Rally' (Oxford: Oxford University Press, 2005), p. 109 –110.
15. Haraway, p. 15.
16. Scarry, p. 37.
17. Beauman,, p. xiii.
18. Allen, p. 33.
19. James Joyce letter to Grant Richards (publisher of *Dubliners*), 5 May 1906. *Selected Letters of James Joyce* ed. by Richard Ellmann, [1966] (London: Faber and Faber, 1975), vol. 2, p. 134. p. 64.
20. Beauman, chapter 4, 'Domesticity,' p. 94–120.
21. Beauman, p. 178, p. 237.
22. Kynaston, p. 109.
23. Horner and Zlosnik, quoted In 'The Ghost and the Omnibus: The Gothic Virginia Woolf' in *Gothic Modernisms,* ed. by Andrew Smith and Jeff Wallace (Hampshire: Palgrave, 2001), p. 62–77.
24. Sceats and Cunningham, p. 83.

25. Wolff, 1990.
26. Smith and Wallace, p. 86, p. 91.
27. Virgina Woolf, 'Mr Bennett and Mrs Brown,' *Selected Essays* (Oxford: Oxford World's Classics, 2008). p. 32–36.
28. EUL MS 144/1/1/1, p. 14, courtesy of Special Collections.
29. Roehberger, 2011, p. 10.
30. Bordo, p. 25.
31. Holstein, p. 3.
32. Bair, p. 62.
33. Woolf, 'Mr Bennett and Mrs Brown.' p. 32–36.
34. Roehberger, p. 2.
35. Kynaston, p. 109.
36. Grosz, p.12.
37. Grosz, p. 2–3.
38. Reyes, p. 170.
39. *OED* 2 on CD-ROM, version 4.0.
40. Armstrong, p. 27–28, pp. 218.
41. Grosz, pp. 4–5.
42. The November 1942 Government report on 'Social Insurance and Allied Services,' better known as the 'Beveridge Report' (London: His Majesty's Stationery Office, 1942). Sourced at http://www.bl.uk/onlinegallery/takingliberties/staritems/712beveridgereport.html [accessed 2.11.21].
43. Henderson, p. 165.
44. Haraway p. 8.

Chapter Three

'The Blue Lenses' [eyes] (1952)

'The Blue Lenses' represents the ocular in du Maurier's literary embodiment of cultural and social themes. *Blacks Medical Dictionary* states that the eyes are a delicate structure and 'many of its disorders cannot be cured or can be remedied only to a small extent [. . .] Most of the diseases are intricate [. . .] requiring the highest degree of skill in handling.' Eyes are one of the boundaries between the world and the inner self. Seeing clearly and understanding the *truth of what is seen* are at the core of this narrative which plays with humanity's negation of its animal self. The animal imagery employed represents a baser self, but one that foregrounds an authenticity and unity of selfhood belied by the human masks we habitually wear. Du Maurier uses hybridity—animal and human—to illustrate the risks of inaccurate perception, a significant factor in events both during and after World War Two. Latterly, the Nazis are regarded as 'bestial' because of their brutality and inhumanity, but in their ideological hierarchy 'it was normative to behave cruelly and inhumanely towards polluted 'lower' beings and affectionately and humanely toward morally elevated animals.'[1] One example is Josef Kramer (1906–1945), the Commandant of the Bergen-Belsen concentration camp. His nickname of the 'Beast of Belsen' was a direct result of the cruelty of his regime. Arnold Arluke and Boria Sax explore the ideological basis for how and why the Nazis treated dogs better than people, a fact that has bearing upon du Maurier's choice of beast-hybrids to investigate the blurred area at the very edge of humanity. There was widespread disbelief at the slow spread of news about the concentration camps in Europe and thus, the Nazis have to be 'beasts,' lesser, base, unfeeling, even evil, because we cannot bear the truth that humans can be inhuman. Our ugliest behavioural traits are thus labelled animalistic, a designation that conveniently negates the anthropoid who actually commits the acts. It is telling that 'The Blue Lenses' follows Reyes' pattern that in body gothic texts often 'surgery facilitates an encounter with some people's "true" selves yet is simultaneously constructed as a form of retributive violence,' and that it is Jim the paterfamilias who exhibits the worst excesses of the predatory animal foregrounding what Reyes calls 'the helplessness of the victim, and the inevitability of violence' in 'the antiseptic efficiency of the hospital [and] the operating room.' This is a text that merits close examination by this critical approach in light of reyes accurate insight that, '[s]urgical horror [. . .] places bodies and suffering at the centre of narratives interested in life-changing excisions and creative assemblages.'[2]

In her study of ugliness Gretchen Henderson notes that 'human-animal hybrids have embodied shifting cultural fears at different moments of history'; here, du Maurier plays with the hierarchy of values ascribed to specific animals, and, using a wide range including domestic pets, farm animals and exotic species, she saves the worst for people closest to the protagonist.[3] Animals do not commonly kill for pleasure and what the protagonist sees as loathsome heads are merely animal masks for the greater human ugliness beneath.[4] Mary Ellen Bellanca takes the opposite view of du Maurier's fiction, insisting that it 'places *Homo Sapiens* back in the web of predatory nature that we like to think we have risen above.' What she does not stress is that unlike humans, for many animals survival depends upon predation. This is another du Maurier character searching for self-realisation but as in 'Split Second,' the dangers of knowing the ugly truth make ignorance the safer option. This resonates with the temptation not to see when confronted with fascist brutality in 'a postwar Europe which carries the scars of its history.'[5]

Du Maurier had been brooding over a story set in a nursing home and in an unpublished letter to fellow-author Leo Walmsely in May 1933 she describes the 'funny little petty world' with patients 'all different, all with a separate mental 'something' [. . .] And all of 'em maybe finding out what's out of tune with themselves and their lives while they're lying there.' This insight into the genesis of the story includes descriptions of the staff:

> [T]hat awful breezy nurse [. . .] so horribly disturbing to the nerves, too cheerful, very efficient, but a big fool inwardly and rather a smutty mind—always with a pretended inside knowledge of the Royal Family "They say that Princess Mary isn't King George's child at all" Oh! And the lesbian Theatre Sister with arched eyebrows and no breasts, always a failure with the pretty rather common night nurse on the top floor who is 'soft about Jack Buchanan.'[6]

Du Maurier's detailed exposition of character flaws was written nineteen years before the publication of 'The Blue Lenses' which was first published in *Ladies Home Journal* in May 1959 and is the second story in *The*

Breaking Point [1959] (the story was also published in *Alfred Hitchcock's Mystery Magazine*).[7] In this story she demonstrates Mansfield's gimlet eye for human nature at its worst and demonstrates the skills of a great short story writer. Sarah Sceats and Gail Cunningham posit that '[t]he hospital and psychiatric ward become a familiar setting in the evolution of the ghost story,'[8] and 'The Blue Lenses' exemplifies May's theory of the 'unified' plot in the short story, commenting on the 'plot understood as a pattern or unified plan' and the feature of 'compression and intensity' particular to the genre.[9]

In 'The Blue Lenses' the reader is presented with a tale that harks back to the traditions of medieval bestiaries: where animals are used to highlight the difference between sight and insight. Albert C. Baugh describes the bestiary as a genre including 'fabulous descriptions of animals such as the lion, eagle, serpent, fox, elephant, panther' followed by a 'Christian inscription or moral.'[10] Du Maurier uses animal forms to challenge notions of the singularity of humanness that separate our species from the supposed irrationality of the natural world. This follows the bestiary fable as the story works as a moral edification containing warnings of human deceit disguised, then revealed, by the visual shorthand accuracy of animal forms. This only works if the reader recognises the traits humans commonly (and often unfairly) attributed to animals, often without any basis in fact. Thus the vulture is greedy and rapacious and the snake deceitful, the deer gentle and vulnerable, the dogs simple and faithful.

Of course, humans *are* an animal species but we like to think of ourselves as beings of a higher order, with higher level faculties and superior linguistic skills. In fact, animals prey upon each other to survive whereas du Maurier's short fiction presents humans enacting murders for pleasure. Kelly states that 'Like Jonathan Swift, du Maurier focuses upon the repulsiveness of the human body,' and in Swiftian fashion the bodies of her hybridised humans convey her commentary on corruption, hypocrisy, and weakness.[11] The snake (Nurse Anselm) and the vulture (husband Jim) are examples of Henderson's argument that '[a]cross history, human animality has posed a seeming threat that nature and culture can deviate or otherwise deform an idealised human into an 'ugly' beast.' From her altered perspective Marda West does not want her newly zoic husband to touch her and 'conflate[s] "bestial" with barbaric, diseased, retrogressed and full of vice.'[12] As Reyes comments on cinematic zoomorphs, 'the fact that they are eminently hybrid and therefore resistant to clear-cut categorization, is deeply disturbing and causes mistrust or hatred. The suspicions that something 'other' lies just beyond what the eye can see creates a sense of uncanniness that generates horror; the Beast folk are 'unnatural' and 'repulsive' and eventually threatening.'[13] Du Maurier's beast-folk are initially kindly medical personnel but latterly appear feral and implicitly in search of prey, and finally those closest to her exhibit greed and duplicity and live outside of societal morality.

What Marda does not realise is that increased perception also brings her greater *self*-perception. 'The Blue Lenses' is one example of the hybridised form which recurs throughout du Maurier's stories, and here the focus is on the human/ animal dialectic, a recurrent theme in contemporary moral philosophy.[14] As anthropologist Mary Midgely clarifies: '[t]here is a supposed contrast between man and animals which was formed by seeing animals not as they were, but as projections of our own fears and desires.'[15] Terms such as 'brutal' and 'beastial' encapsulate our very human need to distance ourselves from what is untamed, instinctual, uncivilised and uncontrolled in our being. No matter that this positions animals inaccurately, and as such, 'The Blue Lenses' must be read as an ironic commentary on our uneasy identification(s) with animals as symbols. The text encapsulates du Maurier's habit of asking the big questions of life by utilising various forms of somatic 'otherness' to demonstrate the extremes, and the repercussions, of violent desire. It also continues the debate over what exactly separates humans from animals, and if that is possible, what it is that makes us differently human.

Du Maurier's topical intellectual discussion shows an awareness of Derridean philosophy. Jacques Derrida opines that it is blindness that 'ensures sight its breath,' to him it is, 'an accident that interrupts the regular course of things affecting both Nature and a nature of the will, the will to know [savoir] as the will to see [voir].'[16] He explores the conflation between seeing and knowing and our major assumption that we accurately comprehend because we are able to physically see. So, the loss and the return of sight equates to increased sensitivity and accuracy of the perception of what is seen. Readers are presented with the character of Marda West, a woman who sees differently before, during, and after medical treatment intended to improve her perception. In 'The Blue Lenses' characters present a facade that disguises who, or what, they really are, while their animal totems indicate their true, hidden nature. The scopophilic theme emphasises our choice *not* to see accurately when the view is repugnant.

The thesis of one of Derrida's final projects is that 'the exclusion of animals from the public realm reveals better than any other thought or deed the highly problematic nature of the claims that human beings make about themselves.'[17] Du Maurier's relocation of unpleasant aspects of human nature into the animal kingdom enables a distance between 'us and them' which then invites humour from the reader. In 'The Lordly Ones,' Maurier playfully reverses the pattern by presenting a narrative that twins animals with nurturing traits more commonly associated with people. In this text the beastly caricatures are ridiculous, but they make visible that which we often cannot discern, who to trust and who is a threat, and what type of 'animal' we are ourselves. 'The Blue Lenses' plays with concepts of personal sovereignty versus animal instincts, and as a teller of truths disguised as fiction, du Maurier questions exactly what fictions are necessary for people to live their lives. Her personal philosophy informs the protagonist's dilemma, illustrated in her statement that, 'the evil in us comes to the surface. Unless we recognise it in time, accept it, understand it, we are all destroyed.'[18] As the protagonist discovers, unpalatable truths are all around us if only we can see beyond our cognitive blindness and then we have to decide, 'what is true?' The story is framed by du Maurier's personal life challenges, hinted at in a letter to friend Phyllis Bottome. 'I had been unhappy the winter before living in London, as you knew, and I think this had triggered off the thread or idea of The Breaking Point—perhaps in my case the gulf between fact and fantasy, so that one asks oneself the question "But what is true?" And that although life itself is deeply good, yet the jungle waits to break through.' The final words are an exact echo of Marda's fears in 'The Blue Lenses.'[19]

The plot is simple. At the start of the narrative, Marda, wife to Jim, is in a nursing home recovering from an eye operation. She lies in bed, eyes bandaged, in the care of a doctor who is 'a voice rather than a presence,' asking her 'to surrender herself to him' (46). Blue lenses have been fitted to protect her eyes and her head is swathed in bandages. Marda can only hear the voices of her carers and she spends time imagining their appearance and their mannerisms. The surgeon is 'brisk and efficient,' the daily nurse is a 'person of sunlight' who exudes a 'daytime brightness,' and during the long nights Nurse Ansel brings 'consolation,' 'quiet encouragement,' and a 'special secret sympathy' (45–47). The nurse's unusual surname echoes the medieval archbishop St. Anselm who famously protected animals and is another connection to the Anglo-Saxon fables which tend to imply their morals indirectly. The content of the conversations between Marda and Nurse Ansel is paramount, as is the tone in which it is uttered. The contrast between visual and aural information is striking as du Maurier questions the avenues we use to establish veracity in the world. In common with medieval hagiography here animals are metaphors that can facilitate greater understanding if read correctly, or disaster if ignored. The bestial serves as humanity's metaphorical shorthand.

It is made clear to the reader that the patient is responsible for the failure of the lenses to bestow clearer sight. In his study of constructions of blindness Edward Wheatley notes that, 'to some extent in modern medicine and to a greater one in medieval Christianity, there is an implicit attitude that somehow the disabled person is himself to blame for resisting a cure.'[20] If Marda's operation is a failure, it will not be because the medical team are inept or Jim is a neglectful husband, it will be because she did not try hard enough to get well.

When she is told that the operation is successful, no date is given for when her sight will be restored, and this leads her to attempt to 'trap' nursing staff and 'catch them unawares' into confirming a date when she will see again.

> Nobody said, 'on the fourteenth of the month you will have your eyes.' And the subterfuge continued, the pretence that she did not mind and was content to wait. Even Jim, her husband, was now classed in the category of 'them,' the staff of the hospital, and no longer treated as a confidante. (44–45)

Before the operation, Marda's loving relationship with Jim ensured that, 'every qualm and apprehension had been admitted and shared' but that was 'long ago' (45). In her initial fear of being 'helpless and maimed' she clung to him but though the fear of blindness remains, it is the nurses who reassure, while Jim is distanced 'for no known reason' (45). Marda is having an operation that she does not understand, and may not need, and she is thus already vulnerable and bedridden as the 'helpless object of the medical gaze.'[21] Jim's warm voice is less valued than the 'calm, comfortable voice' of Nurse Brand, an aural panacea which convinces Marda West that 'she could not lie' (45). This phrase repeats a line from 'The Doll' [1928], another story in which one woman's physical pose symbolises truthfulness for the other characters. In both stories physical position and veracity are interconnected in lexical choices and the agency of female characters through which lying down is equated to lying.

Small details of atmosphere and dialogue foreshadow impending trauma and the first two pages place the protagonist firmly within the context of deceit, both practised upon her, and by her. The surgeon states, '[w]e would not lie to you Mrs West,' and Marda continues her own subterfuge by pretending that she does not mind the uncertainty of her fate (44). Gender is a vital component of the plot, as the female body is now under scrutiny, it is lacking and broken, and it is ready to be 'fixed' by the male mechanics of the body, doctors. As Grosz states,

> Sex is not merely a contingent, isolated, or minor variation of an underlying humanity. It is not trivial to one's social and political status in a way in which it is conceivable that eye color is: it is integral to the status and social position of the subject. [. . .] ones sex makes a difference to *every* function, biological, social, cultural, if not in their operations than certainly in significance.[22]

The disruption of the natural order within this text—patriarchal, marital, economic—says as much about Marda West's artful ignorance about herself, as it does her lack of insight regarding others. Caught up in the cultural complexities of the relationship between physical sight and truth, she literally cannot believe her eyes.

In an unpublished letter to Garth Lean, Du Maurier outlines her thoughts on the connection between ill-health and psychological and emotional anxiety. Lean was a friend and member of the Moral Rearmament Association (MRA), an evangelised Christian group with which du Maurier had been involved. The personal subtext is her discovery of husband Tommy's infidelity and his subsequent breakdown. 'It's odd, Garth, but it's my old Daphstein thing of the physical malaise showing up the inner distress. When a person feels sick it means there has been something in his life that he can no longer stomach—of which he must rid himself. It's as simple as that. Like my short-sightedness: not being able to see what went on under my nose! [. . .] I will not be gentle to the point of complaisance or "shutting eyes" which I see now was my fearful mistake.'[23] Not facing up to the truth is a personal crusade for the author, and it has broader implications as can be seen in the variety of self-deception practised by characters in the short fiction, and her corpus in general.

In this story the reader vicariously experiences the disempowered isolation of a patient, and the first introduction of Marda's husband positions him among the group of medical practitioners whose words articulate comfort, but cannot be trusted. The reader never knows exactly why Marda West has to have the operation that she describes in a curious choice of words as a 'miracle upon the membranes and the tissues which were her *living eyes*' (46, my italics), the adjective highlighting how blind eyes are dead eyes.

Marda's auditory sensitivity is superseded when her bandages are removed and a frightening new vision of hybridised womanhood in beast-human form presents itself.

> Yet, incongruous, absurd, the head with the uniformed cap was not a woman's head at all. The thing bearing down upon her was a cow . . . a cow on a woman's body. The frilled cap was perched upon wide horns. The eyes were large and gentle, but cow's eyes, the nostrils broad and humid, and the way she stood there, breathing, was the way a cow stood placidly in pasture, taking the day as it came, contented, unmoved. (52)

Everyone around Marda West now has theriomorphic heads, defined in the *OED* as, 'Having the form of a beast; also transf. of or pertaining to a deity worshipped in the form of a beast.'[24] The animal variants are consonant with the personality of the lower body that remains physically human. The sinister adder and vulture are respectively her night nurse, Nurse Ansel, and her husband; surgeons are dependable dogs and the rest of the nursing staff are a variety of other animals. At first Marda West thinks it is a practical joke, then later surmises that the animal heads are masks, until finally deciding that it is a conspiracy. In this narrative the reader only 'sees' through the eyes of a person with serious vision impairment: is this paranoia or insight?

Du Maurier uses mythic symbols in her fiction and Marda West has acquired second sight in a literary tradition linking her to the Delphic Sybil Cassandra and Tiresias. Scholar of myths Marina Warner, describes how the Sibyl 'fulfils a certain function in thinking about forbidden, forgotten, buried, even secret matters' and her myth resonates as much about listening and believing, as talking: "[b]y my voice shall I be known."'[25] Echoing the goddess Hera's vengeful transformation of Tiresias into a woman, Marda's 'gift' of sight is also accompanied by dramatic physical change. Yet, the gift parallels Cassandra's as she sees the inner ugliness of grotesque hybrids that she, and others, would prefer to ignore. No other character sees what she sees and no one confirms her vision as accurate. Marda's repeated attempts to communicate her perceptions are dismissed by authority in the guise of the nurses, the surgeons and her husband. The plot is also in dialogue with D. H. Lawrence's 'The Blind Man' [1922], in which Maurice Pervin's blindness imbues him with an instinctiveness and an earthy sensualism that makes him closer to animals than people.[26] Again, authenticity is under discussion. Here, du Maurier's treatment of sensory deprivation makes it clear that blindness is a different matter depending on the gender of the afflicted individual. Lawrence's character of Maurice Pervin is sensualised and animalistic, his blindness does not equate to castration whereas Marda West is physically disempowered yet psychically gifted. While she fears dependency her inner sight offers the possibility of freedom through revelation, undisclosed light as understanding. It is worth noting in passing that while there are no direct references to Lawrence's work in du Maurier's accessible letters, the authors are linked in discussions concerning gender in middlebrow literature.[27]

In his history of cultural attitudes towards the lack of sight, Wheatley says that in medieval Christianity blindness was a 'religiously constructed disability as a spiritually pathological site of absence of the divine.' In this model, blindness can be the Christian punishment for sin, or it can be restored by Jesus' healing which places it as a catalyst for 'divine intervention and miraculous cure.'[28] There is the sense that the disabled or blind person has somehow been chosen by God for spiritual testing and therefore they function as a site for miraculous healing, thus demonstrating God's temporal power in a biological context. Marda's test is clear but her response is not, the open-ended narrative elides a definitive conclusion and du Maurier challenges her readers to discern their own blind areas.

Blindness as bodily incompleteness also evokes associations with psychic potential as in the west the removal of physical sight traditionally enables second sight. Wheatley states that a person's sight did not belong to them in medieval England, much as Marda West's eyes belong more to her husband and her doctors than they do to her. 'Blindness as punishment very concretely demonstrates that in medieval society a person's *sight* did not entirely belong to him either.' Marda West submits to a risky eye operation at the insistence of male authority figures for unstated reasons in events that occur before the story begins. To lose her eyesight would be to lose her autonomy of movement, her financial control, and her independence. It is unclear whether her doctors are curing her blindness or causing it. Wheatley outlines how blinding as punishment was habitually carried out by Norman colonisers of Britain and, as such, the disability was read by the English at one time as 'evidence of admirable political resistance rather than criminal activity.' From this perspective Marda West is a subversive agent whose blindness is lawfully sanctioned violence carried out by the legitimate authority of her husband and male doctors.

The focus of du Maurier's narratives is always the less attractive aspects of the human condition and this story pierces the thin veneer of civilisation to reveal our primal, and putatively unattractive lower selves. Her animals are never cute and fluffy as illustrated by other short stories, for example the inexplicable avian aggression in 'The Birds,' and cygnine family violence in 'The Old Man.' 'The Chamois' conflates sexual predation with an animal hunt, and 'The Lordly Ones' is a Swiftian-style critique celebrating the equine parenting of a human child. 'The Blue Lenses' can be read as a textual variant relating to Ovid's *Metamorphosis*, Aesop's fables, and Circe's enchantment of Odysseus' men in chapter 10 of Homer's *The Odyssey,* where the sailors' porcine behaviour is matched by the pigs they become. Ovid's work is dated to the first century B.C., Aesop's fables to the sixth century B.C., and *The Odyssey* to the eighth century B.C. In parallel with modernist writers Hilda Doolittle and Virginia Woolf, du Maurier engages with the oldest texts of the Western canon. In one sense 'The Blue Lenses' follows Aesop's cautionary tales but in du Maurier's reworking of the genre—no moral is offered. Now, the boundaries of change have blurred so far as to include the alteration of humans into hybrids resembling the centaurs and satyrs of Dionysian troupes, inter-species mongrels whose composition predicts genetic chaos. The diversity of animals mentioned in the text indicates a mutability that Warner identifies as informing the heterodox and the dangerous. 'Bird, amphibian, lizard, serpent, the diabolical mutates into many guises, perhaps because a lingering platonic correlation between beauty and form influences Christian images of the monstrous.'[29] Certainly the choice of animals to characters is pertinent, and renders a powerful commentary on control and dominion.

Christina Bacchilega's observations on postmodern fairy tales note the inclusion of the metamorphic tradition.

> The encounter of beast and beauty, human and other, woman and man is enacted in every room: as the masks peeled off in one scenario are refracted differently in another, suspicion lingers but the dynamics shift. [. . .] Shifting and slippery forms in themselves convey that chaos is evil, and, in the Judeo-Christian tradition, sexuality offered the principal site of danger.[30]

The heterosexual union is the 'site of principal danger' here, human faces disguise while bestial ones reveal nightmarish clues suppressed under the medical cant offered by authority. The text abounds with the terminology of physical sight and truthful comprehension, and plays with the ironies and inconsistencies between the two, Marda's 'new found sight and knowledge' is corrected by the 'proper lenses,' which, while re-presenting the human as human, also render her prey for carnivores and carrion eaters. Her totem animal of a nervous deer clearly positions her as a potential sacrifice for husband Jim and co-conspirator Nurse Anselm, whose realm is the night watch, the most vulnerable time for patients.

As the plot develops Marda West realises that she is the only person to see things accurately in a world which cannot, or will not, recognise what she sees as authentic. There is no evidence that other characters see the animal-headed humans and this suggests they are mental projections from her unconscious mind. Phil Mollon usefully lists the ways in which people flee from facing emotional truths. Among what he calls the 'mechanisms for defence' are repression, projection, rationalisation, splitting, and manic defences. In the lexicon of psychoanalysis projection is the unconscious transfer of desire or emotion onto another person, or thing, and it is one of the defence mechanisms used by the brain when faced with a reality that is impossible to bear.[31] This suggests Nietzsche's inversion of the idea of a cure for disability using the grounds that 'the social ostracisation of the blind, [. . .] shields them from the horrific sights of human atrocity.'[32] In considering Marda's lived experience as perceived by her unconscious mind, Freud's observation that, 'the unconscious pays no regard to external reality but represents internal psychical reality' appears accurate. To Marda West, whose metaphorical blindness to her marital situation is now literal, the horrific 'hallucinations are perceived as real' and would be better not to see them.[33] Since there are hints that Jim and Nurse Ansel have engaged in illicit behaviour, Marda is now directly confronted with facts she may previously have chosen to ignore. Her bald choice is whether to be predator or prey.

'The Blue Lenses' privileges motifs of altered perception and modes of sight both literal and symbolic. Abi-Ezzi posits that du Maurier's life and writing are identified by a 'rejection of the prevailing social order,' citing E. T. A. Hoffmann's story 'The Sandman' and arguing that an individual's perspective, or imaginary life alters their 'reality.' Although Abi-Ezzi claims that when du Maurier's 'inner, or imaginary, world comes into play' it only 'distorts the real,' 'The Blue Lenses' offers a clearer and more candid vision of the actual.[34] However, it is true that Marda's mental and emotional state is a catalyst for isolation and madness, and another step towards the full dependency on husband Jim and Nurse Ansel that the text implies is potentially fatal. Du Maurier's fiction does not offer a simple reading of binary constructs but rather delivers an ambiguous tension between the real and the imaginary. David Punter challenges dichotomous interpretations of plots that hold this tension: 'Gothic vision is in fact an accurate account of life, of the ways we project our fantasies onto the world and then stand back in horror when we see them come to life.'[35] As a seer, Marda now has comprehension beyond that of ordinary mortals, and the medical establishment's denial of her vision is a metaphorical refusal to look at life from another perspective: something du Maurier constantly compels her readers to do.

Marda tries to piece together the events that led her to the operation and her convalescence, but after five weeks her memories of arriving at the hospital are now vague. The traditional fairy-tale plot positions the heroine as about to be disinherited by the powers of evil, and she must change her fate using only her courage and her wits. 'It was a strange thought how memories of coming into the nursing-home were now blunted. The staff who received her were dim shadows, the room assigned to her, where she still lay, like a wooden box built only to entrap.' (46) Marda is aware of the dangers of her situation: the 'wooden box' symbolises a coffin for a woman with dead eyes. She spends weeks wondering whether she will ever see again and the un-bandaging is the culmination of a lengthy period lying in the 'anonymity of darkness,' with nothing to do but reflect upon her own helplessness. Despite the success of the operation, the semantic field remains one of deceit and danger: 'trap,' 'entrap,' 'subterfuge,' 'lie,' 'maimed,' 'helpless' (44–45), and later the blunt confirmation of the subtext in the word 'conspiracy' (71).

The morbid imagery of imprisonment and death indicates Marda's unconscious recognition that her present vulnerability may lead to further powerlessness. Her role as patient is foregrounded, and her helplessness is heightened by the lack of sight which makes her dependent on the nurses for everything. To be a patient is to be infantilised; the individual's mental state is subject to the authoritative pronouncements of carers and family members, and liberty is therefore predicated upon the judgement and the interests of others. Wheatley separates the condition of blindness from the lived experience of the condition, commenting on the 'distinction made in disability studies between impairment and disability: impairment is the particular physical condition (in this case visual impairment), while disability is constituted by the restrictive social and political practices that construct the environment of a person with an impairment.'[36]

Marda seeks constant reassurance from the nursing team and medical experts. There is a tender, loving relationship between her and the night nurse, an intimacy demonstrated by Nurse Ansel's anticipation of her patient's needs. This emphasises the power of the carer to give, or to withhold, kindness and attention. Marda is increasingly referred to as 'the patient' as the narrative progresses. As she loses her name—her personal referent—she begins to lose her individuality and her autonomy, her power to shape events, her mental stability, and lastly her judgement. This echoes the handling of the character of Mrs Ellis in 'Split Second' (see chapter 2), another text highlighting du Maurier's concern with the presence and absence of personal monikers. It is unclear whether the character of 'Mrs Ellis' is accurately designated or is someone else entirely. In this story it is questionable whether there is more agency for Marda in the initial role of wife, or the later role of patient.

Like most humans, Marda West is attached to her illusions and does not let go of them easily. It takes two operations to do so: one to reveal her dangerous predicament and one to replace the fiction that has enabled her to live with it. As sole signatory on a trust fund her medical predicament and consequent vulnerability has far reaching implications. Is Jim an adulterer conniving to steal her money on legitimate grounds? Or is he a loving and supportive husband, even to the point of signing legal and financial documents for his blind wife? In du Maurier's exploration of altered perception every person has a darker side, thus it is doctors who 'steal eyes,' nurses who steal husbands, and all hitherto trusted people have secret desires and motivations. 'The voice that once seemed so tender was over-smooth and false. How deceptive are ears, thought Marda West, what traitors to truth. And for the first time she became aware of her own latent power, the power to tell truth from falsehood, good from evil.' (74)

Marda's seduction by Nurse Ansel's 'soft, beguiling voice' is halted by the sight of her through the blue lenses which reveal her snake's head: '[d]ear, comforting, bewitching Nurse Ansel. [. . .] Was she also in on the conspiracy?' (62). Voices remain a vital component of this story about sight indicating another level of complexity concerning the veracity of what we see versus what we hear. Each time Marda cannot bear to look she closes her eyes and listens instead to the comforting lies of whichever voice is talking to her. The 'looking glass' of fairy tale is mentioned in passing early in the story, as Marda checks her reflection for the animal's head she fully expects to be wearing but does not see in the mirror. It is also the final object handled by the protagonist at the end when she looks at her reflection and sees herself clearly for the first time. Both times Marda is watching herself closely for visual clues as to her animal self, and thus to knowledge of her true nature. Freud refers to the delusion of being watched as the most striking symptom of paranoia. He defines the scopophilic gaze as, 'taking other people as objects and subjecting them to a controlling and curious gaze.'[37] Nurse Ansel is first seen in its reflection, 'grotesque and horrible,' and her forked tongue and hooded eye connote deception with particular regard to the serpent in the Garden of Eden (63). Yet Marda now recognises her ability to differentiate between benign and dangerous characters and for the first time she feels powerful, but is she powerful enough to make choices? 'It slid slowly into view, the long snake's head, the twisting neck, the pointed barbed tongue swiftly thrusting and swiftly withdrawn, it came into view over her shoulders, through the looking-glass. [. . .] Marda West could see people as they really were. And those whom she had loved and trusted most were in truth a vulture and a snake. . . .' (63–74).

Marda is an Alice-in-Wonderland figure: things in the mirror are reversed and the distortion of normal referents confuses her. While Hoffmann's tale concentrates on wholeness and fragmentation within an individual, Nathaniel, 'The Blue Lenses' is a meditation on self-knowledge, and the gradual maturing of a protagonist towards potential autonomy.[38] In this open-ended text du Maurier characteristically leaves the reader to decide which path Marda West will choose: to protect her autonomy and her independence from Jim and Nurse Ansel, or to remain passive as her life is subsumed into theirs.

Following an attempt to escape the nursing home, Marda's lenses are replaced with a new set. Both sets of lenses provide valuable information about character and motivation, and the difference between what is true and what is false. The isolation and powerlessness of the central character becomes ever more apparent as du Maurier heightens the suspense and compels the reader to 'see' other people as Marda does. In this story the reader's experience of reading the story mirrors the experience undergone by the lead character as we first encounter other characters as voices before their animal heads are revealed. The first set of lenses reveal personality traits, for example the surgeon is a dependable Scottish dog and the matron is a sheep-like follower; the second set indicates Marda herself as a subject lacking agency regarding her own care, home, or money.

Douane refers to this mode as 'the emergence and disappearance of female subjectivity, the articulation of an "I" which is subsequently negated.'[39] For du Maurier the childless or childlike woman is a recurrent motif and Marda plays the child to her husband's patriarch, immediately calling him for reassurance when the lenses are wrong. But Jim's time has economic value and 'she knew from the tone of his voice that he was busy, very busy, and she had chosen the worst time to ring him up' (60). Instead of prioritising her needs during a crisis, she blames herself for picking the wrong time to call, and by taking responsibility she acknowledges that her needs are subservient to his and reifies her role as victim. Her subservient status is shown by her inner life: 'The utter hopelessness of her position was like damnation itself. This was her hell. She was quite alone, coldly conscious of the hatred and cruelty around her.' (71)

Although Marda feels her emotional dependence as a wife and practical dependence as a patient, she is economically independent and the private nursing home—and we suspect the West's lifestyle—is paid for by a trust fund that is only in her name; an issue that Jim will shortly attempt to rectify with legal 'safeguards' giving him co-director's status, a move he frames as recommended by a team of lawyers. Marda controls the couple's money, thus making Jim financially dependent, which challenges the traditions of patriarchy. As the breadwinner in the Browning household, du Maurier was well versed in this aspect of sexual politics and the scene between unequal marital partners reads convincingly. The backstory of Jim pressuring Marda to make him co-signatory appears more sinister when his animal totem manifests as a vulture complete with bloody beak; a beak with which he immediately kisses her. Chillingly Marda can feel that, '[t]he vulture's beak was sharp' (68).

> The door opened, the familiar umbrella and bowler hat the first objects to appear round the corner, then the comforting burly figure, but—God . . . no . . . please God, not Jim too, not Jim, forced into a mask, forced into an organisation of devils, of liars . . . Jim had a vulture's head. She could not mistake it. The brooding eye, the blood-tipped beak, the flabby folds of flesh. (68)

The ridiculousness of his transformation evokes a temptation to laugh but in fact only one physical aspect, here the beak, differs from the description of a middle-aged city gent. The comedic possibilities of the alteration of the human body to a beast links most obviously to the character of Bottom and the ass's ears in *A Midsummer Night's Dream* and here again, the silly and the serious are entwined in an analysis of power. Marda's predicament is a play on the way that 'bodies construct and in turn are constructed by an interior, a psychical and signifying view-point, a consciousness or perspective.'[40] Despite the strong parallels with Body Gothic, this story is only one illustration of du Maurier as a non-gothic author, and one in which she invites the reader to share the joke while they gasp in shock. Reyes states that Body Gothic texts follow the way '[t]he gothic often relies on the grotesque, which, as opposed to the carnivalesque, is unredeemed by laughter, and often uses mutilation in conjunction with images of bodies that have been modified and no longer appear strictly human.'[41] While there are modified bodies in this story, the increasingly ludic situation invites laughter and horror as Jim's character expresses mirth: 'He laughed. And turning to the sound, she saw the beak open. It gaped like a trap, and then closed again' (70). Marda's fixation on the beak is explained by the nature of the bird's predation. The vulture is a creature that menaces the defenceless and weak: the vulnerable are circled as they lie dying long before the final swoop in for the kill. Jim's hunched shoulders in the business suit evoke large, feathered wings and the vulture's as carrion-eater suggests the avarice necessary for success in business.

> If she kept her eyes averted she need not see the vulture's head. The voice was Jim's, steady and reassuring.
>
> 'The trust fund papers Forbes and Millwall gave me. They suggest I should become a co-director of the fund.'
>
> The words struck a chord, a thread of memory belonging to the weeks before her operation. Something to do with her eyes. If the operation was not successful she would have difficulty signing her name.
>
> 'What for?' she asked, her voice unsteady. 'After all, it is my money.'
>
> He laughed. [. . .]
>
> 'Of course it is,' he said. 'That's not the point. The point is that I should be able to sign for you, if you should be ill, or away.' (70)

Each time Marda sees her transformed husband, or now-sinister nurse, she turns away, closes her eyes and uses their voices to take her back to a time before she saw them clearly. This tactic fails when she harbours suspicions regarding Jim's motivation for becoming a co-signatory on her trust fund on the doubtful basis that she may be 'ill or away' (70). These sinister implications are reinforced when Marda suspects that vulture and snake, ergo Jim and Nurse Ansel, are sexually intimate and mistrusts a convalescence plan involving Nurse Ansel staying at the West residence. Nurse Ansel is transformed from trusted friend into deceitful serpent.

> Now, watching the smooth snake whose adder's V was hidden beneath the nurse's cap, she knew why nurse Ansel wanted to return with her, and she knew too why Jim had not opposed it, why in fact he had accepted the plan at once, had declared it a good one.
>
> The vulture opened its blood-stained beak. 'Don't say you two have fallen out?' (70)

Marda's sense of being cared for is now replaced with fear for her safety: 'Yes, but once at home, once back there, with a vulture and a snake, would she not be more completely at their mercy than she was here?' (71). Even Jim's habit of paring his nails is now laden with significance and, interpreted through his hybridised form it becomes threatening as Marda knows 'a vulture need[s] sharp claws for tearing its victim (71). In her weakness she fails to cancel the convalescence plan which will leave her at the mercy of the human-animal hybrids. During her foiled escape attempt she expresses her terror at the unintelligible and unarticulated language of animals in a dystopian vision in which 'the world was theirs, there was no human left.'

> The bodies changing too, hands and feet becoming wings, claws, hoofs, paws, with no touch of humanity left to the people about her. The last thing to go would be the human voice. When the human voice went, there would be no hope. The jungle would take over, multitudinous sounds and screams coming from a hundred throats. (70)

Marda West wakes to find that new—and permanent—lenses have been fitted. The bandages are removed and there are no masks, medical or animal. 'Where are your masks?' asks the patient with consummate irony. For if the animal heads were motivation unmasked, then perhaps a human resemblance is the true mask. Likewise, it is the words and the voices that bely hidden motivations of greed, lust, violence. Now there are no visual clues to human character Marda's cognitive blindness is restored.

Humans are creatures romanced by their visual sense. Sight is our dominant mode of understanding the world and anything that masks, blinds, distorts, or disguises, destabilises us beyond measure. 'Normal' sight is restored to the female protagonist at the denouement. Human bodies have human heads, perception is reordered according to accepted norms and the visual aberration is eliminated forever. But if this is Gothic horror's 'gradual transition from the marvellous to the uncanny—the history [. . .] is one of progressive internalisation and recognition of fears as generated by the self.'[42] Thus, the final scene of this self-referential story is when Marda looks into a mirror only to see the reflection of a doe with large eyes and a head lowered 'as if for sacrifice' (82). This illustrates Abi-Ezzi's comment on du Maurier's world as 'the bifurcation of existence into a world of outer tangible reality and one of inner subjectivity.'[43]

Du Maurier's short stories display an insistent return to the presence and absence of body parts, a return that encourages reflection on the broader meaning of corporeality. This is highlighted by Grosz who states:

> [T]he body provides a point of mediation between what is perceived as purely internal and accessible only to the subject and what is external and publicly observable, a point from which to rethink the opposition between the inside and the outside, the private and the public, the self and other, and all the other binary pairs associated with the mind/ body opposition.[44]

The Gothic mode is induced in this story of monstrous sight and it is notable that latter-day Gothic has taken up residence within the self and the monsters are now self-induced rather than external and 'real.' As we see in 'Split Second' and will see in 'The Apple Tree' there can be no escape from these demons as they are self-created and self-inhabiting. It is only when Marda's blue lenses are changed and the 'pressing nerve' is relieved by the surgeon that she sees her inner self revealed, neck 'already bowed' (82).

Kelly is right when he states that this is a text that 'acknowledges the workings of the unconscious mind,'[45] and Marda's lesson is that the timid and the meek are destined to serve the interests of the powerful and the strong. Marda's situation invites the application of Thomson's work on freakery whereby '[e]nfreakment emerges from cultural rituals that stylise, silence, differentiate, and distance the persons whose bodies the freak-hunters [. . .] colonise,' represented in this story by medicalisation and the blurring of a 'freak of nature' into a 'freak of culture.'[46] The fairy-tale looking-glass delivers unpleasant news and Marda receives confirmation of her victimhood in a loaded visual metaphor. Douane interprets this as '[t]he ever-present sense of being on display for the gaze of a judgemental other is symptomatic of another condition within our culture — that of femininity.' This connects to Douane's work on female spectatorship in film, including du Maurier's *Rebecca* in which '[p]aranoia is the appropriate and logical obsession. For it effects a confusion between subjectivity and objectivity, between the internal and the external, thus disallowing the gap which separates the spectator from the image of his/her desire.'[47]

In 'The Blue Lenses' du Maurier centralises the visual, which we can only 'see' through her description and the eyes of the narrator, thus couching a visual spectacle in a 'non-visual textual medium.'[48] This plays with the tropes of myth and fairy tale and is an inversion of the motif in which the queen asks the mirror for confirmation of her supreme beauty only to find that another is more beautiful. Marda's reflection shows her as a victim incapable of escaping sacrifice. Warner's comments on postmodern fairy tales resonate in any discussion of du Maurier's shorter fiction, for these are disturbing fables that reinstate the mythic element. In this analysis the stories 'are themselves magical shape-shifters, dancing to the needs of their audience.'[49]

Du Maurier's preoccupation with human and animal shapeshifting goes hand in hand with the ambiguous handling of morality and this accords with moral philosopher Mary Midgeley and Gilles Deleuze's view that 'the beast is utterly incapable of bestiality.'[50] Derrida's words neatly summarise this stance: '[b]y contrast, no animal is capable of *bêtise*, just as no animal is capable of a beastly act, that is to say, of wilful cruelty or hair-raising perversion. The beastly and the asinine, the base and the brutal, are qualities or modes of behaviour proper to a ratiocinative humankind [. . .] *bêtise* [. . .] is in fact the truth of the human condition.' Krell considers Derrida's final seminar 'The Beast and the Sovereign' in which the philosopher defines the act of separation between humankind and animals as one which signifies 'bêtise' as the 'very authenticity of humankind.' For Krell, '[i]t is the presumption of humanity that troubles Derrida principally.' Thus, the artificial separation of human and animal into discrete categories is destabilised and du Maurier shows how the animal is beast but not bestial. Her narratives carefully reserve that aspect for human behaviour. This story uses animals to signify corporeal and psychological harmony whereby the synthesis of outer image with inner corruption illustrates the moral degeneration so evident in Europe in the post-war years.

In 'The Blue Lenses' animals are used as vehicles for truth, and this reinforces Lacan's view that the animal, unlike the human 'can never feign to feign, can never pretend to be merely pretending, and can therefore never properly prevaricate and deceive, never erase its traces and dissemble, which is something that the human being [. . .] can do exceedingly well' (16–17). Du Maurier employs specific animals to illustrate particular traits, for example the vulture which cannot escape its nature and must behave like a carrion-eater to survive. In Lacanian terms she 'affirms the classical Cartesian distinction between the fixed animal reaction and the flexible human response,' whereby 'the animal merely *reacts*, never *responds*.'[51] The ambiguity of the ending leaves small hope that Jim *may* shed his vulture tendencies and Marda *may* finally escape her fate as his victim.

Du Maurier's heroines pursue escape and freedom with a fervent desire that speaks to Patricia Duncker's theory of 'motifs of entrapment.'[52] When her female protagonists find themselves within confining parameters they often find ways of eluding them and achieving fulfilment. However, this text offers no clues as to whether Marda does, or does not, escape from the path laid out for her by the putative conspirators. This drama of visual aberrations and bodily metamorphosis is contextualised by social institutions and economic realities. It supports the argument that, '[b]odies are always sexually specific, necessarily interlocked with racial, cultural, and class particularities.'[53] The human trait of transposing evil onto the Other is utilised in this story to create the mirror into which, like Marda West, we do not wish to look. Marda's rebellion within the text is brief and the end of the story finds her silently gazing at a theriomorphic reflection she cannot identify with, forced back into an image of herself as victim, by which she may be finally, and fatally, framed. The story rewards a close reading and the ending takes the reader back to the somatic issue which kickstarted the plot. Du Maurier's delight in unexpected endings is clear in an unpublished letter to friend and fellow author A. L. Rowse, where she comments on Kipling: 'I loved the story of 'The Gardener,' that subtle touch at the end which really came as a complete surprise, so that one had to turn back to the beginning—I love doing that in a story.'[54] An examination of endings in these texts shows authorial patterning in the small touches of the unexpected in the final lines and another example is the next story under examination, 'The Lordly Ones' (see 'The Little Photographer,' 'The Alibi').

'The Blue Lenses' illustrates entrapment and freedom for female protagonists proves elusive. Marda West enacts a silent response to trauma that continues in the third story under analysis, 'The Lordly Ones.' This narrative focuses on the tongue and the inability to speak out against oppression in a culture which privileges vocal (self) expression. A child protagonist exemplifies the vulnerability of the voiceless and symbolises the marginalised masses whose stories remain untold. Authority figures abuse power, and violence is regularly carried out on the bodies of the powerless. Continuing the theme of trauma mapped on the human anatomy 'The Lordly Ones' infers Elaine Scarry's study on pain by showing how '[torture] bestows visibility on the structure and enormity of what is usually private and incommunicable, contained within the boundaries of the sufferer's body.'[55]

NOTES

1. Arnold Arluke and Boria Sax, 'The Nazi Treatment of Animals and People' in *Reinventing Biology: Respect for Life and the Creation of Knowledge,* ed. by Lynda I. A. Birke and Ruth Hubbard (Bloomington: Indiana University Press, 1995). p. 253.
2. Reyes, p. 18, p. 27.
3. Henderson, p. 26.
4. Mary Ellen Bellanca, 'The Monstrosity of Predation in Daphne du Maurier's "The Birds" in *Interdisciplinary Studies in Literature and Environment* 18:1 (Winter 2011) p. 26–46, p. 28.
5. Horner and Zlosnik, p. 76.
6. Du Maurier letter to Leo Walmesley, 26 May 1933 (p. 2–6) EUL MS 206, courtesy of Special Collections.
7. *Alfred Hitchcock's Mystery Magazine*, 40: 9 (September 1995) ed. by Cathleen Jordan (Dell Magazines). All subsequent references are to *The Breaking Point* (London: Virago, 2009).
8. Sceats and Cunningham, p. 83.
9. May, Introduction, *The New Short Story Theories*, p. xvii.
10. Albert C. Baugh 'The Middle English Period 1100–1500,' *A Literary History of England* 2nd edn (London: Routledge, 1967), p. 161.

11. Kelly, p. 137.

12. Henderson, p.18, p. 33.

13. Reyes, p. 4.

14. Midgley, 'Animals and the Problem of Evil,' *Beast and Man* (London: Routledge, 1995) p. 24–42, and Haraway, p. 7–20.

15. Midgely, p. 24, p. 26.

16. Jacques Derrida, section 2: 'Blindness,' 'Memoirs of the Blind: The Self-portrait and Other Ruins,' quoted in *A Companion to Derrida,* ed. by Zeynep Direk and Leonard Lawlor (Chichester: Blackwell, 2014), p. 12.

17. Derrida, 'Introduction', *The Animal That Therefore I Am* quoted in David Farrell Krell, *Derrida and Our Animal Others: Derrida's Final Seminar, "The Beast and The Sovereign"* (Bloomington: Indiana University Press, 2013), p. 3.

18. Du Maurier letter to Maureen Baker-Munton, 4 July 1957. Cited in Forster, pp. 420–25 (p. 424).

19. Du Maurier letter to Phyllis Bottome, 6 June 1959. P. 70. Vol. 30. (ff.201).1. ff 1–33, courtesy of The British Library.

20. Edward Wheatley, 'Medieval Constructions of Blindness in France and England' in *The Disability Studies Reader*, ed. by Lennard J. Davis, 3rd edn. (New York: Routledge, 2010), p. 63–76 (p. 65).

21. Mary Ann Doane, *The Desire to Desire: The Woman's Films of the 1940s* (Bloomington: Indiana University Press, 1987), p. 174.

22. Grosz, p. 22.

23. Du Maurier letter to Garth Lean, 29 October 1957, p. 2. .EUL MS Add 5, courtesy of Special Collections.

24. *OED* 2nd edn, on CD ROM, version 4.0.

25. Marina Warner, 'In the Cave of the Enchantress *From the Beast to the Blonde: On Fairy Tales and Their Tellers* (London: Vintage, 1995), p. 11.

26. Lawrence, *England My England and Other Stories* ([n.p] Erik Publications, 2015), p. 53–73.

27. Christoph Ehland and Cornelia Wächter eds. Introduction, *Middlebrow and Gender, 1890–1945* (Lieden: Brill, 2016), p. 6.

28. Wheatley, p. 64–71.

29. Warner, p. 125.

30. Christina Bacchilega, *Postmodern Fairy Tales* (Philadelphia: University of Pennsylvania,1999), p. 141.

31. Mollon, pp. 14–15.

32. Friedrich Nietzsche, 'Montaigne's "Infinities of Formes,"' *Thus Spake Zarathustra* and Nietzsche's 'Higher Men"' in *Narrative Prosthesis: Disability and the Dependencies of Discourse* ed. by David T. Mitchell and Sharon L. Snyder (Ann Arbor: University of Michigan Press, 2002), p. 81.

33. Mollon, p. 37.

34. Nathalie Abi-Ezzi, 'An Analysis of the Treatment of the Double in the Work of Robert Louis Stevenson, Wilkie Collins and Daphne du Maurier,' (unpublished doctoral thesis, King's College, University of London, 2000), p. 2. p. 42. Also sourced at collectionbooks.net [accessed 17.11.21].

35. David Punter quoted in Abi-Ezzi, p. 58.

36. Wheatley, p. 63.

37. Laura Mulvey, 'Visual Pleasure and Narrative Cinema' in *Film Theory and Criticism : Introductory Readings*. ed. by Leo Braudy and Marshall Cohen (New York: Oxford University Press, 1999), p. 833–44 (p. 385).

38. Hoffmann, p. 85–127.

39. Douane, p. 174.

40. Grosz, p. 8.

41. Reyes, p. 4.

42. Rosemary Jackson, *Fantasy: The Literature of Subversion* (London, Methuen, 1981), p. 34.

43. Abi-Ezzi, p. 47.

44. Grosz, p. 20–21.

45. Kelly, p. 123.

46. Thomson, p. 10.

47. Douane, p.126, p.174.

48. Mitchell and Snyder, p. 53.

49. Warner, p. xx.

50. Gilles Deleuze quoted in Krell, p. 19.

51. Lacan quoted in Krell, p. 16, p. 18, p. 86, p. 87, p. 169.

52. Patricia Duncker, 'Re-Imagining the Fairy Tale: Angela Carter's Bloody Chambers' in *Literature and History* 10 (1984), 3–14.

53. Grosz, p. 19.

54. Du Maurier letter to A. L. Rowse, 25 September 1967. MS 113/ 3/ D, courtesy of the British Library.

55. Scarry, 'The Structure of Torture: The Conversion of Real Pain into the Fiction of Power' in *The Body in Pain*, pp. 27– 59 (p. 27).

Chapter Four

'The Lordly Ones' [tongue] (1959)

'The Lordly Ones' is the second story from *The Breaking Point* [1959], the 'new stories' du Maurier named after 'the moment in the life of every individual when reality must be faced.' First editions have the distinctive Gollancz yellow dust-jacket and the quotation comes from her introductory 'Note,' positioned before the first story at p. 9. 'Note: There comes a moment in the life of every individual when reality must be faced. When this happens, it is as though a link between emotion and reason is stretched to the limit of endurance, and sometimes snaps. In this collection of stories, men, women, children and a nation are brought to the breaking-point. Whether the link survives or snaps, the reader must judge for himself.' The challenge for the reader is to judge how characters deal with the crisis and whether epiphanies and self-knowledge are attained after reaching the 'limit of endurance.'[1] By centralising heightened perception, 'The Lordly Ones' particularises the public's way of viewing the difference between pre-war idyll and post-war reality, a process contextualised by the experience of a peace that in some ways felt harder than the war. As shown in the last chapter, Marda West's altered vision reflects new and unpalatable truths: a pertinent theme for a nation of readers aghast at increasing reports of wartime barbarity. Here, the legitimacy of sanctioned brutality is questioned in 'The Lordly Ones,' a story in which parental violence leaves physical marks on a child's body signifying an abrupt end to childhood innocence. This echoes another story, 'The Pool' [1959] in which the near drowning of the protagonist signifies her crossing from childhood to physical maturity by violently traversing the threshold state of female puberty. 'Terror' is an early unpublished story following a similar theme concerning childhood fears. To the protagonist, Bridget, the terror(s) are real and present, her imagination fleshes them out and clothes them with definite aspects of claws, and long black hair, and hunchbacks. As in 'The Lordly Ones,' at the denouement and for most of the story, the child is left to deal with her fears and her imagination alone.[2]

The child protagonist is disabled with a congenital condition called tongue-tie that inhibits speech. *Black's Medical Dictionary* describes it as a physical problem whereby, 'the band beneath the middle of the tongue uniting it to the floor of the mouth is either so short, or attached so far forwards, that the tongue cannot be fully protruded from the mouth, and cannot move with the freedom required for speech,' adding that it is 'responsible for childish defects of speech but is more rare than is commonly supposed.' As highlighted in the two previous stories under analysis, this corpus contralizes incorporates the lame, the blind, the disfigured and the mute, not to simply foreground physical ailments but rather social and psychological impairment. Mitchell and Snyder's critical study of disability outlines how when impaired characters are foregrounded in literary narratives they serve to 'exemplif[y] the literary oscillation between micro and macro levels of metaphorical meaning supplied by disability.'[3] And Thomson goes further, arguing that '[b]y challenging the boundaries of the human and the coherence of what seemed to be the natural world, monstrous bodies appeared as sublime, merging the terrible with the wonderful, equalising repulsion with attraction.' In this story the reader is vicariously silenced and this fits with Reyes notion of Body Gothic whereby '[m]orbid curiosity [. . .] charts our interest in forms of violence and radical alterity that are attractive precisely because they often lie outside the remit of our direct experience.'[4] In this reading du Maurier's stories are like a medieval 'Wonder Book,' a collection of marvels and physicalities inviting the reader into experiences of 'awe, delight, terror.'[5] Though avant-garde elements are present in the open-endedness and brutal themes of the texts, the union of the natural and the human world links them to our earliest written texts.

Ben is the child focalizer whose desire for comfort and certainty is found in the company of a herd of horses who offer a haven from the inexplicable adult behavior of his parents. His fears of sudden brutality reflect broader cultural anxieties about the future in a nuclear age and Ben's search for peace and beauty has the higher aim of fairness and justice—the 'symmetry of everyone's relations to each other.' Scary cites John Rawl's definition of 'fairness' in her argument on 'beauty as "fairness" and justice as "fairness."'[6] Rawls is clear on people's singular and collective duty to reinforce what he defines as 'just' arrangements where they do exist and the human responsibility to create them where they do not. In this text of asymmetrical power dynamics, Ben's attempts to correct misunderstandings with truth and compensate marginalised groups fail. His perception of beauty is united with the 'conviction that equality is at the heart of beauty, that equality is pleasure-bearing, and that [. . .] equality is the morally highest and best feature of the world.'[7] In attributing this view to a child, du Maurier is at her provocative best, rejecting human relationships in favour of equine ones, and producing cultural polemic in the tradition of Swiftian satire.

As seen in 'The Blue Lenses,' the combining of animal with human protagonists is a favourite satirical weapon in du Maurier's arsenal. In the post–Second World War period emerging news of concentration camp atrocities raised the question of what constituted uncivilized, inhumane, and bestial behavior: themes that permeate other stories in du Maurier's corpus. Other examples include The Old Man' [1952], 'The Chamois' [1959], and 'The Breakthrough' [1971]. The family in 'The Old Man' (*The Apple Tree*, 1952) is used to illustrate an example of violent homicide and it is only in the dramatic denouement that the reader discovers the 'family' is a sounder of swans. That tale of parental abuse ends in filicide but like Ben's ideal equine family in 'The Lordly Ones,' the fact that the other family are horses is hidden until the denouement. Grosz's study outlines in detail how the body is positioned culturally is a major aspect of these narratives, and her insights provide a useful segue into the story. 'As an organism, the body is a more complex version of other kinds of organic ensembles. It cannot be qualitatively distinguished from other organisms: its physiology poses general questions similar to those raised by animal physiology. The body's sensations, activities and processes become "lower-order" natural or animal phenomena.'[8] The animal families in these two stories serve as a warning and a pattern respectively. However, unlike the plots of 'The Blue Lenses' and 'The Old Man,' here the metamorphosis from boy to foal is a positive blending of human/ animal characteristics where the noblest of traits—sensitivity, loving care, protectiveness—are firmly designated as animal, while the unnatural, unnecessary violent acts, are human.

Of the eight stories in *The Breaking Point* this, the last, is the shortest at sixteen pages, and here, in the words of Mitchell and Snyder, '[l]iterature borrows the potency of the lure of difference that a socially stigmatised condition provides.'[9] This is the only narrative in du Maurier's published corpus of shorter fiction with an infant as focalizer, albeit one who is focalizer not vocaliser. Ben is an only child, with parents whose guilty frustration over having a mute son blights their family life. Ben is also the name of a simpleminded character in *Rebecca* (London: Gollancz, 1938), who knows more about the events of Rebecca's death than the supposedly 'right-minded' wife murderer. Du Maurier revisits the character with the mute, rebellious boy in her novel *Rule Britannia* (London: Virago, 2004 [1972]), this time specifying blithe age and ethnicity. 'Ben was sitting in the far corner of the room on an upturned chamber pot to serve as stool. [. . .] He was ebony black and beautiful, and looked less than his three years. It was not only because of his colour that Mad had adopted him but because, so the authorities told her, there was something amiss with his tongue, he might never learn to speak. He rolled delighted eyes at Emma as she entered, held up two fingers, a gesture taught him by Terry.' (5) Once again, du Maurier displays difference as the harbinger of unexpected gifts of insight and understanding.

The narrative offers views of the impairment from the adult and the child perspectives and challenges Aristotle's argument that 'anyone who does not take after his parents is in a way a monstrosity.'[10] Du Maurier's fascination with the monstrous body is a theme that runs through her fiction from her earliest stories which portray bodies that are congenitally lacking, deformed, or marred by dramatic events. The device is designed to elicit discomfiture in the reader, an aesthetic nervousness that Ato Quayson defines as 'the interaction between a disabled and a non-disabled character, where a variety of tensions may be identified.'[11] This is especially apparent in another early unpublished story, 'Lundy,' which centralises a child who is physically out of scale, mentally impaired and of uncertain gender.

> Lundy's parents were dull, ignorant folk, with no imagination, but when their child began to grow they were shunned by people, and looked upon with horror as the creators of a monstrosity. [. . .] Poor sexless thing, huge of limb and daft of mind [. . .] Lundy the outcast, Nature's freak. The child was of abnormal size, but pitifully weak and fretful. [. . .] She was noted in the parish register as a girl: it was not until later that her parents realised what they had brought into the world. [12]

The story follows the character of Lundy through the experience of difference as an outcast from family and community, suggesting that it is not her physical condition that is grotesque but rather the reactions of others to her. The 'Lundy' text is antecedent to 'The Lordly Ones' but the two decades between the genesis of the stories indicates du Maurier's lifelong fascination with disfigurement, social exclusion, and the human form of ambiguous construction.

In a refinement of the terms of the debate Tom Shakespeare's exploration of social constructs distinguishes impairment from disability: '[t]he former is individual and private, the latter is structural and public. [. . .] Like gender, disability is a culturally and historically specific phenomenon, not a universal or unchanging essence.'[13] To apply the point to this story, Ben's impairment is as invisible as it is unspoken and relegated to the private wherever possible. 'The Lordly Ones,' then, is a story that plays on personal and communal attitudes towards physical difference, the curiosity of strangers and parental shame is played out against the backdrop of Ben's unspoken desire for the loving protection of a close family. Ben is an embarrassment to his parents and he is largely screened from public view. Like Mrs Ellis in 'Split Second' he is at risk of being permanently put away, whereas disabled characters such as Lundy and M. Paul in 'The Little Photographer' are exposed to public ridicule. Du Maurier's employment of disability and impairment as a literary device aligns with Mitchell and Snyder's theoretical literary model in which 'disability pervades literary narrative, first as a stock feature of characterisation and, second, as an opportunistic metaphorical device.' They define narrative prosthesis as 'perpetual discursive dependency upon disability.'[14] 'The Lordly Ones' illustrates how du Maurier's stories continually return to the trope of disability, using it to explore and expose inequalities of gender, power, family, and diverse aspects of cultural norms.

Ben's inarticulate vulnerability illustrates how 'metaphor and reality structure each other synergistically'; as a powerless minor he has no say in determining where, or how, he lives and his tied tongue is the literal symbol of his metaphorical situation. Wheatley states that '[i]n contrast to the social model, the medical model constructs disability as a deficit or a pathology that requires correction or cure,' and the reader swiftly learns that Ben's condition will eventually result in a trip to hospital where 'something could be done' (273).[15] Without the facility of human speech Ben is a dumb animal and is treated as such by his parents. His muteness is felt by them as an undeserved punishment from God 'Why must [my] son be dumb?' demands Ben's father even as he expresses his frustration by savagely beating him (280). In her analysis of corporeal feminism Grosz explains how '[w]ithin Christian doctrine, it is as an experiencing, suffering, passionate being that generic man exists [. . .] moral characteristics were given to various physiological disorders and that is why punishments and rewards for one's soul are administered through corporeal pleasures and punishments.'[16] The confrontation between Ben's lived experience and the culturally sanctioned fairy tale of all children having loving parents, makes 'The Lordly Ones' an illustration of how, '[w]ithin literary narratives, disability serves as an interruptive force that confronts cultural truisms,' and, that 'the interpretation of representations of disability strikes at the very core of cultural definitions and values.'[17] In du Maurier's short stories blindness, lameness, and mutism through biological flaw are all physical manifestations of a broader spiritual and cultural disease. How the disabled are treated is a measure of how far a given society is just, equitable, kind, and fair.

The first line is laden with latent meaning. 'Ben was thought to be backward' raises the question of who thought him to be backward—presumably his parents—and also implicitly declares that this thought is incorrect, and that this thought is no longer open to correction (273). The events of this past-tense story precipitate the change in how Ben is perceived. As readers we are also given insights into Ben's capabilities that characters in the story are not: we gradually learn that he is able to understand facial expressions and tones of voice and fully comprehend the communication and social order of a group of horses. The ability to read facial expressions establishes that Ben is not limited by a number of developmental conditions that are often diagnosed in childhood. However, 'He could not speak. When he tried to form words sounds came, harsh and ugly, and he did not know what to do with his tongue' (273). This description of a character struggling to articulate his own truth and instead producing 'harsh and ugly' communication, perfectly fits du Maurier's gallery of grotesques. Among the questions raised by the story is that of who is the more grotesque—the vocal but emotionally inadequate parents, or the tongue-tied and sensitive child. In her authorial 'Note,' du Maurier challenges us to reconsider the breaking point of vital human connections, but carefully evades responsibility by determining that: '[w]hether the link survives or snaps, the reader must judge for himself' (7).

Survival is core in 'The Lordly Ones,' where permanently pre-verbal Ben dwells in a world of bewildering adult behavior; his condition silences him and he is treated as an object rather than a speaking subject. Thus, he cannot graduate from infancy to adulthood, and being out of the conversation means he is, effectively, outside of the human family. 'Because of his silence they forgot to explain things to him, arrivals and departures and changes of plan, and his world was made up of whims, the whims of older people. He would be told to dress for no reason, or to go out into the street and play; or some toy was denied him that he had been given an hour before.' (273) The description invites the reader back into the experience of being a child subject to adult rules, where power and choice are often denied, and motivations incomprehensible. The actions resulting from the frustration of the inarticulate powerless Ben seem inevitable.

Disability or impairment is commonly characterised by the individual's experience of it rather than as a state that affects everyone in the community. Ben's parents are mortified by his inability to speak and violently react to the inarticulate 'noise' he makes: strangers are curious, pitying or dismissive. Again, the plot of 'The Lordly Ones' echoes that of 'Lundy' where the parents experience shame and punish their offspring for what they perceive as a necessary and enforced seclusion from the community:

> It was in this atmosphere of sullen shame that Lundy lived, neglected by a father and mother who considered their child as a bar to their happiness, shutting them off from the rest of the world. [. . .] The creature was very tall, nearly six feet high, with huge bones and an awkward ambling gait. her hands were of an abnormal size [. . .] and brown, with curious blunt-shaped fingers. Her head was set on a massive pair of shoulders, bent in a perpetual stoop. There was nothing remarkable in her solid, heavy face except her eyes. They were brown and very gentle, the eyes of a hunted deer. [18]

Lundy is an isolated figure, shunned and rejected by those most capable of supporting her. The mention of 'the eyes of a hunted deer' serves as an implicit link to 'The Blue Lenses' where the temporarily blinded character of Marda West is finally confronted with the reflection of herself as an animal with 'doe's eyes, wary before sacrifice.' Like Ben, Lundy has little facility for speech, and du Maurier uses free indirect speech to convey, at least partially, the lived experience of the characters. Thus the reader too is positioned as vicariously marginalised, expelled from the community and doomed to live an existence impaired by physical limitation, a limitation that enforces separation from the human family and the community. This is an uncomfortable experience fortunately confined for most readers to the duration of the story.

A child is made from genetic material from parental bodies and thus for parents to harm or reject the child is in one sense to reject their own selves. Grosz suggests the necessity for difference to demarcate the limits of the known, and, the difficulty in parenting a child singled out by a negatively perceived physical difference.

> Fascination with the monstrous is testimony to our tenuous hold on the image of perfection. The freak confirms the viewer as bounded, belonging to a 'proper' social category. The viewer's horror lies in the recognition that this monstrous being is at the heart of his or her own identity, for it is all that must be ejected or abjected from self-image to make the bounded, category-obeying self-possible.[19]

Mitchell and Snyder comment that although 'we are trained to compartmentalise impairment as an isolated and individual condition of existence [. . .] disability provides an important barometer by which to assess shifting values and norms imposed upon the body.'[20] In 'The Lordly Ones,' as in 'Lundy,' the human facility for verbal expression is a fundamental aspect of du Maurier's critique of proper social institutions such as marriage, the family, and the state. These are shown to offer no protection for those exhibiting difference, instead rejecting the vulnerable who suffer a downward trajectory towards violence and imprisonment. This is the fate of both Ben and Lundy who as children with impairments are among the most defenceless in society.

This is further illustrated by the child's lack of human sounds. There are few clues to Ben's age, for example he 'dressed slowly, not yet accustomed to doing it quite alone' (282). Although his age is unspecified he is treated as an infant, ignored, ordered about, and continually denied toys, attention, and importance. Ben's feelings of vulnerability and fear lead to frustration and when this is unbearable, 'he opened his mouth and the sound that came out of it alarmed him even more than it alarmed his parents. Why did it rise? How did it come?' (273) His powerlessness is vented in rage expressed in 'alarming' animalistic noises that he feels come from outside of him: '[t]he noise would not be quelled. It did not belong to him.' The noise Ben makes from the back of his throat is always described as if it is something exterior as 'the sound,' a living entity that will eventually 'die away.' He does not see 'the sound' as a part of him, or as something he can control, but acknowledges to himself that its eruptive power cannot be denied: 'The anger was a force that had to have its way' (273). This is echoed in a subsequent scene where his father's fury is expressed in pitiless ferocity on Ben's small body. Du Maurier contrasts Ben's wrathful cry with the uncontrolled rage felt by his father as he beats him. Both cry and beating are fuelled by frustration but Ben utters 'the sound' out of stress—the stress of inexplicable commands, adult whims, and the knowledge of draconian punishments to follow. When he utters the cry his parents panic and violent chastisement follows: a hard smack, a shove, or a beating. Often, Ben's animal cries are punished by incarceration in the under-stairs cupboard where he fears he will be forgotten by his mother. Although he is sensitive to parental moods, continual appeasement is impossible and he is always in trouble. 'The way to ensure against their anger was to please his parents, but this could not always be done, for the strain was too great. In the middle of play, absorbed, he forgot their commands' (273–74).

The lexical choices are redolent of dictatorial anger and violence, and the inscrutability of adult behavior to young children and vice versa. Like her literary heroine Katherine Mansfield, du Maurier gives the reader a child's eye view of adult inadequacy and invites judgement on the abuse of power in an unequal relationship. The character of Kezia in 'Prelude' (see *Bliss and Other Stories*), is one example of Mansfield's preoccupation with marginal perspectives on normative social behavior. Du Maurier admired and emulated this focus in her own short fiction. In a continuation of free indirect thought du Maurier privileges Ben's worldview by establishing his opinion of his parents' volatility, quietly undermining assumptions of adult behavior as intrinsically rational. The story foregrounds the linguistic anxiety that lies at the core of post-structuralist thought, emphasising Ben's life outside of social discourse and his need to identify and name things for himself, to 'make' his world. The horses are the signifier of family and home, a disruptive force that explodes the nature/ nurture binary of structuralist thought. Thus, the title of the story is the title Ben gives to the horses, a term only expressed in his thoughts and one which both defines and constitutes them as lordly, with all the noble connotations of power and grace. 'They were all of one company, these moors, not the band of brothers he had imagined, but a family, a tribe, belonging one to the other. He would never leave them, the lordly ones.' (285) Tragically, it is in identifying the horses as semi-divine beings deserving of his gifts and affection, and awarding them with an appellation equivalent to their importance, that Ben comes to suffer the loss of the thing he most desires: a loving family. Du Maurier delays the reader's realisation that they are a fraternity of horses, not gypsies, in a manner akin to the plot twist she admired in Rudyard Kipling's story 'The Gardener' [1926].

Ben's parents move the family to Exmoor, 'starting *the* new life' (italics mine). The use of the definite article indicates their limited options and a desperate need to escape the pitying stares of neighbours and strangers. Ben does not understand his parents' behavior and nothing is explained to him, not even moving house: 'cajolery and threats were combined: one day he was to be lucky, another he had better not get out of sight once they moved.' He is used to rough treatment from his parents who habitually 'seize' and 'drag' him, and when he unwisely '[f]orget[s] caution' and defies them on the train journey, his mother 'smack[s] him hard' (274). Corporal punishment from parent to child was unremarkable when this story was written but changes in cultural mores have rendered this unacceptable and the disciplining of children through violence is now prohibited in law (Section 58, Children Act 2004, UK). The mother's shove coincides with the entry of the train into a tunnel which evokes the darkness of the locked cupboard. When he makes 'the sound' in fear it makes his mother shout, go red, and remove him from the carriage and the curious stares of passengers.

The lack of communication in the family is contrasted with the horses who seem to easily comprehend Ben's guttural noises. His utterances allow him to ask to feed from the mare and he and the foal are constantly 'calling to one another' as they play (286). When the mare hears Ben cry with pain from the beating she slows her walk in apparent empathy. In the night Ben spends with the horses, the two stallions fight and as the pretender triumphs, Ben sees a 'time of anger, and stamping feet and strangled sobs' that echoes the earlier episode on the train where violence is the only human communication. 'Rage and fear made him stamp his feet [. . .] The sound coming from his belly ceased; only the gasp for breath, the stifling sobs, told him that the pain was with him, but for what reason he could not tell.' (275) Like any vulnerable creature Ben's survival depends on his ability to gauge the behavior of dominant animals, consequently he is adept at reading adult faces, tone, and moods. Despite his immaturity and lack of social status his interior voice is the most sophisticated in the story and it delivers complex thoughts in precise language. Ben's cognitive ability belies his pre-verbal state and in parallel with the idealised horse family it also challenges assumptions and conflations about who is civilised and who is inhumane.

This silenced and abused boy initially appears to be a victim of fate, a boy Philomela, the nightingale figure from Greek myth as told by Ovid whose tongue was removed to keep her tale of abuse from being related, like her Ben is unable to save himself or tell his story.[21] Unlike Philomela Ben is not taken to the forest, but to the moors, where, instead of being eaten, he is beaten. His childish response to adult labels leads him to use adult language and define the 'moors' as 'terrible thieves' as he tries to understand a world that is, inexplicable to him, and unexplained by others. 'So the moors were robbers. A band of robbers wandering by night. Ben remembered the comic paper his father had bought him, with the ogre's face upon the cover. Yet they could not be like that, for the woman was saying something about their fine looks. 'They won't hurt you,' she said, 'they're friendly enough.' This to Ben, who watched her, puzzled.' (277) Like the child, the reader finds the normative roles of expected care and kindness belied by actions, and once again outward appearance and inner values clash together in crisis.

The contrast between the ogre's face on the comic's cover and the description of the fine looks of the moors, parallels Ben's experiences of parental monstrousness in image and demeanour. The lesson for Ben is that while the outside often belies the inside—sometimes things and people *are* exactly what they seem. The foreshadowing violence of the smack on the train, and his mother's hard shove in the car, continue at bedtime in the new house where Ben's parents become ever more monstrous. This occurs at bedtime when, 'his mother helped him to undress, but she was rougher than usual. Her nails got caught in a button and when he whimpered she said sharply, "Oh, be quiet, do." The candle, stuck in a saucer, threw a monster shadow on the ceiling. It flounced his mother's figure to a grotesque shape.' (279) The escalating tension finds outlet in Ben's escape from his family; once again du Maurier reverses expectations, trauma and violence are at home, security and safety are found in unexpected places.

On this evening there is no escape from paternal violence for Ben and here the unpalatable warning—a literary echo from Grimm's 'Hansel and Gretel' and other fairy tales—is that parental love often manifests as cruelty. In 'Hansel and Gretel' children are abandoned by their parents because of a lack of food, the topic is similar here as adult needs have primacy. When the mother returns upstairs, '[s]he threw open the door and stood there, holding the candle, the monstrous shadow behind her. "Did you touch the tea things?" she said' (280). The mother's actual scale is ominously enlarged to indicate her power over the child as frighteningly immense, and this clearly signposts du Maurier's intended reading of parental behavior. The sudden strangeness of the mother in the new setting starts earlier in the narrative as they leave the old house where Ben was born, with her wearing of an 'ugly' hat changing the 'shape of her face': the start of her metamorphosis into the rejecting, aggressive, child-(b)eating mother (274).

Although the family is geographically relocated they do not escape their personal, historical context as determined by Ben's physical condition and supposed backwardness. The parents retain their habitual 'awkward and embarrassed' stance and, on arrival, metamorphose almost immediately into their monstrous selves expressing guilt and rage. The unfairness of the beating is clear in the description as the father 'stumps'— as heavily footed as a fairy-tale ogre and eater of children—into the bedroom, ready to 'hit hard.' It is at this point that, '[d]espair seized Ben. Explanation was beyond him. It would mean a whipping. He began to cry. He heard his father stump up the stairs and come into the room, his shadow monstrous too. The pair of them filled the small, unfamiliar room.' (280) The father speaks in the terminology of power: 'He must know who's master,' but to Ben his 'face was ugly, worn with fatigue.' As power declines into weakness and he gives his son the brutal beating his frustration demands, the father pleads: 'Why must [my] son be dumb?' (280) Ben is helplessly dumb so the phrase '[e]xplanation was beyond him' is a physical fact not a metaphorical statement. He literally cannot explain his motivations to his parents but when he 'makes the noise they knew as a denial,' indicating intelligence and communicative ability—he is ignored anyway (280). As Scarry notes, 'physical pain—unlike any other state of consciousness—has no referential content. It is not *of* or *for* anything. It is precisely because it takes no object that it, more than any other phenomenon, resists objectification in language.'[22] In a sense Ben's wordless protests and his father's inarticulate rage are the same: they are both the expression of a pain that cannot be framed in words.

The mother, a punitive rather than a protective agent, is only concerned at the neighbours overhearing Ben's screams and warns: 'There's neighbours across the green. We don't want trouble' (280). Ben's parents show their power through violence but the horses only use violence as a show of leadership, not as a disciplinary measure for their offspring. The moors show their power benevolently and are like the woman who greets the human family at the new house—she is large, welcoming and maternal, and offers milk to Ben on arrival, as the equine mother does later in the story. The way Ben's parents write out their vengeance on his small body is couched in provocative lexical choices evoking the Old Testament God, Jehovah: 'Eye for eye, tooth for tooth, hand for hand, foot for foot' (Exodus: 21). 'The relentless hand, so large and powerful, *smote and smote* again' (my italics). The use of this verb is startling in Du Maurier's depiction of the physical aspects of family dynamics. The etymology traces the verb back to the Old English word of Danish origin 'smītan' meaning 'to smear, or blemish.' Ben's punishment is an illustration of the displaced emotions of his parents, who feel guilt and rage over their son's disability, and the horrific beating only ends when the father's 'own hand ached with the force of the blows' (280). The first section is saturated with the language of violence and vulnerability, and ends with Ben in pain, facedown on his bed, desirous that 'nothing come.' Scarry outlines the way that bodily suffering demands total attention and removes the sufferer from all other concerns.

'As in dying and death, so in serious pain the claims of the body will utterly nullify the claims of the world.'[23] The casual inclusion of the phrase 'Ben was used to darkness,' is a reminder that this is a child who spends considerable periods of time in a cupboard, subject to parents who cannot govern him, even as they cannot govern themselves (279). The darkness he experiences serves as a metaphor for confusion, emotional absence, and isolation. In essence, it is a living death.

Section 2 of the story covers the rest of the night which Ben spends with the 'lordly ones,' waking to find them outside on the green before the cottage: 'The white night showed him the wonder. The thieves were there, the lordly ones. Not as the woman had described them, but more beautiful. A little group intent upon his offering' (281). Ben identifies the family relationships in terms that are familiar to him, mother, father, brothers, aunt and 'gran.' But unlike his immediate relations, the interactions of the horses are marked by loving kindness. Their inclusion, affection, and fellow feeling comes to represent the light that has been lacking for Ben. The father figure, whom the reader will later come to recognize as the stallion, is 'not angry like Ben's father' he is 'beautiful and wise' and his move away from the food is seen by Ben as him selflessly offering the food to his 'son.' The child recognises the care between fellow creatures and he makes no distinction between human and animal relationships or virtues. Unlike human relationships which are regarded as based almost entirely on verbal communication, their silence is inclusive and suggests to Ben a 'contempt of authority. They made their own laws' (282). This is paralleled by the contempt for the law that Ben has already shown by taking the last of the bread from his human parents as a gift for his new family.

Ben places a feast for the moors on the green before the cottage to prevent them stealing from the cottagers dwelling in the hamlet. He describes this food as 'an offering' and it is here that the 'moors' first become the 'lordly ones,' an aristocratic title bestowed by the child that connotes noble conduct and which positions them highly in his taxonomy: his instinctive version of the Elizabethan concept of the great 'chain of being' whereby the human is the apogee. The 'terrible thieves' become a 'band of brothers powerful and friendly' (277). Clues as to Ben's choice of their chivalric and courtly designation comes in his perception of their qualities of pride, beauty and protectiveness. These qualities date from the introduction of Breton 'lays' by Norman troubadours into English courts centralising the chivalric code of honour, with boys adopting the role of Squires before becoming knights. The feeling of adoration Ben has for the grace and majesty of the horses is in clear contrast to the base motivations of the human family members. In this reading 'The Lordly Ones' is a re-visualisation of the Yahoo/ Houyhnhnm binary in

Jonathan Swift's *Gulliver's Travels* [1726], in which the child envisions an alternative social grouping incorporating care and respect for young and old, an order that separates him from his human family. It also speaks to an earlier story by du Maurier which presents an idealised community: 'Monte Verità' [1952], whose plot presents a mountainous community of androgynous other-worldly beings where cooperative living minus any greed or violence mimics the customs of Ben's peaceful 'Moors.' Like Gulliver, he feels more akin to horses than people as, '[l]ike Ben, they did not speak. They talked by signal' which 'pleased Ben, for it was something he understood and shared with them.' In common with the Houyhnhnm, Ben sees the horses as superior beings who are preferable to 'the parents who did not love him' (283–284), and faced with the evidence, the reader will struggle to disagree.

However, unlike *Gulliver's Travels*, 'The Lordly Ones' is not just satire, it is a critique of parenthood: a vision of despotism without end. This inversion of structures is problematic as it challenges a hierarchy of moral qualities, placing adult, physically able people at the apogee, with children below, and animals at the bottom. In his essay on 'Freaks in Space' Jeffrey A. Weinstock identifies the troubling issue that the apex of evolutionary humanity in science fiction texts is invariably the white male. 'Synonymous with goodness, decency, integrity, ingenuity and compassion, "human" serves not simply as a biological destination, but as a moral marker.'[24] 'The Lordly Ones' confounds reader expectations by departing from predictable patterns of human social grouping to portray the harmonious interactions of a superior group in another species.

Ben's parents ignore or misunderstand his denials and cries of rage as defiance or stubbornness. The boy wants to cuddle the horse mother but he is uncertain about her reaction, 'Would she be angry? Would she push him away?' (285), a reaction derived from previous rejections from his actual mother. His attempt to suckle from the mother (mare) is a cross-species instance of miscegenation. The horse father is protective, a 'guardian' to his sons, the horse mother empathetic, warm and caring, an idealistic maternal figure with whom the boy becomes close: 'Ben closed his eyes, eased by the warmth, the comfort, the tender understanding of the mother and the reassurance of the father, still watching the far hills' (285). The failure of human communication contrasts with the horses whose silent communion is harmonious, only interrupted by the periodic progression from mature stallion leader to youthful challenger—the natural order of progression. Ben regards their customs as strange, but in childlike fashion he adapts fast and makes an intelligent and informed choice about how, and with whom, he wishes to live. Yet, like Gulliver who is eventually expelled from Houyhnhnm society, the choice is not Ben's to make.

It is the reciprocity between the horses and the child that renders the communication striking. To a child there is no difference between animal and human communication—both are language, and both are vital for offspring learning the social rituals necessary for survival in a group of their own kind. Ben recognises the horse whinnies as speaking and murmuring, and his sensitivity to body language, facial expressions and gestures enable him to sufficiently comprehend horse communication: 'The pain made him cry out, and the cry startled the golden mother, who, staring at him, spoke to him. Was she asking him a question? Ben did not understand her language. He thought that the noises in his throat must have told the mother that his back was stiff, for she seemed reassured and slowed her walk to his. Ben was relieved.' (284)

'The Lordly Ones' is an Aristoteleian tragedy that highlights the frequently arbitrary distinctions between the categories of human and animal: verbal/ non-verbal, conscious/ instinctive, moral/ amoral. In this narrative the animals are gracious, generous, inclusive, controlled and predictable. Humans are aggressive, cruel, exclusive, volatile and irrational. Twelve lines before the end of the story Ben finally enjoys emotional security, 'all that mattered was to be warm and sheltered, protected and cherished by the one he loved' (289). With childish simplicity he regards the mare as his mother and the foals as his brothers, accepting a broader family group as including an aunt and gran. Another structural echo occurs as the horses flee from the 'men with sticks' and their unnatural violence, even as Ben has fled from parental tyranny. When he finally speaks it is his first and last utterance, a total, defiant negative against human violence, the 'shouting and yelling' of the angry men which scares the herd of horses away for good. It is only when Ben is at the height of his identification with the equine world that he finally utters one single human word. The mute becomes vocal: '[h]e heard the cry tear his chest and he shouted, 'No . . . no . . . no . . . 'for the first and the *last* time, and he fell face downwards in the snow' (289, italics mine). Ben's utterance is addressed directly to the persecutors, a response which is, to use Mikhail Bakhtin's definition, 'a living rejoinder.'[25] The child makes the word his own as he cries out with intention and expression. Ben's 'No' is a protest against cruel domination and imprisonment in an unjust system.

The final scene epitomises Mitchell and Snyder's 'forward reading of disability as a narrative device upon which the literary writer of open-ended narratives depends for his or her disruptive punch.' The dramatic linguistic articulation renders Ben's previous refusal to communicate a change from a (purported) physical disability into a refusal to engage others in speech. Mitchell and Snyder state that '[b]ecause disability represents that which goes awry in the normalising bodily schema, narratives s[eek] to unravel the riddle of anomaly origins,' and Ben's final utterance raises questions beyond his physical ability to speak.[26] Questions such as, has this child chosen to be silent until a point of desperation when he is finally compelled to make a verbal intervention? As Mikhail Bakhtin comments in his work on dialogism: 'The importance of struggling with another's discourse, its influence in the history of an individual's coming to ideological consciousness, is enormous. One's own discourse and one's own voice [. . .] will sooner or later begin to liberate themselves from the authority of the other's discourse.'[27] Ben only finds his voice in protesting against the behavior of others, and finally speaks when he has something important to say. The story ends without confirmation that his ability to speak is permanent or simply one defiant cry against injustice. This open-ended narrative 'not only deploy[s] but explicitly foreground[s] the "play" of multiple meanings as an effect of [its] discursive production.'[28] Ben may be choosing to remain mute rather than join a discourse he rejects as totalitarian, ignorant and unjust. The tragedy is that while his trajectory as protagonist involves learning and development, the aggression his father exhibits towards the horses suggest that his parents remain as ignorant as they were before events in the story.

'The Lordly Ones' develops the theme of inter-species comparisons that subject heteronormative patterns to close scrutiny, and which was first mooted in 'The Blue Lenses.' It is also evident in several other stories such as 'The Birds,' 'The Old Man, and 'The Chamois.' The animal kingdom is mined for metaphors that symbolise the elements necessary for a discussion of the most disconcerting of human actions. In this way du Maurier indicates a world of reality beyond the information the senses provide, what Roehberger calls 'potentiality' versus 'actuality.'[29] Roehberger's theory applies to this story as Ben is successful in finding a surrogate family that accepts him but this is denied by human laws that determine a child's place as with its biological human parents. His search for love ends on the moors, where he finds a family which accepts him as one of their own but staying with them is impossible. The difficulty of finding an adequate sign to communicate this complexity has led du Maurier to use the allegory to communicate her vision—these are stories born out of pain that must be articulated differently. Mitchell and Snyder's work on 'narrative prosthesis' designates this as demonstrating the 'arbitrariness of linguistic sign systems as a characterising feature of their plots and commentaries.'[30] Du Maurier articulates what the boy cannot, through challenging reading, and the purpose of this study is to take those thoughts, like Ben, out of the cupboard so they can be 'heard.'

In 'The Lordly Ones' du Maurier foregrounds the consciousness of a child in a salute to Katherine Mansfield whose short stories were a lifelong influence. Mansfield's novella 'Prelude' [1922] also starts with a house move that has a major effect on each character. The text echoes Mansfield's technique of free indirect speech indicating the significance of Ben's body as the site of contested power. His muteness has a symbolic as well as a narrative function and the thrust of the story is his interior life rather than the house move with which the narrative begins. The family unit, with particular focus on the bodies of those within it, are the canvas for du Maurier's exploration of domination, brutality and escape, aspects of national life brought to the level of the individual and exposed to scrutiny. Her private observation to close friend Leo Walmesley in 1958 encapsulates this mode: 'I think one has to bring suffering into the family circle to experience it in full intensity, however selfish this may seem.'[31]

This portrayal of the love and brutality of family life parallels the issues surrounding du Maurier in the post-war years.[32] Tommy 'Boy' Browning's mental and physical scars surfaced early on in the marriage and du Maurier regularly had to comfort the 'sobbing creature' who awoke from nightmares of his war service experience in two world wars. Forster writes that du Maurier 'preserved intact the facade of contentment' of a happy marriage but the private nickname of 'Moper' she gave her husband suggests he was not the 'utterly self-reliant war hero' du Maurier thought she had married. What Patrick Macgrath calls the 'reverse anthropomorphism' of this story draws attention to human artifice and one family's doomed attempts to conceal shame and ugliness.[33] As a mute, Ben is a thinker who cannot communicate his interpretation of events unless the author reveals his thoughts. Unlike Gulliver, he is not gulled into loving the horses; du Maurier mocks the narrow-minded thinking of adults, not the open-heartedness of the child. Parental aggression against a child is only justified in as much as the killings in other stories are justified (see 'Kiss Me Again, Stranger' and 'The Little Photographer'). Du Maurier consistently problematizes ideologies that justify violence and the *breaking point* of this story is helpless inarticulacy in the face of a brutal regime. Ben's epiphanic moment comes when he finds his voice and can finally protest. However, in typically mordant du Maurier fashion 'The Lordly Ones' leaves the reader with a final unanswered question: if Ben does talk, will he be heard? The short fiction presents epiphanies whose cruel timing often combines a character's realisation with limited, or doomed, potential for change. Ben said 'No' for 'the last time' (289).

Having read Gollancz on the nuclear deterrent in *The Devil's Repertoire* (1958), du Maurier responds: 'What then is the ultimate answer to fear? Love of course but how does one show it to the greatest effect?' This polemic is subtitled *Nuclear Bombing and the Life of Man,* and du Maurier's 'shocked' response is framed in a letter full of concerns over totalitarianism and indoctrination in European countries: 'by all means fight the idea of doing away with the H. bomb, and indeed every other bomb, but attack at the same time evil ideas of indoctrination from whatever source they should spring. Like you, I get fed up with any patting on the back and chitter about the "free world"—the U.S.A. is not free because they are so terribly tied to ideal plumbing and making more money than anyone else'[34]

The next chapter takes us to the area of the human genitals, literally and symbolically. Here du Maurier exemplifies Conrich and Sedgwick's observation that '[t]he gendered human exhibits anatomical differences across the sexes which Gothic fiction exploits.'[35] The violence in 'Monte Verità' intensifies the corporal punishment initiated in 'The Lordly Ones' until the body is fatally wounded. This chapter reconsiders lives that were broken during the war in the post-war period, how human beauty and peril are aligned, and how the body, that 'most contracted of spaces, the small circle of living matter' is the unlikely site for a cosmic contestation of morality.[36]

NOTES

1. Du Maurier, *The Breaking Point* (London, Virago, 2009). All further references are to this edition.
2. Unpaginated Notebook, EUL MS 144/1/1/1, courtesy of Special Collections.
3. Mitchell and Snyder, p. 62.
4. Reyes, p. 13.
5. Thomson, p. 3.
6. Scarry, part two: 'On Beauty and Being Fair,' in *On Beauty and Being Just,* p. 93, 115. See also, John Rawls, *A Theory of Justice* (Cambridge: Harvard University Press, 1971), section14, 'Fair Equality and Pure Procedure,' pp. 83–84.
7. Scarry, *On Beauty and Being Just,* p. 98.
8. Grosz, *Volatile Bodies,* p. 8.
9. Mitchell and Snyder, p. 55.
10. Aristotle, fourth book of *Generation of Animals* quoted in Marie-Helene Huet, *Monstrous Imagination* (Cambridge, MA: Harvard University Press, 1993), p. 3–4 (p. 33).
11. Ato Quayson, 'Aesthetic Nervousness,' *The Disability Studies Reader,* pp. 254–65.
12. Du Maurier. EUL MS 144/1/1/1 pp. 4–7, courtesy of Special Collections.
13. Tom Shakespeare, 'The Social Model of Disability,' *The Disability Studies Reader*, pp. 266–73 (p. 268).
14. Mitchell and Snyder, p. 47.
15. Wheatley, p. 64, p. 67.
16. Grosz, *Volatile Bodies*, p. 6.
17. Mitchell and Snyder, p. 48–52.

18. Du Maurier, 'Lundy,' p. 4–19 (of the story), EUL MS 144/1/1/1, courtesy of Special Collections.

19. Grosz, 'Intolerable Ambiguity: Freaks as / at the Limit' in *Freakery: Cultural Spectacles of the Extraordinary Body*, p. 55–68 (p. 65).

20. Mitchell and Snyder, p. 51.

21. Ovid, pp. 134–42.

22. Scarry, *The Body in Pain,* p. 5.

23. Scarry, *On Beauty and Being Just*, p. 33.

24. Weinstock, p. 335.

25. Mikhail Bakhtin, *The Dialogic Imagination: Four Essays* (Austin: University of Texas Press, 1992), p. 294.

26. Mitchell and Snyder, pp. 49–59.

27. Bakhtin, *The Bakhtin Reader* ed. by Pam Morris (New York: Routledge, 1994), p. 79.

28. Mitchell and Snyder, p. 48.

29. Roehberger, p. 6.

30. Mitchell and Snyder, p. 48.

31. Du Maurier letter, 29 April. EUL MS 207/6/4/1, courtesy of Special Collections.

32. Forster, p. 216.

33. Patrick Macgrath, Introduction, *Don't Look Now and Other Stories* (London: Folio Society, 2007), p. xiii.

34. Du Maurier letter, 19 October. (pp. 2–3), MSS.157/3/I/DM/1–43. Courtesy of The Modern Records Centre, University of Warwick.

35. Conrich and Sedgwick, p.1.

36. Scarry, *The Body in Pain,* p. 22–23.

Chapter Five

'Monte Verità' [breasts / yoni] (1952)

'Monte Verità' is the first story in *The Apple Tree: a short novel and several long stories by Daphne du Maurier* [1952]. First published in hardback the original story order is: 'Monte Verità,' 'The Birds,' 'The Apple Tree,' 'The Little Photographer,' 'Kiss Me Again, Stranger,' 'The Old Man.' In the somatic model of analysis the story symbolically embodies the female genitals and mammaries in a plot in which the feminised landscape is a body encountered only through the physical demands of mountaineering. Significantly, it is not a story about sex, although the central symbols are the breasts and yoni, or vulva. *Black's Medical Dictionary* defines these body parts as 'Mammalia, found in the most highly developed class of animals and used for the purpose of suckling the young,' and the vagina as the 'front passage leading from the exterior to the womb.' The actual genitals of the characters within the story apparently remain unused: Anna, the main character, has a husband and a would-be lover in his best friend, but she eschews the fleshly delights of penis and vulva in favour of entry into, and ultimately rule over, a monastic community in the mountains. She does not indulge either of the men or herself, but instead ascends the mountain, literally and metaphorically, to discern and act out her vocation in asceticism, androgyny, and celibacy. Once this is achieved, she is fulfilled and has 'everything' she needs, and is undeterred by a visible illness, the leprosy that ravages her face and body. The full sentence reads: 'And [Anna] smiled back at him, saying she had everything, within those walls, that she would ever need.' (74)[1] One of the things she does not need is a husband, and another is a lover. Leprosy reveals the true face of the female protagonist, Anna, just as her would-be lover chooses to see it as a transfiguration into a mask of ugliness that hides her beauty. Here, the mask of femininity hides the inner self of the female and it is only when it is gone that she can be her authentic self. Conrich and Sedgwich call this allowing the wearer to 'transcend their humanity.'[2]

Like 'The Alibi' story discussed in the next chapter, du Maurier's approach to the body in this story illustrates an absence. Anna's abstinence and asceticism are a comment on the use of the body as a point of entry through which the pious may access the divine or esoteric in world religions; this is evoked as a paradox, wherein the body is at once essential to the processes of piety and also disregarded, diseased, and androgyne. Isobel Armstrong outlines how '[B]eauty belongs to the zone of the genitals because, from the eighteenth century on, the Beautiful was emphatically gendered. [. . .] Women, weak, passive, melting, belong to the genital zone because they arouse sexual feeling, not because they experience it.'[3] The gyno-geography and apparent heteronormative romance plot belie the subtext which indicates a rejection of physical love. The female protagonist is strong, active, obdurate, the direct opposite of Armstrong's associative list for the genital zone. Anna is also potentially a double for du Maurier's own frustrations with the socially sanctioned limitations for women in her time.

This plot revolves around a relationship triangle, a favourite trope of du Maurier's stories and a notable feature of her novels. The plot of *Rebecca* [1938] has two women and one man, and that of *My Cousin Rachel* [1951] has two men and one woman. Once again romance is a disguise as this text centralises how 'bodily practice inform[s] piety and serve[s] as an index of religious formation,' the climax of the plot is spiritual and not carnal.[4] In this story only Anna achieves the summit; indicating an inward journey towards heaven through self-knowledge, as she (a woman) is the only one to successfully navigate the feminised mountains and inaccessible crevices of Monte Verità. The physical signs of femaleness and beauty are reconstituted as androgyne strength as their cultural purpose (heterosexual attraction and procreation) becomes redundant. As Anna becomes closer to the spiritual mystery on the heights of the Mountain of Truth, her beauty falls away and she becomes an androgyne priestess like the other disciples. As a lone climber, she attains gnosis through a self-fulfilling lesbian or masturbatory exploration that fully subverts the colonial image of the male adventurer so central to texts of the 1880s such as Henry Rider Haggard's *She* [1887].[5] The questing adventurer role is represented by the two male characters who fail in both their quest to retain Anna, and to scale Monte Verità for themselves.

In this nested narrative a seventy-year-old man relates the discovery, and subsequent disappearance, of a utopian community sited atop Monte Verità—the Mountain of Truth. The mountain range is located in an unspecified country but was probably based on twentieth-century artistic havens such as the one in Ascona, Switzerland. Du Maurier may have been aware of the community at Ascona, famed for being a 'social organisation based on the co-operative system and through which they strove to achieve the emancipation of women, self-criticism, new ways of cultivating mind and spirit and the unity of body and soul.'[6] The narrator describes events in flashback which cover a forty-year period in his life following his boyhood friendship with Victor, their university years, how they climbed together, and loved the same woman. Although both had the chance neither could hold back Anna whose desire to find the 'peace that passeth all understanding' supersedes any earthly ties (Philippians 4:7). As the story unfolds it is clear that Anna is not regarded with any accuracy by either of the men who claim to love her, although the feminine exterior of her body is prized, the inner self is disregarded and finally eludes a heteronormative union.

The reader learns that the young men first climbed in 'the idyllic days before the First World War' (44), and Victor and Anna's later climbing trip takes place in summer 1913 with temporal clues such as, 'the *Titanic* tragedy still fresh in memory' (54), and mention of The Great War soon to come. Then there is a time shift to post World War Two when the narrator's plane crashes near Monte Verità. He discovers Victor dying, waiting in vain for Anna, and ascends the mountain in search of the truth. He finds Anna diseased but religiously ecstatic. As an outsider to the mountaintop community he is incapable of accessing the source of her joy. The story ends inconclusively with 'nothing more is known,' inviting the reader to find their own solution to the conundrum of Monte Verità. The feminised landscape of crevasses and mountainous peaks suggests the dislocation and dismemberment of desire, and links to Julie Wosk's thesis that, '[t]he women that men manufacture are often articulated creatures, assemblages of disparate parts.'[7] The character of Anna is more the creation of male desires than a living, breathing woman.

The germ of the story came on a trip to the mountains which du Maurier took with friend and explorer Clara Vyvyan and is framed in her comments to friend Peter Howard. 'I shall be off on one of my crazy expeditions in Europe, on my way to climb Mount Olympus. I don't suppose for a moment I shall even get to the foot of it, but I have a new thing about the Greek gods and goddesses and mythology in general, so if you suddenly hear I have been turned into a laurel bush like my namesake don't be altogether surprised.'[8] Vyvyan describes how 'Daphne went off on her own sometimes, exploring, and would return 'in a mood of mountain ecstasy.' Like the main characters in the story du Maurier was exhilarated by the mountains and the travelogue details how Vyvyan 'could feel that Daphne . . . was separated from her everyday self by a new sense of freedom.'[9] 'Swinging along the paths she unzipped the skirt and walked in shorts, then in villages she zipped it back up—"she was feminine . . . [then] on the yonder side up rolled the skirt and she strode forward like a boy."'

Writing to fellow author Oriel Malet, du Maurier expressed the need to find, 'a way of looking at mountains even if I don't climb them. And I am sure I must get that out of my system, the feeling of being near mountains [. . .] But now I think I shan't get my Monte Verità story right until I have been out there. There are twenty pages to do, and it seems Fate I should go out, and then write the last twenty pages afterwards.'[10] There is something keenly direct concerning freedom in the author's unpublished correspondence, supported by Vyvyan's comments on her behaviour and dress during the mountain trip.

'Monte Verità' invites associations with the remote and venerable monasteries at Mount Athos in Greece: they are exclusively male self-governed communities, many of which have remained woman-free since the Byzantine period. As Grosz observes: '[t]here will always remain a kind of outsiderness or alienness of the experiences and lived reality of each sex for the other. Men [. . .] can never feel or experience what it is like to be, to live, as women.'[11] As an experienced and experimental writer, du Maurier swaps the genders and the exclusively male retreat becomes an androgynous realm where traditional femininity is replaced with physical and spiritual strength, self-sufficiency, and a beauty that is non-gender specific. In a letter to Gollancz she hints at her desire for peace and solitude, to the extent of wishing for a Monte Verità for herself: 'being a woman with a family I can't very well do a T. E. Lawrence and lose identity, however much I would like to do so.'[12] In the 1950s Du Maurier continually refers to religion in her letters and this is reflected in 'Monte Verità'and her concurrently written novel, *The Scapegoat* [1957]. 'I confess that churches & a set creed & long prayers would never comfort me, & I suppose some people would say I was an atheist, but I'm not exactly that. I sincerely believe the world is in a state of evolution, and so is everybody in it. Also I think the idea of reincarnation has a lot in it, As for Heaven and Hell and all that rot, it's absurd. Everyone, sooner or later gets punished for their sins, in their own lives, but not by the way priests tell one.'[13] 'I am all *for* The True Faith actually, if people must be brought up to date, though personally the Cretan mother Goddess and her Son, and Horus, mean just the same thing—it's only the development of a universal instinct.'

Du Maurier wanted to stay at a women-only retreat asking Oriel Malet to research one at a monastery she visited in France: 'after Sarthe we *did* visit l'Abbeye de la Grande Trappe [. . .] and I thought you and I must go there some time and find a little hotel nearby.'[14] La Grande Trappe is a monastery in Soligny-la-Trappe, Orne, France, and the home of the Order of Cistercians of the Strict Observance. The retreat was originally founded as a small chapel dedicated to the Virgin Mary in 1122, which links to another story combining the sacred and the profane. 'La Sainte-Vierge' foregrounds the character of Marie, a Breton housewife, who is misled twice, once by her handsome adulterous husband, and then by her faith in a false spiritual vision. Entrapment, imprisonment and freedom are themes that run throughout the corpus, variously seen somatically, psychologically and geographically. Throughout her life du Maurier's desire for the peace and solitude to write competes with her duties as wife and mother. She celebrated her solitude to think, write and create: 'It's all great fun—the sheer selfish joy of living alone and being dependent on no one, as I imagine you relish as well as me!' Du Maurier's escape to Cornwall where she could write in peace, away from London and family, is played out in this story.[15] The character of Anna rejects the gender-defined roles of wife and mother-to-be, by escaping to an inaccessible place and finding fulfilment, without men. The author's letters to confidante Oriel Malet outlines her own desire to escape the mundane: 'I have been reading an interesting book about La Trappe [. . .] it says there is a 'Hôtellerie des Dames.' It surely can't be true? I know men go for a retreat, but surely not women? Could you bear to go and ask? We might have gone together some time! [. . .] And Guinness has just sent me a book called *The Nun's Story*, so all these Catholic people are trying to push me into the Faith. Little do they know my Pagan depths![16] While overtly dismissive of religion, du Maurier's story hints at a deeper, mystical belief system and this is borne out in her unpublished correspondence with Victor Gollancz.

The collectivism of Monte Verità's community with its pooled resources and harmonious rituals is contrasted by the individualistic narrator, who erroneously sees himself as a conqueror, boasting: 'We climbed from desire, because we loved the thing we won' (44). He begins the story referring to the mountain in the possessive as 'my' and 'mine' yet, twice he refuses Anna's invitation to climb it and eventually only does so reluctantly at the behest of his dying friend, her husband Victor. Anna urges the narrator to come climbing with them but he pleads business in New York; when the world and the sublime compete, for him the world wins. '"The Mountain of Truth," she said. "Come with us, do." I shook my head and went off upon my journey' (55). Having chosen a life of material comforts over spiritual 'Truth,' he 'closes his mind' to Anna for twenty years. Žižek cites this story as characteristic of all du Maurier's stories of female masochism, but this is a misreading as it is Anna who shows that she is capable of finding her own way, geographically and spiritually, without male guidance. Arguably it is the male characters who are masochistic in their quest to restore Anna to the woman she was before her ascent. A clear impossibility and something she does not desire. Du Maurier invites the reader to see the gap made by the absence of Anna as wife, mother and lover. And, as millennial women choose more and more not to procreate, and androgyny becomes ever more prevalent as a fashion and a fact, du Maurier's story is incontrovertibly ahead of its time.

Traditional gender roles are subverted by centralising a female on a personal quest, while male characters either wait a lifetime in hopes of her return or wander the world searching for the truth she so easily finds. In an early draft du Maurier went so far as to turn Anna into a man midway through the story, but this was vetoed by Gollancz who had doubts concerning the sexual aspects, 'I don't understand the slight implication that there is something wrong with sex' he wrote. Thus, Anna remains female but single-mindedly pursues her dream over the dreams of others, a feature traditionally reserved for masculine characters and rather more unusual in female ones. Beautiful but reserved, Anna abandons her marriage after eight months to live among the (presumably) celibate community of androgynes in a closed order atop the mountain. Du Maurier is habitually coy regarding explicit intimacy in her fiction, but it is apparent that the community relationships favour a platonic model. Forster concludes that 'the general drift of this highly metaphorical story *is* that there is something wrong with sex between men and women—it spoils relationships, it drains energy, it gets in the way of self-fulfilment.'[17] It is certain that sexual congress is not depicted as a sublime union in any of the stories, but is rather a risky act involving vulnerability and potentially leading to violence.

'Monte Verità' has been read as a tale of wistful lesbianism and whether that was du Maurier's point remains unknown, but it certainly foregrounds freedom and intimacy in the context of spiritual, rather than sensual, love. In one of her few direct references to lesbianism du Maurier reflects the social mores of her time and comments: 'it's amazing how women can fall in it, who have been normal before.'[18] In an essay on the concept of outrage as the central motif in the text Christine Reynier correctly states that 'Monte Verità' is the 'least commented upon and the most cryptic' of all du Maurier's stories, reaffirming Auerbach's definition of them as 'cryptic and many-sided.'[19] In Reynier's analysis Victor displays cultish behaviour in sacrificing his life to his internalised ideal of Anna, in another refutation of Žižek's position. However, Reynier misreads the text by stating that the villagers 'give' their daughters to the *sacerdotesse*, whereas the girls first feel drawn to the community, then slip away in the night and subsequently abandon their families for the ascetic life. The story is a play on Wosk's argument that '[w]omen are often expected to be both artificial and genuine, to wear surface masks of beauty and yet also be emotionally authentic.'[20] Readings of Du Maurier as determinedly non-feminist are problematised by this story which celebrates the androgynous body and mind in a gyno-geographic landscape.

However, mountains and women are explicitly compared in what reads today as misogynism: '[t]he moods of a mountain can be more varying, more swiftly-changing than any woman's, bringing joy, and fear, and also great repose' (44). Du Maurier's favoured device of the isologue is used in the mapping of female physicality onto the mountainous terrain. The isologue is used here in poetry critic Don Patterson's sense of two elements 'mapped together in the text, but not linked by any syntactic comparison, copula or any other unifying formula.'[21] 'Monte Verità' is located within a deep crevice between twin peaks. It is split into two like a divided hand, the two peaks 'seem as one' when seen from the valley and the village, they are like a closed hand tenderly holding, and guarding, the religious order but they are also high walls to deter the uninitiated. Valley dwellers who say that there are no local guides available for the climb as the mountain remains unexplored and savage. Victor considers himself un-lyrical by nature but even he admits that the mountain is 'somehow . . . sublime' as the text highlights the influence of place on emotion (58).

The sexualisation of colonial landscapes is now a common feature of the critical field of this type of literature, but this was not the case when du Maurier was writing this story. Once again the author is prescient as she touches on issues that came to the fore decades after composition. This narrative explores an alternative religious perspective and an alternative social order and du Maurier's letters to Oriel Malet clearly show the direction of her thoughts. 'What interests me, is whether Woman, as such, has been quietly seething to get back to a matriarchal society [. . .] The aim of Society should be to achieve complete balance.' While social balance is disrupted by the order's existence—as it was disrupted in Britain by post-war changes in traditional family life—Anna's self-focused choice prioritises what du Maurier calls the 'correct *balance* of your own individual self.' Du Maurier writes about the 'three female types' of women, the 'ruling type, the ministering type, and the prostitute' and helpfully mentions that: 'Of course, one can change to another.'[22] This can be seen in the next chapter in 'The Alibi' where the female character morphs from prostitute to ministering angel to murderer.

In this plot the villagers explain to the protagonists that the climb is dangerous for girls and women as they cannot resist the spell of Monte Verità where they will embrace immortality like those who are already members of the community, the *sacerdotesse*. Victor dismisses their sombre warnings as 'an African travel tale,' an elliptic reference to classics of the 'lost world' genre such as Rider Haggard's *She,* a text 'Monte Verità' implicitly references. *She* was a popular book in du Maurier's youth and 'Monte Verità' is a literary descendant in several respects. Du Maurier was a prolific reader and may well also have read Rider Haggard's best-seller *King*

Solomon's Mines [1885] where he maps the female body with a mountain range called Sheba's Breasts. This sexualisation of colonial landscapes is a feature of texts celebrating the imperial adventurer as Anne McClintock's study on race, gender and sexuality illustrates.[23] Like Haggard, Du Maurier artfully uses a feminised landscape to echo male fears regarding woman-centred power: the 'two peaks, absolutely bare and naked' (53), and between them the Christian symbolism of the Holy Grail: 'the shape of it was like a chalice held between two hands' (65). The story appears to be continuing in the tradition of Judeo-Christian symbols of sacred female gestation, but Anna denies the role of wife and mother instead embracing heterodox female-centred power.

This non-linear text necessitates examination of character through individual narrative arcs. The promise of eternal beauty and immortality, the androgyne dwellers, and the nude worshipping of the sun and the moon, appear to enact pagan practices but this is fused with a subtext of Christian ideology. In common with Haggard's character Ayesha (the immortal ruler in *She*) the *sacerdotesse* practice telegnosis and are enchantingly beautiful, and Ayesha's horrible death after her instant aging of millennia is another link to Anna's affliction of leprosy. The story acts as a female-focussed adventure tale and the prize is self-actualization and the freedom of selfhood. The gendered lexical choices are deeply significant, the fortress is 'impregnable,' 'stark and savage' with no windows and a tower over a sheer drop, 'a great wall encircle[s] the whole place' and there is no visible entrance (66). It reads as Rapunzel's tower in the woods or Cinderella's castle but Anna has no wish to escape and stubbornly avoids her Prince rescuers.

Like the fortress, the three principal characters each represent a certain impenetrability but only one of them has the qualities to access the mountain retreat. Anna is an orphan who has the physical attributes of a goddess: golden hair, 'incredible beauty,' inner radiance, serenity—her 'blessed healing silence' (45–48). Victor's sparsely furnished house reflects Anna's dislike of possessions, something the narrator finds odd as he expects a woman to bring her 'feminine touch' to a bachelor household. Her room is Spartan: no curtains or carpet, a chair, a table, a narrow trestle bed and one blanket. This reflects the simplicity of her upbringing in the Welsh hills that also elicits her sobering comment that, '"Mountains are very demanding," [. . .] "You have to give everything."' (46) Anna understands what climbing really means. This is reinforced when one evening Victor tells the narrator the tale of a climb up Snowdon where Anna had been constantly ahead and having lost sight of her, he searched frantically until she appeared 'out of the mist like a spirit from another world.' Events on Monte Verità are foreshadowed by his account of how '[s]he went down that blasted mountain as if she had spent the night on Olympus' (53). The same night the narrator wakes, chilled by the extreme cold, and sees Anna barefoot on the frosty lawn in the light of the full moon. He feels that he is watching something 'intimate and secret' that must not be told. The narrator echoes the sense of the mystical observing that: 'this stillness came out of her yet from another world' (53).

Having been adopted into the integrated mind of the community minus sophisticated material luxuries, Anna has everything she will ever need behind the walls of the fortress despite, or perhaps because, there are no men there. This Spartan sense of purity and freedom from possessions is paralleled in du Maurier's correspondence. A decade previously in 1939 she wrote to Maud Whadell: 'We ought to give up trying to make money, trying to be successful, trying to live by the "values" of the world, and get back to simplicity in all things, and simple faith!'[24] As the breadwinner for her family, she felt the pressure keenly to write for popular success and the resulting financial gain. As the years pass Anna protects Victor from the 'truth' of her existence at Monte Verità as if he were a child, while the narrator is stripped of his illusions and naive romantic desires.

The personal and arbitrary nature of truth and lies is demonstrated when the narrator finally climbs Monte Verità years later and meets Anna again, only to find that her 'very perfect' eyes are now blackened holes. 'One side of her face was eaten quite away, ravaged, terrible. The disease had come upon her brow, her cheek, her throat, blotching, searing the skin. The eyes that I had loved were blackened, sunk deep into the sockets.' (110) The contrast between her physical blindness and increased inner perception is marked in the contrast with the narrator, who consistently lacks insight. However, Anna has succeeded in her quest to 'seek [. . .] an answer to eternity' and her inner vision remains greater than her would-be lover's, as his bitterness illustrates (80). Despite the claim that he loves her and that his values have 'all changed,' he does not speak of them being together after he sees her disfigurement (104). For du Maurier, Anna's leprosy had a personal resonance as she considered her beauty marred by the lack of truth in her marriage. In a letter to a friend she outlines the biographical parallel: 'learning the truth can give a person the appearance of disease, and leprosy can eat away the body and the mind. If you try to reach the gods you can destroy the body—leprosy.' Du Maurier's carnographic nightmares explore our physical boundaries only to frame deeper issues about sentience, authenticity, and whether one can ever truly transcend the somatic. They pose 'important questions about the nature of human existence.'[25]

The unpublished correspondence frames both the collection, and the personal context behind this story: 'The only thing to do was then to write out the many problems in yet a different way, and the short stories were written.

Monte Verità is myself and Moper, and myself going to the mountains to learn the truth, and Moper waiting for me, and finally dying without ever having learnt that the person who had gone to the mountains had not the perfect beauty of mind and body that he wanted in his wife but had a leprous face.' 'Moper' was a family nickname for Frederick 'Tommy' Browning, Du Maurier's husband as she unflatteringly describes him to Maureen Baker-Munton in her letters of 1957.[26] The biographical context parallels the locus of this story where the dialectics between truth and ugliness are connected, also beauty and lies, binaries explored in 'Split Second' and 'The Little Photographer.'

The difference between actual sight and metaphorical perception is an issue that threads through du Maurier's corpus of shorter fiction, it starts here with the alteration in Anna's eyes from perfect to possessed first identified by the old man in the village: 'I saw it in her eyes last night [. . .] She had the eyes they have' (64). In several plots eyesight is destroyed, by avian madness in 'The Birds,' by operation in 'The Blue Lenses, or by simply not seeing the facts clearly—'The Doll' and 'The Alibi.' Du Maurier was exploring notions of retribution whereby character flaws were punished in the most direct and apposite fashion, as she outlines in a letter to Malet: 'those who lose their sight do so because they have refused to see clearly what has happened in their own lives. Those who lose their hearing, lose it because they have never developed understanding, and have refused to listen to what went on around them. Those who become paralysed, become so because they did not take action at some vital moment, or crisis.'[27] This disconcerting theory is reminiscent of biblical retribution and underlines du Maurier's short fiction as a space where immorality inevitably results in disfigurement, and frequently with fatal consequences.

It is poetic that Anna's divinity seems to increase in direct proportion to the increasingly abject state of her body. Her beauty is emphasised in the text and when she ascends the mountain she becomes more like a classical Grecian statue, bare-footed and clad in a tunic, a contrast to her leprous state: 'her face was eaten away, ravaged, terrible. The disease had come upon her brow, her cheek, her throat, blotching, searing the skin. The eyes [. . .] were blackened, sunk deep into the sockets' (110). She transgresses societal norms by abandoning Victor and the patriarchal contract of marriage, in an example of how 'transgressions and the attempt to control them obsessively return to somatic symbols.' In Anna's physicality du Maurier revisits cultural assumptions about the beautiful and the ugly, combining them to challenge the way 'the grotesque body stands in opposition to the bourgeois individualist conception of the body, which finds *its* image and legitimation in the classical.'[28] This is a trope she returns to in 'The Little Photographer,' a story concerned with the body in extreme physical states.

At the end of the narrative Anna relates the proverbial tale of the man who requests a ticket to Paradise and when refused by the ticket clerk, offers violence and is subsequently imprisoned (109). She highlights the irony in vocalising a demand for freedom while behaviourally pursuing the opposite. This is echoed situationally in Anna's membership of a closed order, and the occupation of a cell, in a fortress without visible means of entry, on the peak of a mountain somewhere in Europe. The language of secrecy, sinister practices and odd rituals laces the prose. It is 'no common danger' but 'awe and fear' that keeps climbers back yet the dreaded promise of '[f]orbidden walls, dreaded and shunned,' turns out to enclose only disappointing silence, empty cells, and a bare court (43). Grosz comments that, '[d]ualism is responsible for the modern forms of elevation of consciousness (a specifically modern version of the notion of the soul, introduced by Descartes) above corporeality.'[29] In this plot the body is as much the site of conflict as the soul. Victor represents a study in sacrifice and Anna gives everything to attain fulfilment. Both perish for their ideals in a disintegration of their physical selves. This is not a simple tale of marital disintegration after a brief eight months, it is a woman sacrificing one sacred commitment for what she considers to be a superior union—one not physical but spiritual.

Victor experiences anger and grief when Anna abandons him to live a celibate, aesthete's life, and his subsequent nervous collapse is caused by 'stifled rage' that then necessitates a stay in a nursing-home (56). Extreme emotionality is reserved for men in the story, the male perspective is privileged by first-person narration, but as is common in du Maurier's male monologues, it undermines itself with interlocutions and inconsistencies. Within the outer narrative frame there is Victor's post-breakdown tale of Anna ascending and not returning, the villager's stories of women and girls leaving their families for the sect and Anna's parable of the man buying a ticket to Paradise. An evocative nested narrative that raises the question of whether the mountain community is paradisial. Only pubescent girls receive the calling and Anna is thought to be safe from the lure of the sect as she and Victor are married. However, despite being sexually mature Anna is also drawn to Monte Verità and when the narrator sees her after twenty years she is once again exceptional in the role of High Priestess. This instance of what appears to be female power is initially dismissed by Victor as 'cats, broomsticks, and sixteenth century witchcraft,' despite hearing the report from a village girl guided back to safety by the *sacerdotesse*. Like Anna, she dwells high above now, securely isolated from male desire, fulfilled by access to 'everything she would ever need' (74).

Having attained the zenith of community life, High Priestess, it is in her role as the wise matriarch that Anna advises Victor to abandon his annual pilgrimage to the mountain, yet he does not. He accepts the reality of Anna's absence and keeps a lonely vigil with patient resignation. Thanks to his wife and friend he keeps his illusions intact and dies prematurely, but peacefully, and is buried at the foot of the mountain whose summit he never attains. Thus, he figuratively continues to worship at Anna's feet even after death. As he is similarly bereft to many local husbands before him the villagers look at Victor 'with compassion' (111). It is worth noting that although Victor Gollancz may have inspired the choice of the name 'Victor,' arguably its martial overtones of masculine prowess and the contrasting passivity demonstrated by the character of Victor are reminiscent of 'Moper' Browning, du Maurier's nickname for her war hero husband. From one perspective, Anna's smooth path to self-fulfilment reads as a wistful vision of utopia from her author-creator who spent a life preferring solitude to company.

The narrator in 'Monte Verità' is trapped in a single, narrow perspective on life and initially he finds it 'monstrous that an unknown sect, on a mountainside, could [. . .] have such power over a woman, a woman of intelligence and personality' (76). He can imagine only one mode of communion, a heterosexual one, yet his discourse is imbued with the rhetoric of vision and a desire for clear sightedness:

> I like to think there can be no final desecration, that at midnight, when the full moon rises, the mountain face is still inviolate, unchanged, and that in winter, when snow and ice [. . .] make the climb impassable to man, the rock face of Monte Verità, her twin peaks lifted to the sun, stares down in silence and compassion upon a blinded world. (43)

The narrator stands for the values of capitalism and staunchly defends the marital unit (having never been married himself) against the subversion of the collective, a weak defence against the 'collective unconscious' of Monte Verità. Du Maurier places the Jungian model of an integrated mind on to the character of Anna, including the possibility of metempsychosis: 'And we have two consciousnesses. The ordinary, individual unconscious, made up of a sort of second self, [. . .] and a 'collective unconscious' which goes streaming back to old Assyrians and cavemen and people, and we can't *help* that. Of course, this collective unconscious could be a case for reincarnation.'[30] This authorial curiosity concerning the collective unconscious and the mind/ body dialectic is expressed in a later story, 'The Breakthrough,' where another bleak location is the setting for exploratory psychogeography. In this narrative the clues are there from the start as the narrator has suspicions about Anna that the more straightforward Victor misses. In Victor's home the narrator finds something odd as he expects a woman to bring a 'feminine touch' to the bachelor household rather than asceticism.

A discussion of the esoteric leaves the narrator questioning the materialism that has satisfied him thus far in life. 'Now I was not sure that it had any value' (50). Anna incorrectly assumes that they are 'both in search of the same thing, after all' (103), but the narrator prefers the 'glittering fairy-world of fact': New York. This centre of business and busyness is a place that 'holds no tenderness, no quietude,' a place where he 'long[s] suddenly for peace, for understanding' (42). Tragically he realises that, 'in the mountains we come closest to whatever Being it is that rules our destiny' but he is unable to connect in any meaningful way (41). The narrator is haunted by opportunities missed and intimacy denied. 'What I saw and heard and felt was not of this world. I think of the rock-face, with the moon upon it; I hear the chanting from the forbidden walls; I see the crevasse, cupped like a chalice between the twin peaks of the mountain; I hear the laughter; I see bronzed arms outstretched to the sun' (41).

To the narrator recalling events from decades before, the central mystery is what finally happened to those dwelling on the summit. When the fortress is finally invaded by the valley people, intent on retribution for their missing womenfolk, the enclave contains no bodies or clues as to what happened to the denizens. The story is the narrator's search for, glimpse of, and loss of spiritual truth, and it starts with an ending: 'They told me afterwards they had found nothing' (40). In the first edition of *The Apple Tree* [1952] 'Monte Verità' is the initial story and the initial three words of each story are capitalised. The abstract and elusive concepts of truth and freedom are entwined in this text, epitomised in the narrator's fruitless search which leaves him alone at the end of the story in the deserted village watching the 'full moon rising from the dark valley' (113). No mountain is high enough to bring him close to enlightenment and he knows it. 'I was lost in wonder, locked in a dream I could not understand. [. . .] but something indefinable waited to be won. Always it was denied to me, the experience I desired, and something seemed to tell me the fault was in myself' (45). Physical desire and materialist pursuits have cost the narrator spiritual enlightenment and the intimacy of true communion.

He is the outsider denied entry to Paradise and he is full of rage: '[a]nd I knew, in the depths of my heart, why I hated the story of Monte Verità and wanted the place to be destroyed. It was because Anna had found her Truth, and I had not . . . ' (77). During his stay on the mountaintop he realises that he has not been accepted, he remains, 'a stranger from the world below' (106). The horror of Anna's ravaged eyes makes his love a past tense emotion—'loved'— and he looks wistfully at the comforting fires and lighted windows of the valley settlements thinking that: '[i]t was as though all feeling had been frozen' (110). The narrator expresses his failure to join the community in sadness: 'I guessed dimly, with a sort of hunger near to pain, what ecstasy of love they knew, that I had never known' (104). Anna achieves her dream of Truth and sees clearly despite being blind, only the narrator is left dissatisfied. Bemused, 'What could have been the final answer?' he asks himself and dismissing a secret descent or a mass suicide pact as improbable, instead he chooses his favourite theory of immortality for the dwellers at the summit. This despite his last conversation with Anna where she relates how others died of her affliction because '[l]eprosy can come to anyone, even the supposed immortals of Monte Verità' (110). In spite of information revealing eternal life as a myth concealing a more profound bond between minds or souls, the narrator clings to his fantasy. 'The Blue Lenses' serves a partner story in that Marda West's sight is altered but the denouement is ambiguous, and the reader has to decide whether she will act on the new information, or ignore it. There are several other stories where protagonists ignore warnings or visions at their peril such as 'The Birds' and 'Don't Look Now.'

During the period of writing du Maurier was reading *En Route* [1895] by Joris-Karl Huysmans, a novel outlining his struggle with the 'impulses of the flesh' as Catholicism became more central to his life. In this semi-autobiographical account of a conversion to Catholicism, the main character of Durtal goes to a Trappist monastery. Du Maurier was keen to revisit La Grande Trappe, the Order that broke away to become stricter in religious observance of the three rules of monastic life: stability, fidelity, obedience, inspiring other Orders of Trappists and Trappistines.[31] Her correspondence is laced with references to monasteries, retreats and paganism.[32] Although the story frames spiritual freedom, du Maurier's private opinions on religion are ambiguous, as these comments on Catholic and Protestant Christianity to Maud Whaddell illustrate:

> 'I think nuns are either saints or fools; the life is too restricting to give a happy medium. But the whole subject is of great interest. I shouldn't be surprised if the really holiest body of people are not the Quakers. No talk of publicity but always on the scene when there is any distress. So many trappings have grown up round the Catholic Church that it is difficult to find the kernel in the nut, if you understand the metaphor! But I think the old C of E is really worn-out, and utterly lacking in inspiration. I don't know if the new Arch Bish will ginger things up.'[33]

While continuing a discussion that is evidently important to her, du Maurier's amusement is clear as she comments that these impulses are 'always in such embarrassing places, like Mass or somewhere. I should think it was nerves and then his guilt was overwhelming!' This comes through in plot details of a later story called 'The Way of the Cross' [1971], but her preoccupation with religion can be traced throughout this period. To a limited extent it is clear that du Maurier did achieve some catharsis through writing out the events of her personal life and in exploring her spiritual inclinations.

Her comment on the contemporary period is another clue to interpreting the story: 'Everything that goes wrong in the world is through some false emotion—Hitler, strikes, anything.' The stories show a refreshing lack of didacticism as she works through her ideas about life, events, and people, challenging the reader to do the same. However, she has firm opinions and these are embedded in the texts as the following excerpt from her correspondence demonstrates: 'how close hunger is to greed, how difficult to tell the difference, how hard not to be confused, how close ones better nature to ones worst, and finally, how the self must be stripped of everything, and give up everything, before it can understand love. But one can't tell that to the ordinary reader. He that has ears to hear, let him hear.'[34] In the same way, her characters either see and hear clearly, or they ignore the warnings and face the consequences at the breaking point.

Victor sees the narrator as a 'poet,' a dreamy youth who becomes infected with mountain fever, and who is always slow to come out of the trance. At these times the narrator quotes William Wordsworth's lines: 'The world is too much with us; late and soon/Getting and spending, we lay waste our powers.'[35] Other poetic references enrich his comments, and the inclusion of a reference to Edna St. Vincent Millay's poem 'Euclid alone has looked on Beauty bare' highlights the narrator's impoverished spiritual condition even as he encounters his heart's desire.[36] He 'prates' of what he sees while the members of the Order observe silence and his self-regard ensures that he will continue to be one of those who endlessly 'ponder on themselves' (LL 2–4). There are parallels with another of Wordsworth's poems, 'The Solitary Reaper,' in which a male narrator listens to a personal song, sung by a group of women, which is described to readers who will never hear it.[37] Du Maurier's prose mimics music in the way it rises and falls, increasing in tempo and punctuation until the crescendo and the coda which returns us to silence.

> This was their song of praise. [. . .] a murmur came from them, low and distinct at first, then swelling louder [. . .] the sound echoed from the rock-face, rose and fell upon the air [. . .] This was their song of praise. [. . .] the chanting rang in my ears, unearthly, terrifying, yet beautiful in a way impossible to bear. [. . .] Then slowly, very slowly, the great hymn of praise faded in strength. It sank low to a murmur, to a sigh. It hushed and died away. Silence came back to Monte Verità. (96–97)

The chanting of the acolytes is of an unearthly beauty that cannot be comprehended by the male listener. The song of Monte Verità is heard and described by two men, neither of whom can join in, grasp the mystery, or articulate it.

Unlike other stories within this study, which strengthen the connections between human and bestial bodies, this one exhibits Grosz's statement that the body is 'an intrusion on or interference with the operation of mind, a brute givenness which requires overcoming, a connection with animality and nature that needs transcendence.'[38] The narrative arc of 'Monte Verità' engages positively with the female body and the female mind and the intimacy of the relationship between them. Anna survives leprosy longer than the other sufferers of the condition, refuting the assumption that 'women's bodies are presumed to be incapable of men's achievements, being weaker, more prone to (hormonal) irregularities, intrusions, and unpredictabilities.' This theory has only recently been refuted by science and this is demonstrated in collections of academic essays such as *Body Politics*.[39] It is evident that du Maurier had firm views on sexuality and natural bodily processes: 'If only [people] were brought up to know about sex like they know the rain falls from the sky, half the battle would be over. It's all the mystery and giggle-behind-the-hand that causes the trouble. As D. H. Lawrence said, one is brought up in the belief that sex is "natures dirty little secret" and I fear that is how most people regard it.'[40] Grosz traces the blurred edges surrounding this issue:

> The mind/ body relation is frequently corroborated with the distinctions between reason and passion, sense and sensibility, outside and inside, self and other, depth and surface, reality and appearance, mechanism and vitalism, transcendence and immanence, temporality and spatiality, psychology and physiology, form and matter, and so on. These lateral associations provide whatever "positive" characteristics the body may be accorded in systems where it is the subordinated counterpart of mind.[41]

However, Žižek suggests an alternate version of the story, without du Maurier's 'disturbing intrusion[s],' for this critic it is 'a fantasised escape from th[e] misery' of the characters' situations.[42] While this comment is a useful signpost in consideration of *The Apple Tree* in entirety, the problem with this reading of 'Monte Verità' is that Anna is *not* miserable. Žižek's interpretation omits female desire, one of the author's key interests, and when Anna is called to join the community she is privileging her alternative desire rather than fleeing an unbearable existence. Victor relates Anna's promise that she will not climb without him and will not leave him behind. Yet, she does exactly this, literally and spiritually. Men are barred from entering Monte Verità though the narrator is seized from behind the walls as he leaves Victor's final message. He enters the sanctum to behold something he can neither conquer, possess nor share: the woman he has loved, sanctuary from the world below, and the 'peace of God' (101). Unlike Victor who accepts what is irreconcilable and retains his ideals, his friend's tragedy is to witness the mystery yet remain the unworthy outsider: 'I was lost between two worlds. My own was gone, and I was not of theirs. I longed for the sanctuary of the drifting clouds again' (97). His comments frame the paradox in visual terms that convey the additional sense of a lack of understanding: '[f]or the first time in my life I looked on beauty bare' (96), and following this, 'my eyes could not penetrate the depths' (103). Žižek is not the only male to misread the situation: both Victor and the narrator do so.

Behind the characters' struggles with spirituality and the rejection of fleshly desires is the backdrop of World War One with its human carnage, a theme that continues in the next chapter on 'The Alibi,' a story set after World War Two, in which the Armistice is mentioned midway through the text (78). The denial and non-use of female sexual organs in 'Monte Verità' continues in 'The Alibi' where somatic absence also implies presence. The central character finds a creative outlet for his urges and ambitions, citing 'an old war wound' (18) as the explanation for his lack of sexual appetite. There are biographical parallels to the author's own experience of veteran behaviour. Du Maurier's husband Lieutenant-General Frederick Tommy 'Boy' Browning was the veteran of two world wars, Chief-of-Staff with the Mediterranean Fleet, a hero whose regular nightmares showed latent suffering, a fact which may make her non-heroic, non-combatant male characters less surprising.

'Monte Verità' is du Maurier's most woman-centred story dealing as it does with themes of freedom, escape from gender-orientated duties and the attainment of personal fulfilment. Yet, it does not outline a smooth path to independence but rather portrays a heroine who only achieves fulfilment through discarding the 'feminine' aspects of physical beauty, maternity, and connubial partnership. Cryptic is an apt word for the modernist, multilayered plot and in the next chapter on 'The Apple Tree,' torturous gender relations continue to be relentlessly written on the human form.

NOTES

1. Du Maurier, *The Birds and Other Stories* (London: Virago, 2004). All further references are to this edition.
2. Conrich and Sedgwich, Chapter 3, 'Head and Face.' 35
3. Armstrong, p. 28.
4. Richardson, p. 100.
5. Haggard, *She: A History of Adventure,* first serialised in *The Graphic* magazine, 1886–1887.
6. Harald Szeemann. Sourced at <monteverita.org> [accessed 2.12.21].
7. Wosk, p. 5.

8. Du Maurier letter to journalist and fellow MRA colleague Peter Howard 8 April 1955. EUL MS Add 5, courtesy of Special Collections.

9. Clara Vyvyan, *Down the Rhone on Foot* (London: Peter Owen, 1955). Quoted in Forster, p. 263.

10. Malet, p. 9.

11. Grosz, p. 207.

12. Du Maurier letter to Victor Gollancz, 21 February 1955. MSS.157/3/I/ DM/ 1–43, courtesy of Modern Records Centre.

13. Du Maurier letter to Maud Waddell 11 February 1924. EUL MS 207/6/4/1, courtesy of Special Collections.

14. Malet, p. 70, p. 77.

15. Du Maurier letter to Maud Waddell, 2 July 1931. EUL MS 207/6/4/1, courtesy of Special Collections.

16. Malet, letter dated 19 October 1956, p. 81.

17. Gollancz quoted in Forster, p. 257.

18. Du Maurier letter to Maud Waddell, 8 June 1944. EUL MS 207/6/4/1, courtesy of Special Collections.

19. Christine Reynier, 'The Outrageousness of Outrage: Daphne du Maurier's "Monte Verità" 'in Études britanniques contemporaines 20.10.13 Sourced at: <http://ebc.revues.org/683> [accessed 29.6. 2022].

20. Wosk, p. 78.

21. Don Patterson, *Reading Shakespeare's Sonnets: A New Commentary* (London: Faber, 2012), p. 184.

22. Malet. p. 50.

23. Haggard, *King Solomon's Mines* ed. by Dennis Butts (Oxford: Oxford University Press, 2008). McClintock, *Imperial leather: Race, Gender and Sexuality in the Colonial Contest* (London: Routledge: 1995).

24. Du Maurier letter, 17 October 1939, p. 5. EUL MS 207/6/4/1, courtesy of Special Collections.

25. Reyes, p. 25–27.

26. Du Maurier letter, 4 July, quoted in Forster, p. 422.

27. Malet. Du Maurier letter to Malet dated 14 June 1955, p. 51.

28. Stallybrass and White, p. 26, p. 22.

29. Grosz, p. 7.

30. Malet, p. 39.

31. Joris-Karl Huysman, *En Route* ed. by W. Fleming, trans. by David Blow (Cambridge: Dedalus, 2002).

32. Malet, p. 67.

33. Du Maurier letter, 11 June 1942. MS 207/6/4/1, courtesy of Special Collections.

34. Malet, pp. 48–49. p. 81.

35. William Wordsworth, *The Complete Poetical Works* (London: Macmillan and Co, 1888).

36. Edna St. Vincent Millay, *The Norton Anthology of Poetry*, LL 1–8, p. 1383.

37. Wordsworth, 'The Solitary Reaper,' 'Poems Written During a Tour in Scotland,' in *Poems in Two Volumes, and Other Poems* ed. by Jared Curtis (New York: Ithaca, 1983) [1807], p. 184–5 (p. 415).

38. Grosz, p. 4.

39. Mary Jacobus, Evelyn Fox Keller, Sally Shuttleworth eds., *Body Politics: Women and the Discourses of Science* (London: Routledge,1990).

40. Du Maurier letter to Maud Waddell, 30 November 31. EUL MS 207/6/4/1, courtesy of Special Collections.

41. Grosz, p. 14, p. 3.

42. Žižek. Sourced at <https://www.lacan.com/zizdaphmaur.htm> [accessed 29.6.22].

Chapter Six

'The Apple Tree' [limbs] (1952)

This chapter sees the corporeal theme develop through the flight from desire represented by female body parts in 'Monte Verità' to the dismemberment of a marriage in 'The Apple Tree.' The plot has its inspiration in myth and includes some of the literary traits of modernism as listed in the introduction. Of these, the ambivalent portrayal of the central character, the temporal switches that flash back to suggest a full-length life, and the 'reiteration through pattern' illustrated by the seasonal cycle are particularly notable. In the somatic approach the eponymous apple tree evokes human limbs, defined in *Black's Medical Dictionary* as 'outgrowths from the sides of the body [. . .] made up by the muscles or flesh,' incorporating 'bones which give it rigidity' attached to which are arteries and nerves 'embedded among the muscles close to the bones.' The static sapling's development and fruition parallels the life cycles of the female human, its branches are her limbs, its flowers her hair and its fruit her children.

The central symbolism of the tree itself indicates the implicit but unheard voices within the text, a dialogistic form that evokes the work of Mikhail Bakhtin. The anatomic enumeration first developed by Bakhtin and postulated in this analysis is elaborated here by the excessive fertility of the tree which becomes overabundant, and its destruction, which symbolises 'the dismemberment of the body, its rendering apart and swallowing up.' Having iterated the essential themes of this 'bodily life,' Bakhtin further enumerates that '[g]rotesque realism knows no other lower level; it is the fruitful earth and the womb.[1] It is always conceiving.' In the same way the character of the deceased wife is a revenant whose demise in anthropoid form is simply another stage in the human life-cycle and whose return as a fruiting tree indicates the unceasing round of death and life. Limbs allow the body to traverse boundaries while impairment of those limbs prevents freedom of movement.

This is a story that foregrounds limitations in the form of a marriage that circumscribes mobility of all kinds.

Throughout du Maurier's fiction, and in the short stories especially, we see her writing demonstrate a phenomenological worldview which holds that the body is the site of an individual's apprehension of the world (through sense-data) and that the body is the site of an individual's presence in the world (as the locus of capacity to add to or alter the sense-data of other individuals). This is seen in her insistent use of the body as the locus of selfhood, identity, desire, and perception, and amounts to a declaration of a phenomenological position closely related to work by Merleau-Ponty. Maurice Merleau-Ponty is a philosopher whose work is synergic with du Maurier's short fiction in his 'unique account of the bodily basis of perception.' He focuses on the 'four aspects of human existence: embodiment, the advent of meaning, the relation to "otherness" and freedom.'[2] His work privileges the body and reconstructs human corporeity and psychology into a synthesised non-Cartesian whole. The body is a permanent condition of experience, or 'incarnated subjectivity,' in which 'perception and its corporeal basis' find a unified home. The idea that the body and what it experiences cannot be separated from cognition runs through du Maurier's corpus of short fiction and here the dismemberment of a marriage, a tree, and (symbolically) a woman acts metonymically for her broader evaluation of the body in multiple parts, in multiple stories.

Before examining 'The Apple Tree' in detail it is important to note that when considering du Maurier's stories as a whole, unsurprisingly, one finding is that they are thematically interrelated, both within collections and throughout the corpus. Marital dysfunction runs through her material from the earliest composed stories. Although they were printed in 1955 these stories were mainly written when du Maurier was in her twenties (between 1927 and 1937), and they illustrate her revulsion and fascination with the dangers of romantic love and marriage: a dichotomy that is prevalent in her narrative focus and which continues throughout her career. In 'A Difference in Temperament' [1955], there is the line: '[y]ou are such a part of me that to stand alone leaves me dumb, without speech, without eyes. A tree with hatched branches like someone with no hands.'[3] This utterance comes part-way through a fracas between a mismatched couple and has its final echoes in 'The Apple Tree' when protagonists Midge and Buzz irritate each other like the annoying insects for which they are aptly nicknamed. The guilt of their miserable union is a blight which lingers afterbereavement and 'til death us do part' has a grim resonance in a tale where revenge is a dish best served from the afterlife. In her correspondence du Maurier expresses insightful concern regarding family relations post-Armistice, framed in the plot of a play she was writing in 1943: 'I've brought this subject to the fore in 'The Years Between' because I think a lot of couples after the war will find their moods and habits have grown rather apart, and it's not always going to be easy beginning afresh.'[4] As Margaret Forster's biography indicates in her coverage of the du Maurier/ Browning union, this was certainly true of the author's personal experience.

'It was three months after she died that he first noticed the apple tree,'[5] is one of Daphne du Maurier's expertly balanced first lines, and as her editor Sheila Hodges noted, this was a consistent feature of her writing frequently characterised by striking initial and final lines (114).[6] 'The Apple Tree' is the third story and it was included in four separate collections before its title role was replaced with the subsequently more famous story 'The Birds,' in Penguin's 1963 edition. Originally entitled *The Apple Tree* [1952], *The Treasury of Short Stories* [1960], *Echoes from the Macabre* [1976], and *Classics of the Macabre* [1987], these are the collections published by Gollancz which include this story. The Penguin edition is the first to feature the titular change and the new story order. The narrative has been read as a straightforward tale of haunting in the style of Edith Wharton's narratives of ghostly repression. This literal reading is in the tradition of limiting yet another du Maurier narrative in order to classify it to one genre: the ghost story. A quotation from *Women and Fiction in the Twentieth Century* by Sarah Sceats and Gail Cunningham indicates the temptation to categorise and thus reduct:

> Similar difficulties in married life are explored in Daphne du Maurier's ghost stories. Here there is a significant comparison between marriage and courtship. The status of wife appears diminished when privileges held at the beginning of a relationship are recalled. [. . .] in 'The Apple Tree' du Maurier locates the spirit of a widower's wife in a tree. The widower recalls his unhappy marriage and reproaches the tree, attempting to destroy it, but is instead killed by it. Ghost stories indeed become a way of re-evaluating memory.[7]

A good example of this type of plot is Mary E. Braddon's story 'The Cold Embrace' [1860]. While it is useful to identify this story as continuing the trend away from the simply supernatural towards the psychological as the site of horror, 'The Apple Tree' has much in common with fairy tale and myth and is a useful example of the author's fascination with both genres. Du Maurier's interest in the mythic is reflected in a postcard to friend Maud Whaddell of two Doric columns and a triangular Grecian pediment: 'Have just sacrificed to Apollo in his temple. I never want to visit another country in the world, it is so beautiful and so just what I expected—and primitive!'[8] The text weaves mythic elements into an ambiguous narrative of psychological realism in which the Greek tragedy illustrates how the husband's mania draws him towards self-destruction.

The plot concerns a recently bereaved widower and, with typical du Maurier subtlety, the reader is encouraged to pity the husband whose wife is presented as a passive/ aggressive drain, a killjoy and an emotional succubus. There are no clues about Midge before she was married except for the tantalising mention of her childhood in India. Using third person narration, the free indirect style brings the events intensely close until the husband's biased perspective dominates all, while his wife's thoughts go unreported. Buzz cannot enjoy his retirement as Midge's continuous domestic chores force him to migrate around a home that appears to have no room in it for him. The emphasis on place, seen so often in these stories, links to Christopher Pittard's work on psychogeography which analyses the influence of location on character, concluding that: '[d]u Maurier's characters are repeatedly enclosed: in their desires [and] in unhappy marriages.'[9] This plot questions the gendering of territories wherein domiciliary revenge is practised on a husband who embraces retirement in full view of a wife with unending domestic duties. Midge occupies the traditional wifely domain of the home and garden; her duties concern the kitchen and social life. In his professional persona Buzz makes regular forays into the business world, spending only limited time at home. Like other du Maurier protagonists he did 'war work of a sort' (122), but the suspicion is that he did not have a 'good war' because he did not see any military action. In 'The Alibi' the character of James Fenton also mentions a war wound which serves as an excuse not to engage in physical and sexual activity. Like Buzz, Fenton's cowardly and self-serving nature is the antithesis of the necessary qualities of a martial hero. Like Fenton, Buzz is not a military victim but rather regards himself as a marital one engaged in hostilities over household dominion. A further battle over territory outdoors between Buzz and Willis the gardener mirrors the growing animosity between the married couple, presented in flashback.

This pattern of the disintegration of domestic harmony seldom includes the latent female power to cause discomfort; something du Maurier observed at first hand in her own family and transposed into her stories. She was never close to her mother Muriel, a strong character well able to disconcert those who opposed her, such as her husband Gerald whose adulterous inclinations resulted in the occasional crisis. This is detailed in chapter 3 of Forster's biography and certainly resulted in du Maurier's jaded view of heterosexual relationships.[10] The female-centred power inflicted by Midge upon her husband is humorously outlined by novelist Jeanette Winterson, with regards to her own 1950s upbringing: '[My mother] held him in contempt (and that wasn't fair), but she called him the head of the house (and that wasn't true). That marital/ domestic pattern was repeated everywhere I looked.'[11] It is depicted in this narrative arc as Buzz sees Midge as disapprovingly resentful, full of silent reproaches that form a constant mental whine like the hoover she uses every day. Midge is du Maurier's mocking response to the idealised wife as immortalised in Coventry Patmore's poem 'The Angel in the House' (1854–1862): an ideal of femininity who served as a pattern for the model Victorian woman.[12] The 'Angel' is a self-sacrificing female, who sits in a draught and eats leftovers, and is finally 'murdered' by Virginia Woolf in an essay in 1924, even as Midge's death is ensured by Buzz's neglect.[13] Everything about Midge irritates her husband; from the way she reads the newspaper—smearing it with jam and creasing it—to her constant sniping at other people's good fortune. Even her yawns and sighs exasperate him. He retreats to his study to get away from her company, feeling a 'hopeless sort of anger' (129). His impotence and incapacity to deal with his wife, and his frustrated desire for freedom from the marital union, underline the unevolved nature of his character.

And yet, in another passage of free indirect style, Buzz critically describes the Midge of courtship days as 'anxious to please,' 'eager yet uncertain' and, above all 'desperately anxious to attract' (135). Once married, attention, interest, intimacy, and passion are gone, never to return. Buzz recalls their return from a party in the early years celebrating the longevity of theirs, and their friends,' marriages:

> When he had put the car away in the garage and gone into the house he had found her waiting there, in the living-room, for no reason at all. Her coat was thrown off to show the evening dress, and the smile, rather uncertain, was on her face. He yawned, and settling himself down in a chair picked up a book. She waited a little while then slowly took up her coat and went upstairs. (136)

Like George, the husband in Ernest Hemingway's story 'The Cat in the Rain' [1925], Buzz is more interested in his reading about other people's lives than he is in his wife whose implicit demands for affection and attention are brutally ignored. Unlike Midge, Hemingway's American wife is explicitly demanding but the end result is the same: invisibility. Her pleas for attention are pathetic and childlike: 'Anyway I want a cat,' she said, 'I want a cat. I want a cat now. If I can't have long hair or any fun, I can have a cat.' George was not listening. He was reading his book. His wife looked out of the window where the light had come on in the square.[14] The female form is redundant emotionally and sexually and masculine non-engagement appears feeble. George and Buzz behave like boy-men without insight, without empathy, without responsibility.

The American husband spends all of the story reading. The light 'coming on' in the square may indicate the wife's growing realisation that the desired attention from her husband will never come. The private act of reading enables George to have experiences excluding his wife, something Buzz desires and achieves when he is free to do so after Midge's death. He too hides in the book-lined study to avoid the companionship of his wife. Until Midge dies her presence denies him, and her absence absolves him of conjugal duties. He rejects her tacit advances and by taking up a book he ignores her until she tires of waiting and goes silently to bed. Passivity is a repeated trait in du Maurier's characters but when action does occur and if they do find agency, the result is violence.

To Buzz, Midge is a woman without beauty, intelligence or charm, and she seems to keep busy in order to justify an existence that ceased to be relevant to her husband long ago. In a vignette of their post-marital life he chides her for initiating his nickname, deems that her best green dress turns her skin 'sallow' and finds her smile 'too eager.' His thoughts reveal him as a misogynist who wants her to be the perfect servant, obedient and discreet:

> The ideal life, of course, was that led by a man out East, or in the South Seas, who took a native wife. No problem there. Silence, good service, perfect waiting, excellent cooking, no need for conversation, if you wanted something more than that there she was, young, warm, a companion for the dark hours. No criticism ever, the obedience of an animal to its master, and the light-hearted laughter of a child. Yes, they had wisdom all right, those fellows who break away from convention. Good luck to them. (134)

If Buzz had met Midge in the East he might have lived that way himself: the lord of his domain, with a wife who was always submissive and pleasing. Midge was born in India but she lacks the 'native' submission his racist stereotype celebrates. In retirement, the dynamic is changed and now Midge displays her own form of power within the domestic realm. A power to render life as difficult and unpleasant as any office despot or colonial administrator intent on terrorising the natives.

She dies swiftly after a typically pointless gesture of martyrdom: tying back the Michaelmas daisies in torrential rain leaves Midge with fatal pneumonia and a husband eagerly anticipating his freedom. The newly widowed Buzz throws a photograph of her in the fire and like a tragi-comic Cheshire Cat, her 'vivid smile' is the last part to burn. The representation of the image in photography and the moving image is a recurrent theme from du Maurier, steeped as she was in the complexities of theatricality and authenticity. In an unpublished text called 'Study of an Old Man,' another unnamed character brutally disregards sentiment: 'In the centre was the photograph of his wife, who had died twenty years ago, and another of his dead brother. If their portraits had not been there to remind him he would have forgotten their faces.'[15] Du Maurier references photography in several stories including 'A Border-

Line Case,' 'Kiss Me Again, Stranger,' 'The Little Photographer.' Destroying the photograph is a callous act by Buzz and is suggestive of his general behaviour as a husband, he rejects everything about his late wife, even her photographic facsimile. The influence of Robert Browning's poetry is also apparent here, there were few smiles in the marriage and like the character of the murderous husband in 'My Last Duchess,' even the image of Midge's smile must be destroyed, just as the dead Duchess' painted smile is hidden behind a curtain: '[t]hen all smiles stopped together.'[16] And, like Browning's newly widowed Duke, Buzz is also free to execute new plans. With Midge gone he 'could breathe, he was free, and [. . .] he had not felt so well for years' (133). This ecstasy is checked, however, as the hoover 'whines, gasps and dies'—merely the first of the continuous reminders of absence that imply Midge's presence (117). With misplaced sympathy for his bereavement the doctor comments, 'it takes time to get over these things,' but Buzz's chronic guilt is deeply repressed and not something easily resolved (133). Du Maurier's characters seldom get to enjoy peace and psychological health as the author excels at identifying our ugly human flaws without providing any hope for improvement. Buzz will be the architect of his own downfall.

Midge dies in December and according to Buzz, he does not think of her for thirteen weeks, until the apple tree reminds him of her habitually dispirited demeanour. Like his wife, every aspect of the apple tree is out of kilter and guaranteed to displease. The blossom is too thick, 'like a mop,' a description that echoes his comments on Midge's hair: 'that fluffy mop, much too thick and bushy for her face' which was 'long and narrow even then' (135). He ascribes human emotions to the anthropomorphized tree, describing it as 'gloating and triumphant,' it becomes a 'perpetual reminder of all the things he most detested and always had, he could not put a name to them . . . ' (144). But he *has* named them constantly in his narrative: all of the aspects of Midge, from her smile to her speech to her manners to her dress. The story is loaded with all of the things he detests about her and, as usual with du Maurier plots, the truth is in plain sight but unseen by the flawed character whose self-centeredness disregards others feelings but not their physicality. Midge's mortal life is over but the tree symbolising her body must be killed before she can be truly gone.

Unlike 'The Blue Lenses' where people are seen to have animal heads pertinent to their characters, here women from Buzz's past return as appropriately designated plants. The nubile Land Girl takes the form of young apple tree that 'stand[s] modest and demure' versus an older tree, a 'freak which did not know its texture or its shape, but thought to please,' just like Midge, a woman minus elegance or allure (139). Buzz remembers that the Land Girl he kissed during the war had skin 'like a very young apple' (122). He immediately associates the other tree with Midge: 'the likeness was unmistakable.' A passage of insistently dispiriting adjectives underscores the point:

> The tree was *scraggy* and of a *depressing thinness*, possessing none of the gnarled solidity of its companions. Its few branches, growing high up on the trunk like *narrow* shoulders on a tall body, spread themselves in *martyred resignation*, as though *chilled* by the fresh morning air. The roll of wire circling the tree, and reaching halfway up the trunk from the base, looked like a *grey* tweed skirt covering *lean* limbs; while the topmost branch, sticking up into the air above the ones below, yet *sagging slightly,* could have been a *drooping* head poked forward in an attitude of *weariness*. How often had he seen Midge stand like this, *dejected.* (114, italics mine)

The parallels to his wife's form and attitude are marked, exactly echoing descriptions of her, one of which is from the photograph Buzz examines and the tree is described in the medicalised terminology of degeneration and disease.

> the small brown buds had unfolded themselves, had ripened into flower, and now spread themselves above his head into a fantastic cloud of white, moist blossom. It grew thickest at the top of the tree, the flowers so clustered together that they looked like wad upon wad of soggy cotton wool, and all of it, from the topmost branches to those nearer to the ground, had this same pallid colour of sickly white. (138)

The lexicon also evokes a bridal gown and although Midge is dead and mute, her palpable unhappiness pervades the story with the bitterness of Miss Havisham's rage over her own romantic rejection. Buzz sexually rejects Midge's body while she lives, burns the photograph of her smile after her death, and enacts uxoricide through his felling of the tree that he thinks resembles her. Yet, while the image of the older tree powerfully conveys misery, Midge's dejection is written so as to invite laughter, not pity. The unrelentingly pessimistic description indicates one of du Maurier's trademark isologues, in which the adjectival treatment of an object—here a tree—signifies a character's attitude towards a person, in this case a deceased wife. The unwitting Willis the gardener asserts that the old tree had 'been barren as long as I've worked here.' The infertile middle-aged wife who, like the fruitless apple tree, never blossomed and is now 'humped, straggling and thin,' is consigned to useless old age (122).

This echoes the fact that in Western culture femininity, morality, and sterility permeate the ageing process for women with a gradual but palpable lessening of social status corresponding to increasing age. According to Marina Warner: '[d]ecrepitude encipher[s] ugliness, ugliness unloveliness, unloveliness unwomanliness, unwomanliness infertility: a state of being against nature.'[17] An ironic comment considering that ageing is itself a natural process. The 'knowing look' in Willis the gardener's eye precedes a passage of free indirect thought from Buzz, reminiscent of a similarly humorous passage in 'The Alibi' where Fenton inwardly registers shock and secretly accuses Anna of offering her son as his first murder victim. Like the character of Fenton, Buzz has no self-knowledge, only self-consciousness. He is paranoid that Willis has perceived his intent to destroy the apple tree and connected this to his feelings about his dead wife: 'What did the fellow mean? It was not possible that he had been struck also by that fantastic freak resemblance —no, it was out of the question, indecent, blasphemous; besides, he had put it out of his mind now, he had not thought of it again.' (124) Buzz is the master of self-deception, since recognising it he has thought of little else but the tree and its uncanny resemblance to Midge, and now he reflects upon it to the point of obsession.

The widower initially appears delighted at being single and answerable to no one. He is an immature, high-strung man whose lack of emotional intelligence will ultimately bring him to disaster. Buzz's inner ruminations make it clear that everything reminds him of his late wife and the pretty Land Girl. He wakes newly alone in the marital bed and looks out of the window to see how 'the moon shone upon the withered branches, and they looked like a skeleton's arms raised in supplication.' The branch he felt a 'queer distaste' to touch the previous day, falls, and points towards the young tree 'as if in accusation' (126). A stolen kiss with the Land Girl is a cherished memory and now the two trees are indelibly associated with her cheery, girlish self and his morose, mature wife. He hopes the old tree is dead; '[a]nd a good job too' (134). The trees are the living embodiment of two dead women, and in psychological terms they represent the unfinished business of the repressed as du Maurier continues to ramp up the tension.

On one level the narrative reads as a shorter version of Molly Panter-Downes' novel *One Fine Day* (1947): a critique of a post-war society in which middle-class women endlessly struggle to adjust to running a household with no domestic staff. Midge ties back plants, puts photographs in albums, sees to the flower garden, buys food, mends clothes and cleans while Buzz enjoys retirement: trips to London, his Gentleman's Club, and the cinema. What her husband regards as the tiresome legacy of marital bliss includes rooms that are scrubbed and straight and 'much too tidy,' a shed that has everything in its place, and the 'bother of cooking and washing up' (133). None of this is missed or regretted until much later in the story. During the war it is Midge who supports the home front, joins the Red Cross, and goes to endless meetings, while there is the deliberately vague mention that Buzz merely does 'some kind of war work' (124). After Midge dies he takes a longer holiday than was customary, driving for six weeks through Europe rather than their habitual duty visit of a month in Norfolk with his mother. Freed from wifely concern over his fitness, he drinks and puts on weight, dances with young girls having not done so 'for years,' and thinks: '[t]his was the life, no worries, no cares' (141). He fails to recognise that Midge managed the worries and the cares, it was she who made their domestic and social life run smoothly and closely monitored his physical health.

Du Maurier's shorter fiction presents the hazards rather than the rewards of love and this device is also evident in 'The Doll' where like Buzz the narrator elides what he does not wish to face. An apparent focus on heterosexual intimacy belies the constant subtext of confinement and escape, a factor which applies to either gender in many of the stories. Du Maurier is not generally regarded as a feminist writer despite her recent inclusion in *The Encyclopaedia of Feminist Writers*. To facilitate her writing she engaged female staff to cook, clean, and nanny, ensuring that she had time to create and she was a member of the privileged classes where females could pursue ambitions (such as writing) that were often unavailable to other women. However, her short fiction presents an equal ratio of male to female narrators and the themes offer no single reading or simple argument about gender relations in the early twentieth century. The complexity of the material however, does underline the necessity of realigning du Maurier's position to that of an early twentieth-century exponent of the anti-romance genre. It is this encoded model of subversive plot within apparently romantic literary tropes that renders her storylines subtle and anarchic.

Despite this serious agenda du Maurier's mordant sense of humour is most apparent in the stories in which comedy is closely interwoven with the politics of the personal. In common with the majority of her male characters, Buzz is a thoroughly unpleasant man and the reader can enjoy his suffering in the knowledge that it is well deserved. He is a self-deceptive liar and his view of events has no veracity as it is invariably inaccurate and distorted. Though outwardly confident, he is afraid, filled with nameless foreboding that centres upon the apple tree, the blossom, the fruit, and even the smoke from the fallen branches now turned into apple logs:

> Suddenly, for no reason, he was seized with a kind of fear, a feeling of panic almost. What if the smell filled the whole house through the night, came up from the kitchen quarters to the floor above, and while he slept found its way into his bedroom, choking him, stifling him, so that he could not breathe? the thought was ridiculous, insane—and yet . . . (131)

Each time he considers the tree his thoughts trail off into an ellipsis. As his mania escalates his drinking increases, his behaviour becomes increasingly erratic, and he is sharp with the servants, yet the doctor still sees him as a grieving widower. Buzz is aware of the irony: 'At least he himself had the honesty to admit that he did not miss her at all' (133).

Comically unaware of the torturous undercurrents, Willis the gardener continually refers to the tree by the feminine pronoun and soberly determines that: '[i]f *she* doesn't bear fruit, we'll have *her* down next winter' (125, italics mine). He does not see the 'martyred position,' the 'weary branches [. . .] like wispy hair,' or hear the tree's unspoken judgement which (the increasingly paranoid) Buzz recognises as directed at him: 'I am like this because of your neglect' (115). Instead, Willis regards the fresh apple blossom as a 'treat' and directs his master to 'take a look at her directly' and enjoy the sight. The small, brown, blemished, dry, dusty, buds of the old apple tree are promising to Willis who 'has hopes' for future fruit but, in a phrase which echoes his repulsion towards his wife, Buzz feels a 'queer distaste to touch them' (124). The use of adjectives denoting aridity, ruination and worthlessness continue the text-long isologue representing Midge and reveals Buzz as a husband who did not 'touch,' or rather enjoy, his wife sexually or otherwise. This follows fairy-tale conventions in which 'the body of an infertile woman, when invoked in any way as a body, expresses perforce a perverted dimension of the natural, becomes transgressive in itself, open to derision as well as fear.'[18] It is plain to the reader that minus fecundity Midge's ageing body serves no marital purpose and du Maurier slyly omits the issue of Buzz and his fertility entirely.

This complex narrative explores and disrupts the dialectical oppositions of beauty/ grotesqueness, youth/ age, fecundity/ nullity. In examining representations of beauty and du Maurier's heroines, Margaret E. Mitchell states that beauty's function is an ethical one.[19] Mitchell's theory however concerns the novels; the shorter fiction explodes her argument. In 'The Apple Tree,' the pretty Land Girl displays questionable morals by kissing a married man, but it is the young apple tree that 'hadn't a fair chance' as the older tree shadows its sunshine. It is Midge who does not stand a chance in competition with youthful beauty of the Land Girl as her husband's flirtation demonstrates. Likewise the fey and lovely character of Rebecca in 'The Doll' displays a disregard for conventional morality, in common with the alluring Marquise in 'The Little Photographer' (and the eponymous Rebecca in the novel). Du Maurier's characters upset the norms of the romance trope in proffering the ugly as benign and the attractive as malignant.

As the plot develops the trees continue to evolve in fecund echoes of the two women: one 'modest and demure [. . .] her soft flowers reaching to the sky, the old tree a 'freak' with petals of a 'wilting, dingy white.' The old tree remains a reminder of Midge, ever 'reproachful, anxious, desirous of an admiration that he could not give' (140). The emphasis is firmly on the rejection of her body but we are not encouraged to speculate on the reasons behind Buzz's frigidity. The tree becomes increasingly grotesque: '[i]nstead of blossoming to life, to beauty, it had somehow, deep in nature, gone awry and turned a freak' (139). This supports Grosz's theory of how '[w]omen's bodies are often regarded culturally as uncontrollable, with surprising and sudden emissions of bodily fluids, too close to our bestial origins, frail and unreliable compared to male biological consistency.'[20] The word 'freak' is significant and informs the narrative development in various ways: the tree is abnormal in appearance, i.e. a monster in nature, and Buzz continually exhibits whimsical and freakish behaviour with regards to it. A freak is something aberrant to normal life and as the story illustrates through vegetative rather than the more common bestial symbolism, therefore it must be attacked, expelled, destroyed.

At page 150 Buzz irrevocably commits himself to cutting down the old apple tree by offering the logs to the landlady at the pub, enjoying the secrecy of his private plan which he frames as, 'an act of mercy really. Never had he seen anything so wretched as the apple tree. There couldn't be any life left in it. Not a leaf remained. Twisted, ugly, bent, it ruined the appearance of the lawn. Once it was out of the way the whole setting of the garden would change.' (151) Or rather, the whole setting of his life? He happily organises his sharpest tools in preparation for the act, and the combination of methodically brutal practicalities and his sense of satisfaction at the destruction to follow, chillingly conveys the preliminaries of a ritual killing. The staccato quality of the initial sentences and the repetition of the personal pronoun indicates the inexorable quality of his actions: an irony that is uppermost in *his* mind:

> He took down the saw, the wedges, and the axe. He might need all of them. He ran his thumb along the edges. They would do. As he shouldered his tools and walked back to the front garden he laughed to himself, thinking that he must resemble an executioner of the old days, setting forth to behead some wretched victim in the tower. (151)

By cutting down the apple tree Buzz thinks he will have peace and like his life, the garden is blighted by this twisted memento of his dead wife. Buzz is not a wise man and characteristically he is determined to do this job without help, alone and at night, after a visit to the pub and a heavy drinking session. While he works on by moonlight, he is oblivious to the moon, to the symbolism of female deities such as Diana, protectress of virginity, childbirth and death, and the night's beauty cannot distract him from his destruction of the apple tree.

In order to complete the process he hacks frenziedly at the tree, destroying the 'rubbery flesh' in a fit of hysterical derangement reflected in the pace and syntax, verbs, and ellipses: 'Now she's groaning, now she's splitting, now she's rocking and swaying, hanging there upon one bleeding strip. Boot her then. That's it, kick her, kick her again, one final blow, she's over, she's falling . . . she's down . . . damn her, blast her . . . she's down, splitting the air with sound, and all her branches spread about her on the ground.' (152) In shocking language Du Maurier serves up the bitter rewards of old age: withered and cold and dejected are epithets describing an older wife in an unhappy marriage who is considered a burden now she is no longer fecund. 'After all I've done for you' and 'the best years of my life' are the proverbial reproaches of the abandoned and rejected wife. Yet as this story illustrates, this kind of (frequently) female self-abnegation is a bind in which both genders are caught, both partners imprisoned.

Midge the patient martyr should ideally be rewarded for her selflessness, but her spirit remains reproachful, and readers are not convinced that she is admitted to Paradise despite her self-sacrificing ways. As a living woman Midge had physical needs for love, attention and sex, that were ignored. Yet even as a dryadic inspiration for unwanted memories she must be erased as Buzz favours a type of woman without demands for affection and attention. Julie Wosk's study of female replicants in literature includes the comment of a male creator on his female automata: 'she is a non-consuming woman, a safe one for me to have around,' and this confirms Buzz's ideal of a safe female partner as one without physical or emotional needs.[21] Du Maurier's deftly ironic touch is again apparent when Buzz repeats Midge's catchphrase when he hears of the untimely death of May the land girl. 'Oh well . . . he smiled. Was he going to make use of that expression now? Poor Midge!' (125)

The next night the apple logs do not burn, instead they fill the house with sickly greenish smoke and have the appearance of human limbs. 'The logs lay there [. . .] one charred limb above another, black and huddled, like the bones of someone darkened and dead by fire. Nausea rose in him. He thrust his handkerchief into his mouth, choking.' (131) Now desperate, he throws the logs into the field where he hopes they will, 'rot and perish, grow sodden with rain, and in the end become part of the mouldy earth; he did not care. The responsibility was his no longer. They were out of his house, and it did not matter what became of them.' (132) The denial of responsibility parallels his resentment against Midge who also became a liability, a denier of pleasure and a reminder of toil and dependence. His hopes of freedom from responsibility morph into hatred for the apple tree logs which literally embody her memory. Buzz takes the 'bones' outside of the house and garden, now solely his domain, and leaves them to decompose in the neighbouring field. Once relocated, they continue to cause mayhem as a foal trips over them causing aggravation between Buzz and the farmer who owns the field. The unburied logs, or rather bones, serve as a Freudian symbol of the repressed and an indicator of psychological, though not literal, murder. He wonders if he is going mad, there is both time and occasion for it, and his increasing isolation cements his conviction of being haunted. As Winterson opines: 'Going mad takes time.'[22] Du Maurier may have read Charlotte Perkins Gilman's novella *The Yellow Wallpaper* [1892]. On one level this story is a reworking of the plot whereby a woman living a restricted life becomes obsessed with the wallpaper in her room which eventually symbolises her own incarceration by contemporary personal and societal restrictions. Here, the story continues after the woman's death and her vengeance is purely psychological.

The choice of fruiting tree is significant as regards gender relations. The apple is present in mythic, biblical and fairy-tale stories, representing the dangers of temptation, destruction, and expulsion. In Greek myth the Garden of the Hesperides had an apple tree with golden fruit and the goddesses made Paris choose the most beautiful among them in order that the winner claim a golden apple; a choice that catalysed the Trojan War. Although originally 'apple' was a general word for fruit, Christian tradition generally holds that the forbidden fruit of the Garden of Eden was an apple and in western culture it is synonymous with illicit sexual knowledge, especially pertaining to women and female curiousity. 'Of the tree in the garden thou mayest freely eat, but of the tree of the knowledge of good and evil, thou shall not eat of it'(Genesis 2.16–7). However, the proverbial phrase 'the apple of your eye' also has a biblical origin and contrastingly conveys feelings of great love and admiration, feelings that Buzz has for the Land Girl, not his wife (Deuteronomy 32.10). In du Maurier's short fiction, symbolism is seldom straightforward.

Temporally the narrative covers the natural seasons of dormancy, fecundity, fruition, and decay—represented by the apple tree's development: budding, blossom, apples, and stasis. But every aspect of life is crippled in this latter-day Aesop's fable: the beauty of blossom and fruit is rendered ugly. The old tree 'laden, bowed down under her burden of fruit,' the apples are personified as 'clamouring brothers and sisters [. . .] split open and rotting.' Their vegetative silence is a parallel to Midge's unspoken reproaches for her husband's neglect. The hyperbolic language heightens into 'monstrous,' 'frightful,' the tree is in 'agony and torture,' 'groaning' under the weight of the rotten apples it carries. Buzz describes the fruit of the old tree as '[f]ilthy-tasting things' which are '[s]tringy, beastly,' '[t]he thing was rotten'—like his marriage (143–44).

In the story the apple occupies the equivocal role of a positive, and a negative symbol and illustrates both the beauty of youth and the decay of age. It was the bite of an apple that sent Snow White into a deathlike slumber and we learn that the Land Girl named for the spring month of May has already passed into the land of perpetual winter. Killed in a motorbike accident months before her marriage, Buzz laments that now there will be, '[n]o more curling hair, blowing about her face, no more laughter.[. . .] he had put his arm about her and kissed her for one brief, fleeting moment. May, the Land Girl with the laughing eyes.' (157) Unlike Persephone, May cannot return from the underworld, and it is directly after learning the news of her death that Buzz goes out into the snow suspecting that for him spring will also never come. The garden is hushed and still, 'as though some spirit had come and put a spell upon the place' and he touches the dormant young tree no longer shadowed by the old apple tree he chopped down. He touches the young tree, seemingly a thing of 'fantasy and ghosts' checking for signs of life in the hope that, 'in the spring *she* would blossom once again' (157–58, italics mine). Unlike Willis, his hopes are all for the young tree, he never saw the older tree's buds as potential fruit, and for him there was no miracle in the older tree's renaissance. The warning is clear: once relegated the wife/ tree is doomed, and, without clear sight and decent values the husband/ gardener is also lost. The story ends with Buzz outside in the cold darkness, helplessly caught in the 'clutch' of the apple tree stump. 'He sank deeper, ever deeper into the snow, and when a stray piece of brushwood, cold and wet, touched his lips, it was like a hand, hesitant and timid feeling its way towards him in the darkness.' (159) In this chapter the deconstruction of the patriarchal traditions of marriage are symbolised by the dismembered limbs of the unwanted body of the wife. The end of the marriage through the death of the wife is swift and calm, but the end of the story is bloody and brutal. In 'The Apple Tree' the protagonist disintegrates physically and mentally as he is haunted by memories of a loveless marriage, and as predicted in the marriage rites—there is to be no swift severance of husband from wife, or limbs from the trunk of the apple tree. 'And they twain shall be one flesh: so then they are no more twain, but one flesh./ What therefore God hath joined together, let not man put asunder' (Matthew 19.1–12). Du Maurier allows Midge to have the final revenge upon her husband and it is the attitude of timidity characterising the branch/hand that settles the case. Whether psychologically or literally haunted, Buzz cannot be separated from Midge. Her limbs embrace him even after death, an ending which has never seemed actual in a text dominated by the deceased.

Du Maurier offers a lively anti-romance to amaze and amuse us and this dark fable inverts Aesopic conventions and blurs the borders of human physicality in common with stories such as Franz Kafka's 'Metamorphosis' where the reader encounters the human as hexapod. As in that story, here the action is solely interpreted by Buzz—Willis, for example, is involved in the events throughout, but does not understand them in any way that is recognisable to Buzz. The widower is unrepentant, unenlightened, and treats the tree with the same hostility and neglect that Midge received in life. When we are told that Buzz 'felt,' 'thought,' or 'sensed' something, the lower-order conceptual thoughts are that this is, firstly, true, and secondly, Buzz's interpretation of the world.

To follow the movement of unreliability further, we proceed past true events and honestly reported thought into the realm of the narrator imposing the experience of Midge's endless survivance via the tree on Buzz as a punitive measure. The narrator is visiting a haunting upon Buzz by manipulation of his thoughts, in a clear act of vengeance. Midge's survival and actions towards Buzz are not perpetrated by the unwitting apple tree, whose avatar status exists solely in the mind of Buzz, but by the narrator who relates the events. This leads to the conclusion that, most unusually, 'The Apple Tree' is a ghost story told from the perspective of the ghost—the disembodied and re-embodied ghost of an embittered, long-suffering and still-suffering wife.

In the previous story, 'Monte Verità,' Anna and the other acolytes escape the confines of the body, in this story marriage is the basis of a union where the death of one does not preclude an aftermath of physical consequences on the anatomy of the other. The 'unfinished business' of the dead and the living blurs the distinction between anatomy and presence and 'enforces the idea of the continuingness of human activity as well as the boundarylessness.'[23] This aspect ties in with the gothic but du Maurier frames the text with her personal brand of retribution. Seen from this perspective 'The Apple Tree' is an object lesson in the Old Testament principle of 'an eye for an eye' demonstrating that the most suitable punishment is that which is physically enacted upon the human body. As expressed in Deuteronomy 15.12–18: 'Eye for eye, tooth for tooth, hand for hand, foot for foot, Burning for burning, wound for wound, stripe for stripe.' Regarding her notion of ideal punishments du Maurier outlines that in her system, '[e]ach murderer would be treated [. . .] in the light of the murder that he or she had committed. The treatment would always be individual, and always *creative*, because the murderer's fault was that he or she destroyed.'[24] This quotation is from a four-page letter on capital punishment issue and alternatives to life imprisonment to Victor Gollancz. However, contemporary reviews of du Maurier's stories decry them as the malformed products of a diseased mind rather than as a rich source of cultural commentary. In the *Daily Express* Nancy Spain lambasted *The Apple Tree* as a collection of narratives defined by 'malformation, hatred, blackmail, cruelty and murder.'[25] In response to Gollancz's staunch defence she stated that '[a]nyone writing such stories was surely sick.'[26] Spain's literal reading misses the allegorical framework, mistaking an interrogation of normative values for gratuitous violence. The dangers of missing the evident is a motif that continues in the next story, 'The Alibi,' in which James Fenton's 'failure to look at what women see' dooms all the characters in the text ('Don't Look Now,' 52). Their fates continue du Maurier's concept of punishments that fit the crime, and indicate that for her, moral turpitude enacts sterility upon the body of both perpetrator and victims.

NOTES

1. Bakhtin, 'Popular and Festive Forms,' *Rabelais and His World,* trans. by Helene Iswolsky (Bloomington: Indiana University Press, 1984), p. 197–220.
2. Rosalyn Diprose and Jack Reynolds, eds., *Merleau-Ponty: Key Concepts* (London: Routledge, 2014), p. 10–13.
3. Du Maurier, *Early Stories* (London: Todd, 1955), p. 28.
4. Du Maurier letter to Maud Waddell, 20 December 1944, EUL MS 207/6/4/1, courtesy of Special Collections.
5. Du Maurier, *The Birds and Other Stories* (London; Virago, 2011). All further references will be to this edition.
6. Sheila Hodges, 'Editing Daphne du Maurier' in *The Daphne du Maurier Companion*, ed. by Helen Taylor (London: Virago, 2007), p. 25–43 (p. 34).
7. Sceats and Cunningham, p. 81.
8. Du Maurier postcard to Maud Waddell, 17 May [n.y]. EUL MS 207/6/4/2, courtesy of Special Collections.
9. Christopher Pittard, 'Time, Space, and Psychogeography in *Castle D'Or*' in *Women: A Cultural Review*, 20:1 (2009), 57–73.
10. Forster, 'The Golden Girl,' p. 43–60.
11. Jeanette Winterson, *Why Be Happy When You Could Be Normal?* (London: Vintage, 2012), p. 131.
12. Coventry Patmore, 'The Angel in the House' [1854–1862]. Sourced at <http://www.gutenberg.org/files/4099/4099-h/4099-h.htm> [accessed 29.6.2022].
13. Virginia Woolf, 'Mr Bennett and Mrs Brown' [1924].
14. Ernest Hemingway, *The First Forty-One Stories* (London: Arrow, 2004), pp. 157–60.
15. Notebook, EUL MS 144/1/1/1, courtesy of Special Collections.
16. Robert Browning, 'My Last Duchess,' *Dramatic lyrics* [1842], *Norton Anthology of Poetry*, p. 1013.
17. Warner, p. 44.
18. Warner, p. 48.
19. Margaret E. Mitchell, '"Beautiful Creatures": The Ethics of Female Beauty in Daphne du Maurier's Fiction' in *Women: A Cultural Review*, 20: 1 (2000), 25–41.
20. Grosz, p. 12.
21. Wosk, p. 137.
22. Winterson, p. 171.

23. Smith and Wallace, p. 64.

24. Du Maurier four-page letter to Victor Gollancz on capital punishment, 14 November 1955. p. 3. MSS.157/3/I/DM/12, courtesy of Modern Records Centre, University of Warwick.

25. *The Apple Tree review,* 'Nancy Spain Cries How Improper, Daphne!,' 7 May 1954.

26. Quoted in Forster, p. 260, no details provided.

Chapter Seven

'The Alibi' [phallus] (1959)

'The Alibi' is the first story in *The Breaking Point: Short Stories*, a collection introduced by du Maurier with an invitation to the reader to judge the characters, and by implication, to examine themselves, as seen in the prefaratory note quoted in full later in this chapter.[1] The plot foregrounds the impotence of the male protagonist to realise his desires, both psychologically and emotionally, in a barren marriage and has a subtext that infers the physical dimension. Gollancz often promoted an upcoming collection by running a story in a periodical and *John Bull* magazine advertised their 'sensational' new Daphne du Maurier serial on the front cover in May 1959.[2] The front cover reads: 'Begins today *The Alibi*, sensational new story by the author of *Rebecca* and *Frenchman's Creek*: Would you refuse to help a policeman?' The magazine ran from the early 1940s to the 1960s featuring writers including Agatha Christie and H. E. Bates. This story may itself have been inspired by Agatha Christie's play 'Alibi.'[3] A pamphlet compiled for Hampstead Museum with a cover drawing by George du Maurier, includes the information that '[i]n 1928 Gerald du Maurier was engaged to produce "Alibi," the first Agatha Christie play, and it was suggested to him that [Charles] Laughton should play Hercule Poirrot, the detective.' Christie and du Maurier were in correspondence and there is further research to be done on du Maurier's literary influences and the historical context of her work. The magazine cover is a hand drawn colour illustration of a boy and a girl smiling at each other while another boy holding a cricket bat scowls at them. The explicatory summary runs: 'Of course, it isn't exactly cricket, but this is one of those moments in life when rules don't count—and it's every man for himself.' The 1950s pictorial idyll of children playing cricket, a quintessentially English game synonymous with patriotism and honour, is a curious contrast to the serial within its pages. *John Bull* magazine also includes many advertisements for domestic products such as hoovers, linoleum, and Triumph cars accompanied by large photographs of happy mothers and children, with capitalised strap-lines such as 'More time . . . with HOOVER freedom' and 'SHE'S FULLY INDEPENDENT' highlighting the 1950s consumerist idyll with its concomitant associations of domestic contentment.[4] Du Maurier's ambiguous relationship with traditional gender roles has been covered elsewhere but her alter ego Eric Avon (an imaginary Eton schoolboy) and contemporary males were trained in the values exemplified in Sir Henry Newbolt's well-known poem 'Vitaï Lampada' [1892], which has a repeated refrain of 'Play up! play up! And play the game!' (L8). The code of masculine behaviour summed up in Newbolt's poem, namely selfless duty, commitment, and fairness, is the antithesis of du Maurier's portrayal of twentieth-century male behaviour as portrayed by the character James Fenton.

The abridged magazine version of her story skips the two pages of framing introduction and begins by outlining the plot: 'Quite suddenly, Fenton had gone mad. In cold blood he was going to murder a woman and her child. Already the child was strapped to a chair, waiting, unsuspecting . . . ' Reassuring images of young Britons enjoying post-war prosperity surround this grim story set in a hellish locale where nothing and no one is stable or trustworthy. However, in the accompanying images middle-aged Fenton is attractive and smartly dressed, refugee Anna Kaufman is a red-lipped, exotic brunette, and dull-witted Johnny is a cleanly dressed, alert little boy. The illustrations are by Robert Fawcett (1903–1967) who portrays Fenton as looking like Hollywood film actor Cary Grant.[5] There is no evidence of the 'squalor' and 'shambles' of number eight Boulting Street as described in the text and the pictures offer a more palatable vision of the horrors to follow (7).

'The Alibi' conveys the austerity endured by a nation slowly recovering from war: the drab streetscape, derelict houses and desolate bombsites are the material representation of psychological dis-ease. Yet the story is framed by advertisements and editorials conveying the delights of a period when Prime Minister Harold MacMillan claimed '*most* of our people never had it so good' (italics mine).[6] The ideology of nationalism and patriotism is at odds with du Maurier's portrayal of slum denizens without hope or comfort, whose only apparent escape from suffering is self-destruction. It is predictable that the reviews by Nancy Spain in *The Daily Express* describe du Maurier's work as 'improper' and 'revolting' as she comments, 'I have noticed with despondency and alarm a growing morbidity in the work of Miss du Maurier.'[7] Du Maurier's plot notes for The Alibi can be found in a small brown leather notebook written in du Maurier's handwriting, together with pencilled notes for 'Ganymede' and 'The Tinted Spectacles,' an early title for 'The Blue Lenses.'[8] The choice to present the untold side of warfare is a bold and deliberate choice and one that appears to be at odds with du Maurier's position as wife of a major player in World War II

The plot centralises impotence, defined by *Blacks Medical Dictionary* as 'the inability to perform the sexual act. It may be partial or complete, temporary or permanent. [. . .] Of the many classifications of this not uncommon condition, the most satisfactory is probably that which divides it into two main groups: *organic* and *psychological*. [. . .] Among the psychological factors are ignorance, fear, weakness of sexual desire or abnormality of such desire.' The damaged dwellings of Boulton Street are metaphors for the minds and bodies of the characters. The female protagonist Anna Kaufman is isolated and weak. Apathetic from suffering she is unable to protect herself, her son, or her unborn baby—all are dead by the end of the story. James Fenton, the other major character, is emotionally detached and a compulsive liar. Du Maurier conspicuously dislocates desire from particular and genital origin, instead portraying the lusts and impulses of male characters as literally impotent. This compels Fenton, Buzz ('The Apple Tree'), and Victor ('Monte Verità'), to seek unorthodox and even disordered releases for their desire including fetishisation, delusion, and murder. Sexual practice is not erased but rather suppressed and redirected into fixations that motivate the characters. In 'Monte Verità' another character called Anna finds spiritual release is a sensual experience involving the renunciation of marital ties for life in an austere Trappistine community on a remote mountaintop. In 'The Alibi' an example of this is James Fenton's refusal of sexual contact with Anna Kaufmann even when she initiates intimate relations and clearly offers him intercourse. He shuns her advances on the basis of his impotence—'an old war wound . . . I've had to put all that sort of thing out of my life long ago'—instead he maintains the power relation that is already established and that he finds so enthralling (18).

In an attempt to escape his dull existence James Fenton starts a double life; randomly picking a house he plans to murder its occupants, a single mother and her son, but instead finds release by painting them in oils, before eventually confessing their murders—of which he appears to be innocent—to the police. These are themes du Maurier spent a lifetime returning to in her short fiction. A notebook in the archives (dated 1926) includes an early draft of 'The Story of a Weak Man,' an unpublished story about another of du Maurier's insecure, middle-aged, male narrators. The nameless man tells his life story to a stranger in Leicester Square. He lived in a bungalow in Beachcombe with his wife until she had a baby and he, 'made a fool of himself over some girl' (Notebook, 2). Nothing is his fault as no one has understood him since his mother died: 'I hate ties in any form, I must be independent' (4). He exhibits the same physical inadequacies as Fenton: 'You see, I'm not a very physical person, and unless I have someone who is sympathetic, who understands my countless little changes of mood, it's hopeless—hopeless. I suppose she was disappointed in me' (2–3). The final line is typical of du Maurier's manipulative males: 'If you could possibly lend me five pounds . . . '[9]

'The Alibi' bookended a decade that began with the execution of Timothy Evans in March 1950 for the murder of his infant daughter—a miscarriage of justice based on a false confession and poor judicial practice that led to a posthumous pardon in 1966. This was followed by the conviction and hanging three years later of the real killer, his landlord, John Christie, who was found to have murdered at least eight women in west London. Decades later du Maurier describes an abiding interest in forms of punishment including incarceration. She states her enjoyment of the books Gollancz regularly sent her: 'I enjoyed *Break Down the Walls*—when I say enjoyed, I mean I was very interested, always am in anything to do with prisons.'[10] 'The Alibi' uses a murder plot as a vehicle for a grotesquely funny exploration of self-deceit, an exposé of bourgeois rituals, and an affecting tracing of the life of one immigrant among multitudes in post-war London. In a postmodernist reading the text is a merciless dissection of the relations between personal power and fame, and between image and the interior life.

In a letter to fellow author Phyllis Bottome, du Maurier describes how the themes of the collection had 'lain dormant for years' and how: '[s]omeone in the *Sunday Express*, describing Alibi, got the whole point wrong. Of course, Mr Fenton did not seduce the girl or murder her. Painting had been his therapy. He cracked at the non-belief of his wife and the world, and because he had once thought guilty-wise became guilty.' This comment indicates the author's concerns with the mind leading the heart and the body into vice, a theme revisited in 'The Apple Tree' and 'The Doll' where ennui leads to obsession and savagery. Her own unhappiness is entwined in with the narrative theme of the collection as she informs Bottome: 'So delighted to [. . .] hear your reaction to the stories and indeed the basic themes of a few of them had lain dormant for years, but I had been unhappy the winter before living in London, as you knew, and I think this had triggered off the thread or idea of The Breaking Point—perhaps in my case the gulf between fact and fantasy, so that one asks oneself the question "But what is true?" And that although life itself is deeply good, yet the jungle waits to break through.' That 'jungle' reference is of course to the animal-faced ferocity implied in 'The Blue Lenses' and the truth du Maurier seeks remains elusive as the denouement of 'The Alibi' shows.[11]

Readers first encounter Fenton disposing of his wife into a cab 'watching a phase of life that had gone forever,' freeing himself to pursue a power game of violence and intrigue in which he plays a merciful destroyer with the power to choose life or death for others (2). As real-life serial killer Christie commented after his conviction: 'I gave them a merciful end, the mob should remember that.' But Christie's habitually violent misogyny clouded his superficial sympathy, as seen in his comment that, '[y]ou can't help feeling that women who give you the come on wouldn't be so smug if helpless, or dead.' The psychologist at one judicial hearing described him as a 'self-righteous prude. A moraliser, and a killer of women. He feared women and their criticism, and hated their sexuality.'[12] Like Christie, the character of Fenton despises Anna and deeply resents his wife—desiring her admiration even as he deceives her. Deluded by his self-image as a Nietschean Übermensch, Fenton's charity only extends as far as his self-serving motivations allow. Du Maurier's fictional doppelgänger reifies Christie's role for our amusement. 'They don't know' he thought, 'those people inside, how one gesture of mine, now, at this minute, might alter their world [. . .] according to what I will, what I decide, their whole future will be decided. Faces smashed in. Sudden murder. Theft. Fire. It was as simple as that.' (4) The human need to feel powerful and in control initially makes this character appear threatening and sinister, yet the story finally renders Fenton a pathetic creature, minus family, home, talent and power. Caged and solitary he will face the death penalty for murder.

Du Maurier interrogates the motivations of characters indicating predatory actions that invite destruction without directly authoring it. The narrative guides the reader firmly towards violence from the outset as James Fenton, would-be psychopath, gets his wife out of the way so he can capriciously select a victim to murder. The apparent randomness of the way Fenton decides which house, and which victims, convincingly portrays the behaviour of a pathological psychotic and reveals the influence of Robert Browning on du Maurier's characterisation. 'He decided to work on a system of numbers. He would walk down three more streets, and then, depending upon the name of the third street in which he found himself, and how many letters it contained, choose the number of his destination. [. . .] The name was Boulting Street. Eight letters meant number eight.' (4) This callous plan reads as chillingly as anything from the characters in *Madhouse Cells* [1842], Browning's collection of confessional lunatics. As he works out which house to call upon in his self-imposed guise as the Angel of Death, Fenton tells himself 'No cheating' with a soberness that highlights the curious morality of those with murderous intent. (4)

Du Maurier's dramatis personae are not inmates but they are denizens of particular landscapes. The houses have 'lost caste' having suffered bombing and neglect, and Fenton's confidence contrasts with the 'drab' stairs, 'the unpainted gates, the lowering basements, the air of poverty and decay': number eight is 'even shabbier' than the rest (4). The lengthy description of the Victorian villa utilises du Maurier's trademark device of the isologue, an under-examined but efficient means of character delineation through the illustration of location or material things. This device is used in multiple texts including 'Split Second' and 'Monte Verità.' The tone of hopelessness continues with the 'white-faced, blank-eyed' three-year-old boy 'tied in some strange fashion to the mud-scraper so that he could not move,' a defunct doorbell, and the pallid, expressionless, lank-haired Anna. Even the stray cat has a wounded paw. 'The apathy of Sunday lay upon the streets. Houses were closed, withdrawn' (4). Like her son Johnny, Anna is tied into a situation where she cannot move, literally or metaphorically, circumstances that will also hold true for Fenton at the denouement. Du Maurier challenges her readers to consider the possibilities for change, and the constraints that govern our lives.

The slum is home to Anna Kaufman and her son Johnny, unwitting models for the 'art' of Fenton's planned homicides, executions that form an exciting and dramatic contrast to his humdrum existence. In keeping with du Maurier's emphasis on place and time, this story offers two locations that are equally repulsive: the condemned slum of post-war London, home to tragic events, and the Fentons' elegant Regency square townhouse where 'bright front doors and window-boxes' belie the stifled, miserable lives within (4). On his canvasses Fenton creates for himself a vividness and vitality that are conspicuously absent from his everyday life.

> and now all was riot—sunsets that had never been, and unrisen dawns. The Venetian red was not the Doge's palace but little drops of blood that burst in the brain and did not have to be shed, and zinc white was purity, not death, and yellow ochre . . . yellow ochre was life in abundance, was renewal, was spring, was April even in some other time, some other place . . . (21)

There are notable similarities between du Maurier's description of Fenton and the police profile circulated in the manhunt for Christie. Both depict an average-looking man who seems 'In many ways [. . .] incredibly ordinary.'[13] The police report for the missing John Christie reads: 'Aged 55, height 5 ft. 9 in., slim build, dark hair thin on top, clean shaven. Sallow complexion, long nose, wearing horn rimmed spectacles, dentures top and bottom, walks with military bearing. Wearing a dark blue herringbone suit, brown leather shoes, fawn belted raincoat, and brown trilby hat.'

Anna meets Fenton on the threshold of number eight but '[t]he effort to size him up was beyond her—the tweed suit, appropriate for London or the country, the trilby hat, the walking-stick, the fresh-complexioned face, the forty-five to fifty years' (6). Fenton is at once both externally nondescript and internally singular. His average body disguises an interiority coloured by violent rage and the urbanity of his clothes is a clue. Nina Auerbach comments on the trilby hat as symbolic in du Maurier's work as regards sinister intent: 'Trilby hats bob through Daphne's later tales like a sinister joke; invariably they portend disaster.'[14] Auerbach is right when she surmises that the inclusion of trilby hats in du Maurier's fiction is a tacit salute to the author-grandfather from whom Daphne was thought to inherit her literary talent. In George du Maurier's novel, *Trilby* [1895], the eponymous heroine and artist's model turned singer is mesmerised by Svengali and cannot perform without him. She is ultimately rescued but dies soon afterwards. Fenton evokes George du Maurier's character Svengali in that he does not seduce Anna, but without him she cannot survive.

The story serves a protest against mediocrity as Fenton determines to find fame and awe others with his talent, rejecting his former life as 'an insignificant little man,' also a common description of John Christie by those who knew him according to Oates' biography. He declares himself to Anna who sees his ambition as artistic in origin.

> 'When I was younger,' he said aloud, 'I had so much ambition.'
> 'To be a great painter?' she asked.
> 'Why, no . . . not particularly that,' he answered, 'but to become great. To be famous. To achieve something outstanding.' (24)

The psychologist's report describing Christie as 'weak and immature' could easily serve for du Maurier's grotesque yet pathetic figure of Fenton, a man whose search for excitement ends with Anna, the boy, and the house, *ergo* the mundane, the dull, and the quotidian. Christie is described as: 'An intelligent man who suffered from anxiety, not insanity. [. . .] he is a man of weak character, he is immature – certainly in his sex life he is immature; he is a man who, in difficult times and in face of problems, tends to exaggerate in an hysterical fashion.' This description perfectly illustrates the hyperbole in Fenton's expressions on his art. In fact, Fenton is a composite of *both* suspects involved in the Christie case, Du Maurier gives his character the ambitious and sly mind of Christie and the '[s]ordid, yet commonplace' fate of the lodger, Evans.[15]

'The Alibi' is one of the many du Maurier stories that incorporate themes of freedom and escape, with violence as a key element and examples include 'The Lordly Ones,' 'Monte Verità,' and 'The Apple Tree.' Initially Fenton is a man living a life that no longer feels real, acting out a pretentious round of middle-class social rituals that neither satisfy, nor comfort. Dinner and drinks with the Althussons is a leitmotif in Fenton's thoughts as is his subsequent glee at escaping. On a walk with his wife he suddenly sees everyone as 'puppets manipulated by a string. The very steps they took were jerking, lopsided, a horrible imitation of the real thing, of what should be' and this epiphanic moment is the start of his psychopathy (1). The breaking point is reached almost immediately as Fenton cries out: 'I can't go on.' Something has to change and as so often when ennui is depicted in the short fiction, the change is a negative choice that leads to destructive forces.

Henri Bergsen's essay on laughter provides an insight into the beginnings of Fenton's psychosis.

> We should see that this movement of relaxation or expansion is nothing but a prelude to laughter, that the laugher immediately retires within himself, more self-assertive and conceited than ever, and is evidently disposed to look upon another's personality as a marionette of which he pulls the strings. In this presumptuousness we speedily discern a degree of egoism and, behind this latter, something less spontaneous and more bitter, the beginnings of a curious pessimism which becomes the more pronounced as the laugher more closely analyses his laughter.[16]

Both du Maurier's theatrical background and the influence of Mansfield's writing can be discerned here, Fenton's aghast reaction to what he perceives as masks and marionettes ruled by a 'master-hand,' reads as ambivalently towards God, as it does to pretence. Mansfield's comments to her husband, John Middleton Murray in 1917 are indicative of the compulsion to hide the secret self: 'It's a terrible thing to be alone. Yes, it is. But don't lower your mask until you have another mask prepared beneath—as terrible as you like—but a mask.'[17] Both writers share an interest in layers of artifice and the enjoyment in the psychological protection of a mask, the resulting stories illustrate what happens when the mask slips. Even 'Mr Sims,' the false name Fenton assumes for 'the lovely duplicity of a secret life' is a misnomer: there is nothing simple about him or the situation he engineers (22). Again, Christie's comments on his own actions are chillingly apposite for Fenton as self-appointed judge, jury and executioner: 'It was thrilling because I had embarked upon the career I had chosen for myself—the career of murder.'[18] 'The Alibi' continues themes of artifice and authenticity presented through the lens of the human body initiated in the much earlier story, 'The Doll' (1928). In both stories Grosz's summarisation of the possible interpretations of the bodies around us is pertinent: '[o]ther bodies may simply be complex automata, androids or even illusions, with no psychical interior, no affective states, no consciousness. Consciousness becomes, in effect, an island unto itself.'[19]

Du Maurier specialises in a particular type of male narrator, exemplified by Fenton who places himself at the centre of events with the doomed quality of Samuel Taylor Coleridge's Ancient Mariner. Fenton's self-pity is boundless and although it is his actions that engineer the tragic events the reader knows he will continue to deny responsibility despite his final defiant confession. Du Maurier specialises in male characters whose style of unreliable relation betrays their sinister motivations and true character. Fenton's determination to be seen by others as he sees himself leads to verbal enrolment that only works with the apathetic Anna, not the police, nor his wife Edna. Nicholas Royle links this aspect of the first-person voice to a Freudian impulse whereby 'the uncanny seems to be bound up with a compulsion to tell, a compulsive storytelling.'[20] Fenton divides the world into his godlike figure dispensing justice and favour at will, and subhumans who deserve to die for 'grimacing and jumping on their string [. . .] jiggling and smirking.' A case of kill or be killed. Despite his egocentric impulses, his desperation to escape banality is genuine as shown by his thought that: '[t]he drowning man who sees the pattern of his life pass by as the sea engulfs him could at last be understood' (3). The solipsistic drama of his thought processes continues when Anna is ill after her miscarriage and instead of a human empathetic response, Fenton is full of resentment over his unmet needs.

With resignation implying a lifetime of disappointments, Anna appears unsurprised that he is not, after all, her friend and protector. This episode has a direct effect on how Fenton regards his painting and foregrounds the relationship between muse and artist centralised in Wilde's *The Picture of Dorian Grey* [1891] and George du Maurier's *Trilby* [1895].[21] Trilby was published serially in *Harpers Monthly* magazine in 1894 and tells the story of Trilby O' Ferrall, an artist's model in Paris, who falls under the spell of the compelling Svengali, a musician who trains her voice through hypnosis and turns her into a singing star. The pair travel throughout Europe on successful concert tours, Trilby as La Svengali, the famous singer, and Svengali as the accompanying orchestra conductor. When Svengali falls ill and dies, the spell is broken, and Trilby loses her voice. Likewise, without Anna, Fenton's inspiration is gone and his art suffers: '[b]ack in the studio, he pottered with the final touches to the self-portrait, but concentration was difficult. Nothing worked. The thing looked dead. She had ruined his day' (30). Anna's dismissal of his self-portrait as inaccurate is pertinent despite her apparent lack of insight: the facsimile image is a true reflection of the 'sick man.' In addition, the reader is reminded that this is a painting of 'Mr Sims,' not James Fenton.

> The self-portrait was absorbing. Madame Kaufman had found a mirror and hung it on the wall for him, so the start was easy enough. But he found he couldn't paint his own eyes. They had to be closed, which gave him the appearance of a sleeping man. A sick man. It was rather uncanny . . .
>
> 'So you don't like it?' Fenton observed to Madame Kaufman, when she came to tell him it was seven o'clock.
>
> She shook her head. 'It gives me what you call the creeps,' she said. 'No, Mr Sims, it's not you.' (28)

He 'smile[s] in fantasy' as he considers his work triumphantly exhibited in a gallery and expresses with devastating emotional illiteracy the thought that, '[a]lthough unfinished, that self portrait of a man asleep, it had significance' (31). Fenton hopes to have significance in the world while knowing that he does not. The relations between truth and art climax in a jejune bourgeois artist faking the primitive mode but revealing more than he intends, or could appreciate. As ever, du Maurier's mirror reflects the ugly truth and the protagonist remains unwitting while the reader enjoys the show. On another level the story works as a personal homage to du Maurier's grandfather. In addition to being an author, George du Maurier was a well-known illustrator for *Punch* magazine.

Fenton's sense of marital life imprisonment crystallises when his wife Edna innocently asks 'Which way?' as they stroll along the Embankment. He receives the question in a cosmic sense, unintended by Edna, as a result of which he literally and metaphorically changes direction with fatal consequences for everyone because, 'for him everything had changed. He was aware of a sense of power within. He was in control. His was the master-hand that set the puppets jiggling.' (3) Again, Bergson confronts the relationship between the body and laughter, naturalism, and mechanisation, offering insight into the mind of a psychopath.

> THE ATTITUDES, GESTURES AND MOVEMENTS OF THE HUMAN BODY ARE LAUGHABLE IN EXACT PROPORTION AS THAT BODY REMINDS US OF A MERE MACHINE. [capitalisation in original][22]

The crushing denouement sees Fenton in police custody, potentially on his way to a cell for the condemned. The brutal consequences of the revelation that caused him to 'step out of bondage into a new dimension' have, however, also freed him from his identity, from Edna, from the Althussons, and from the tedium of bourgeois Sunday rituals and his quotidian existence (4). The contrast between the central characters initially appears stark but both are trapped and neither escape successfully. Through Fenton's eyes we see Anna Kaufman as a blank-stared, 'girl or woman,' a refugee with a life as derelict as her demesne, trailing an infant as passive as herself through serial encounters with abusive men. With no family, partner or friends, her fate is a matter of unconcern in a London teeming with post-war human debris. While her relentlessly apathetic demeanour is mordantly funny this does not eclipse her despair: 'If you hadn't appeared . . . I don't know what I might *not* have done' (11, italics mine). Since we cannot know what Anna did before the story opens her comment supports the interpretation of her death as suicide. It may also refer to prostitution as a necessary means of survival for a poverty-stricken single mother.

Du Maurier shows how poverty and dislocation are mapped on to the female body and the disposable aspect of certain lives is the darker theme woven into the story. The parallels to the Christie case continue. Ruth Fuerst was the twenty-one-year-old Austrian who was Christie's first victim: 'the disappearance of a single foreign young woman, with fourteen addresses in four years, without close friends or family, was not remarkable, especially because there was no suspicion of foul play.'[23] It is clear from du Maurier's archival correspondence with her publisher and others, that she paid close attention to current affairs in which the little lives of ordinary folk are seldom represented. 'The Alibi' presents the reader with an uncomfortable reminder of the all-too-recent gas chambers in which countless 'non-persons' died; the full horror of which was still fresh when she wrote this collection as the post-Holocaust world reluctantly accepted the grisly realities of the Nazi regime. It is the very ordinariness of the victim and the assailant that adds veracity and power to the plot.

Appropriately Anna lives in the old servant's quarters in the basement of the house, and the description of the 'mute, drab villa' equally fits the abandoned mother and child. Du Maurier is scathing regarding the hypocrisy of contemporary attitudes towards unmarried mothers: 'People don't see anything wrong with one married woman having ten children—but if one poor unmarried mut has one! Oh, isn't it all unwholesome? The little more, and how much it is!'[24] Although she is not known as a feminist sympathiser, the author shows her awareness of the inequity of gender relations in her times and offers the silenced a chance to appear centre-stage, albeit arguably as victims rather than agents of their own fates.

Fenton's delight at finding the Kaufmans is expressed as he departs with the 'jaunty step of someone at the start of a great adventure,' a piquant contrast to Anna's invariable inertia. 'Her apathy was just what he needed. He wondered if she slept very heavily, or was even drugged. Those dark shadows under the eyes suggested drugs. So much the better. And a foreigner too. There were too many of them in the country.' (7) This throwaway comment on a throwaway person connects to philosopher Hannah Arendt's identification of a debate both ancient and current on how the 'distinction between man and animals runs right through the human species itself.' In 1958 in *The Human Condition* she notably wrote that those who 'constantly prove themselves to be the best (aristeuien) [. . .] and who "prefer immortal fame to mortal things" are really human; the others, content with whatever pleasures nature will yield them, live and die like animals.'[25] The date of her seminal text is significant and has bearing on this character whose actions and motivations appear simultaneously base and seductively elevated. It is clear that Fenton's philosophy is rooted in Hericlitus as he mentally measures the garden as large enough for a grave, and scopes out the coal cellar for burial possibilities. He is pleased at the isolation of his intended victims. Oates' commentary on Christie's situation is startlingly accurate for Fenton showing du Maurier's knowledge of the case and use of the details in the narrative. 'He had a secure base which he could lure his victim to, where he could kill and dispose of the body safely, and his wife was absent. Finally, the social upheaval caused by war enabled him to meet his first two victims and kill them with impunity (this was also the case for Haigh in 1944).'

Fenton feels godlike through the creation of images of his victims, he despises Johnnie but he 'felt more tolerant about him as soon as he had finished the first portrait. It was as though the boy existed anew through him. He was Fenton's creation.' (23) Likewise, Anna only exists in glimpses and fragments, her body is an assemblage of parts that Fenton restates and reshapes at will.

> It was only in the imagination, or glimpsed in passing or behind a window, or leaning from a balcony abroad, or from the frame of a picture, or from a canvas like the one before him now—he changed from one brush to another, he was getting quite dextrous at this—that a woman had any meaning, any reality. And then to go and tell him that he had given her a mouth like a fish . . . (24)

Like Christie, Fenton chooses his victims from among the 'transient population of London; from among the vulnerable whose disappearance would not be likely to create a stir.' It remains unknown whether Ruth Fuerst saw John Christie as a father figure and protector although as an inveterate liar Christie claimed: 'it was she who suggested that we should become lovers . . . I was rather backward and shy.'[26] It is known that she had a daughterly affection for him and his age supports his theory. Either way, the real-life person of Ruth and her fictional revenant Anna are twin sisters in their poverty of comfort, hope, and aspiration, and in their untimely demise.

Psychologists state that Christie was sexually inadequate and similarly Fenton has no intention of having sex with Anna, though she immediately offers him her body as part of the subletting deal. She decides that Fenton is her friend, but has no illusions left about men, or life. Unbuttoning her cardigan she asks, '[a]nd now Mr Sims, [. . .] which would you prefer to do first? Come to bed or paint Johnnie?' (17) Her reassurance that they will not be disturbed as 'no one will come' and Johnnie will be tied up, suggests what has surely been the repeated act of an impoverished person. The diametric motivations of the characters create much of the dramatic humour of the text as, unbeknownst to Anna, Fenton desires consummation of a violent, rather than sexual, act as his suspiciously swift invention of a war wound shows. 'It's . . . it's extremely kind of you Madame Kaufman,' he said. 'I do appreciate your offer. It's most generous. The fact is, unfortunately, I've been totally incapacitated for many years . . . an old war wound . . . I've had to put all that sort of thing out of my life long ago.' (18) In common with the character of Buzz in 'The Apple Tree' whose London job excluded him from active service, Fenton's war service is doubtful and disguises an impotence that seems as much martial as it is sexual. Calder details how reserved occupations could be deferred by application to special committees and thus 'by the end of 1940 more than two hundred thousand men had been granted deferment at their employer's request.'[27] When he is not enthusiastic Anna utters the sobering comment of a woman well-used to being used, 'It makes no difference to me. I'm at your *disposal*' (17, italics mine). The final word of this exchange iterates the throwaway condition of Anna and Johnnie Kaufman, and everything inside number eight. However, it can also be argued that before James Fenton has a chance to objectify her, Anna Kaufman is taking power herself and this reading is borne out by her final act of self-destruction at the end of the story.

Fenton's inner tirade at women on page 24 illuminates his view that women are usually dissatisfying and therefore lacking in meaning or reality, and may thus be treated accordingly. His thoughts are couched in resentful, angry, staccato language: 'That's right, he thought. Stay put. Keep your place. If there was one thing he could not stand it was a woman who argued, a woman who was self-assertive, a woman who nagged, a woman who stood upon her rights. Because of course they were not made for that. They were intended by their Creator to be pliable, and gentle, and accommodating, and meek.'(24) In another real-life parrallel Oates states that: '[Christie] had a "dread of women" according to psychologists the 'anxiety being mostly centred on sex fears' he would probably be unable to approach normal sexual intercourse at all; and if then, only with considerable fears. [. . .] A sad, unhappy, rather inadequate anxiety ridden man [with] a considerable amount of repression, especially of aggression.'[28] Having provided a lengthy and detailed exposition of the purpose of female humans, with comi-tragic bathos Fenton disappointedly acknowledges that, '[t]he trouble was that they were so seldom like that in reality.'

(24) Du Maurier indicates the breaking point catalyst for Fenton as centred on women, in this case both Edna and Anna.

Later Fenton smiles as he considers how his wife Edna would react to his suggestion of a move to Boulting Street, and contrasts this with undemanding Anna whose sole purpose is to make tea and clean his brushes. His earlier ferocious tirade seems to be aimed at Anna but as she is 'accommodating and meek' the absent Edna is implicitly referenced. Fenton's presumed lack of authority at home and resentment of Edna cannot be expressed to her directly and are externalised as imagined violence towards random strangers. The initial murderous impulse Fenton felt months ago he now recalls as '[s]ome temporary phase of irritation' that has long since morphed into regarding number eight as a place of solace and anonymity. Du Maurier specialises in portraying the egocentric middle-aged male and Fenton's literary 'brother' is Buzz from 'The Apple Tree' whose equally racist and sexist views decree that ideal female behaviour should follow eastern customs. Dunn's rather weak biography includes comments on the author's attitudes towards gender as shown in her writing: '[Daphne du Maurier's] women were only admirable if they were women who should have been men, but even they in the end were thwarted in their lives or ended up murdered. Her men were just as unsatisfactory, either weak and ineffectual or brutish and bullying.'[29] Buzz articulates the brutish view: 'The ideal life, of course was led by a man out East, or in the South Seas, who took a native wife [. . .] No criticism ever, the obedience of an animal to its master, and the light-hearted laughter of a child.'[30] In Fenton's thoughts Anna lacks personhood and he thinks of her merely as 'the woman' (26). Immortalised in his painting as '[t]he first woman, the first child,' Anna and Johnnie are types, sacrificial characters in Fenton's narrative, as the Madonna and child are in the Christian story (42).

Anna dies in a basement of gas poisoning with her infant son and an envelope of money by her side. Fenton reflects on their deaths, musing that '[i]t seemed somehow inevitable,' conveniently (and comically) forgetting his initial plan to gas them himself.

> the narrow trench he would be able to dig for her body—no need to make it deep. Turning towards her, measuring the size of her, reckoning the length and breadth, he saw a glimmer of understanding come into her eye, and he quickly smiled to give her confidence. [. . .]
>
> He glanced round the room again. But there was to be no question of butchery. No blood. No mess. The answer would be to stifle them both in sleep. The woman, and her child. It was much the kindest way. (9–11)

The futility of his own existence pushes Fenton into his one truly exceptional act: accepting responsibility for his part in a tragedy. Yet, this is a story that hinges on the absent wife as Fenton's pathetic machinations are designed to elicit the 'dawn of new respect in her eyes' (31). His need to be acknowledged as a 'genius or a madman' reflects the drama of art that shakes us out of complacency into seeing the world anew, but it also highlights the risk of pretentiousness when the need to shock is the paramount motivation. Contemporary artist Grayson Perry outlines the authentic artistic vocation in *Playing to the Gallery* (2014), a discourse that chimes with Fenton's assessment of the radical nature of his art: 'only by offending or shocking the bourgeoisie does the artist know he is being true to art. Any other path is artistic prostitution. The bourgeoisie seeks comfort. Art must make them feel uncomfortable.'[31] To Fenton, his art is sanctioned by Anna's lack of appreciation, it is Edna's negative opinion that crucifies him.

Ina Habermann identifies another du Maurier character, the Reverend Davey in *Jamaica Inn* [1936], as a 'brutal and pathetic Nietzschean overreacher,' and like Fenton his 'hubris is expressed and deflated' in one sentence in that novel.[32] As Fenton is driven away by the police he murmurs 'She doesn't believe in me—she'll never believe in me,' a reference to Edna's dismissal of his paintings as 'daubs, done anyhow,' which leads to his shouted confession of three murders and intention to commit a fourth—hers (42–43). Habermann's thesis re-examines du Maurier's apparent adherence to conventional forms in the novels as a means of 'recreating the myth in order to explore, and finally to explode it.'[33] What she calls the 'the liberating possibilities of (imaginative) re-enactment and traumatic repetition' are disrupted in du Maurier's version of a fertile chaos that ends the mundane life and the tragic existence of two characters.

When Edna asks 'Which way?' at the start of the narrative Fenton is catapulted into a mythical space, a liminal crossroads between two worlds where his diametrically opposed selves travel towards known, and unknown, futures. He can return to the rituals of middle-class existence and traumatic repetition, or follow the impulses of his anima and embrace the übermensch within. Anna is also caught in the pattern as she invites Fenton inside number eight and begins the events that culminate in her (presumed) suicide and his (probable) execution. Though the latter occurs outside the limits of the story it is clear that Fenton desires respect and fame and failing that, notoriety will do. As Habermann indicates regarding the slaughter in *Jamaica Inn*, it is the mythical dimension of the stories that renders the violence so horrifying. By leaving her front door ajar Anna literally and symbolically invites the Devil in, and though Fenton does not actually murder her, his neglect and abandonment surely kill her. The tragedy is that it is the reminder of how life might have been that leads Anna towards death as the preferred choice, and this promise is personified by the disintegrating personality of Fenton, a human catalyst who is himself on a destructive path.

Fenton's thwarted desire is for the respect of his wife Edna, and he even espouses murder to get her to take him seriously. Distracted by painting he reorders his world and himself through art, hoping she will finally respect him. His failure can only end in self-sacrifice. As Habermann indicates: 'In "The Uncanny" psychoanalysis teaches us how to get from death to Mummy: we move from smothering terror to mothering lechery, tranquillised by the assurance that this terrifying fantasy is "only the transformation" of another, completely un-terrifying fantasy.'[34]

As in 'The Birds,' there is no refuge from oppression and violence, the vulnerable are left to fend for themselves and as usual in du Maurier narratives, 'authority does not look particularly good.' Most notably, the murder of an immigrant mother and child is not sensational in a post-war England still reeling from the slaughter of the previous decade. Nor is the hanging of a mediocre murderer. Though widely reported, John Christie's execution was 'not an event which excited much interest in the world at large and it did not make headlines. A double murderer had been hanged for his crimes and that was that.' The irony is that Fenton/ Sims will not achieve the fame he desires, or the notoriety he would settle for, in confessing to a crime he did not commit, just as in real life Christie was swiftly forgotten. Fleet Street reporter Harry Proctor of the *Daily Mail* commented that the Evans murder case was 'dull, sordid, unglamourous, dreary,' a reflection of the post-war national context.[35]

Du Maurier's friendship with Gollancz ensured a regular supply of prepublished texts on current issues and their letters reveal her thoughts on a range of controversial issues, such as life after death, the nuclear threat, illegitimacy, Apartheid, Vietnam, and the death penalty. Gollancz was a political activist and socialist who founded the Left Book Club in 1934. As Heeley indicates, 'It was into this politically motivated milieu that du Maurier moved when she transferred her allegiance to Gollancz from Heinemann in 1934.'[36] She penned a passionate response to the founding of his Campaign for the Prevention of Legal Cruelty:

> I agree with all you say in principle, and yes, of course the principle must be that we forgive our brethren not only seven times, but seventy times seven, so that no matter if we see a child murdered before our eyes we have got to forgive the murderer [. . .] but you do not in the pamphlet give the practical alternative to the present death sentence. I cannot believe you mean the even more horrible cruelty of imprisonment for life, prison being what it is today [. . .] It seems to me that imprisonment is so much more soul-destroying than the quicker rope, and will continue to be soul-destroying until all prisons are run as places of rehabilitation, and run not by governors or warders, but by monks.[37]

Here du Maurier strongly rejects the death penalty, and imprisonment under contemporary conditions, yet several of her stories centralise crimes that do, or may, result in execution by hanging, examples include, 'The Little Photographer,' 'Kiss Me Again Stranger,' and 'Panic.' In the same letter du Maurier mentions newspaper reports of murderers such as Haigh who dissolved an old woman in a bath of acid, and a certain Mrs Roberts who used rat poison on her seventy-two-year-old employer to obtain money in her will. 1955 was the year Gollancz published *Capital Punishment: the Heart of the Matter* and the year that Ruth Ellis, the last woman to be hanged in Britain, was killed by the public executioner on 13 July. 'The Alibi' is another multivalent story inviting historicist, psychoanalytical and feminist readings, and in a prefatory 'Note' du Maurier outlines the keynote of *The Breaking Point* as climactic states which lead to unpredictable behaviour.

> There comes a moment in the life of every individual when reality must be faced. When this happens, it is as though a link between emotion and reason is stretched to the limit of endurance, and sometimes snaps. In this collection of stories, men, women, children and a nation are brought to the breaking-point. Whether the link survives or snaps, the reader must judge for himself.
> (The unpaginated 'Note' precedes the preface in the Virago edition.)

The significance of threshold moments and personal choices runs through the stories with characters electing to take paths that lead directly to them reaching their 'breaking points.' They can be seen as a bridge between periods whereby the work exhibits both modernist elements and post-modernist anxieties. Du Maurier's 'commingling of the familiar and unfamiliar' is an example of what Nicolas Royle calls 'the critical spectralization of feeling and belief, [where] the uncanny is a key to understanding both modernity and so-called postmodernity.'[38] The story engages with modernism in its use of colour symbolism, fragmentation, the dehumanised self in all of the central characters, and the tracing of psychogeography in parallel with the psyche and the city. The human need to find a lasting home is entwined with a Künstlerroman mockery of artistic pretension and of those who somehow escaped their duty of war service.

As a seventeen-year-old, Daphne du Maurier had been taken to Pentonville Prison by her father, Gerald, who was researching his next acting role as a convicted murderer. Du Maurier's diary describes '[a] sketch of a man being hanged brought a macabre note into the current diary, inspired by a visit to Pentonville Prison with D, who was rehearsing a play called *Not in Our Stars,* concerning murder.'[39] The previous year, 1923, had seen the trial and execution of the infamous lovers Edith Thompson and Frederick Bywaters for the murder of Percy Thompson, Edith's husband, and her execution death throes were luridly described in the newspapers of the time. Biographer Jane Dunn tells how the du Mauriers were shown around the condemned cell and the hanging shed where the drop that killed Bywaters was 'gruesomely demonstrated.' According to Dunn the adolescent Daphne remained calm and stolidly 'digested the images and added them to her already jaundiced view of human nature and the harm people do each other.' They saw the 'locked cells with their miserable inhabitants, the patients in their beds in the hospital wing, the condemned cell and the hanging shed. [. . .] The unmarked graves of the hanged added their own grim melancholy. [. . .] Daphne could not get the images out of her mind and sketched the cell and the hanged man's drop in her diary.'[40] Years later the case of convicted murderers John Christie and Timothy Evans added to the seed already planted in her mind and du Maurier composed 'The Alibi,' a tale of distortion and display in which an unexceptional, unhappy man is revealed to have an unexpectedly murderous streak that blights and ends lives, including his own. In a letter to Gollancz written in 1955 she recalls Christie, describing him as:

> That wretched little man near Paddington who put all those women's bodies in cupboards a few years ago, I forget his name, wait a minute—Christie—must surely have been insane. (I think after being buried alive in the 1914 war. Psychiatric treatment might have cured him, I don't know, but he was hanged.)

She wrote in response to a pamphlet Gollancz sent her on capital punishment, describing what what she considered to be viable alternatives and also what views Christ might have held: 'We are back to the question, what do we do to our murderers? [. . .] I think that for example he would have used other words to the murderer. [. . .] "Restore the life thou hast taken away. [. . .] When thinking of these type of murderers I am thinking of them as predominantly sane. (No murderer can be quite sane.) The truly insane ones can only be sent to asylums, I fear.'[41] In this letter du Maurier mentions Nobel prizewinner Albert Schweitzer, whose 'Reverence for Life' philosophy influenced both her and Gollancz.

'The Alibi' indicates the world of a deeper reality beyond the perceived, something Roehberger calls the difference between potentiality and actuality. In hinting at this unrealised world, the story expresses a yearning for unfulfilled desires. 'Short story writers question the world of appearances and in that questioning cast doubt on the immediately apparent and, at the same time, signify the timeless universals beyond the extensional world.'[42] These desires are illustrated by the pictures that accompany the story in *John Bull* magazine, depictions of an idealised and safe Britain where people with orthodox values live contented lives. They strike a contrast with the sources of fear in 'The

Alibi' itself: impotence, isolation, and irrational violence. This is yet another open-ended text, and its challenge to the status quo is due to a preoccupation with deception and moral decay. This is more apparent because of the story's first appearance in a popular magazine promoting family values and patriotism. The text belies the illustrations. As London is disfigured after the Blitz, and British society is maimed after years of war, Fenton's portraits are unrecognisable: Anna's mouth looks like a 'big fish ready to swallow' yet she remains a marginalised and voiceless person (24).

This exercise in close reading shows du Maurier's insistent practice of writing the violence of the 1940s upon the distressed social tissue of a recovering London. She enacts her insights through the violence of her stories—violence against a non-combatant city population; violence that ended thousands of lives and devastated millions more. The crux of 'The Alibi' is Fenton's impotence as a man, a husband, and a creator, the ensuing frustration motivates him to contemplate violence and leads to his deranged actions. Fenton's character is a composite representation of the impotent governing forces of Britain, unable to protect the population from bombing or foreign belligerence, and innocent bystanders subject to the irrationality of war and post-war aggression. The climax presents the reader with the dead bodies of a mother, a child, an unborn foetus, and the body of Fenton caught by the hangman's noose. Du Maurier takes violence from the battlefield to the domestic arena illuminating the damage on a personal level to ordinary people. The dreadful historic counterpoint to Macmillan's 'never had it so good' is Churchill's 'never in the field of human conflict was so much owed by so many to so few.'[43] The 'few' did not include civilians.

In this story du Maurier interrogates contemporary artistic culture, dwelling particularly on the nature of figurative representation; elsewhere in the stories she turns her attention to cinema in 'Kiss Me Again, Stranger' and 'The Menace,' and photography in 'A Borderline Case' and 'The Little Photographer.' 'The Little Photographer' reworks the corporeal theme through a focus on the body as presented photographically just as 'The Alibi' centralises portraiture as a frame for a discussion of identity, artifice, and authenticity.

NOTES

1. Du Maurier, *The Breaking Point: Short Stories* (London: Virago, 2009).
2. *John Bull Everybody's Weekly* dated 'week ending 30 May 1959.' (Odhams Press Ltd), 2761: 105 (1959). EUL MS 307/2/4/1, courtesy of Special Collections, University of Exeter.

3. Christopher and Diana Wade, *The du Mauriers: A Hampstead Family*, p. 17 ([n.p.] Matthew Norgate, 1984). MS 307/2/4/3/1/ 3, courtesy of Special Collections.

4. EUL MS 307/2/4/1, p. 2, p. 31, courtesy of Special Collections.

5. *John Bull*, p. 20–21. EUL MS 307/2/4/1, courtesy of Special Collections.

6. Prime Minister Harold MacMillan's speech on 20.7.1957. Sourced at <http://news.bbc.co.uk/onthisday/hi/dates/stories/july/20/newsid_3728000/3728225.stm> [accessed 29.6.2022].

7. Nancy Spain, 'Nancy Spain Cries—How Improper Daphne!': 7 May 1954. *The Daily Express,* sourced at *The Daily Express* Online Archive <http://www.ukpressonline.co.uk/ukpressonline/?sf=express> [accessed 5.2.2016].

8. EUL MS 207/6/1/6/1, courtesy of Special Collections.

9. EUL MS 144/1/1/1, courtesy of Special Collections.

10. Du Maurier letter to Victor Gollancz, 21 February 1955. MSS.157/3/I/DM/1–43, courtesy of Modern Records Centre.

11. Du Maurier letter to Phyllis Bottome, 6 June 1959. MSS 78861, courtesy of The British Library.

12. Jonathan Oates, *John Christie of Rillington Place: Biography of a Serial Killer* (Barnsley: Pen & Sword Books, 2012), p. 142.

13. Oates, p. 129, p. 185.

14. Auerbach, *Haunted Heiress* p. 65.

15. Oates, p. 92, p. 155.

16. Henri Bergsen, '*Le Rire. Essai sur la signification du comique'* trans. by Brereton Cloudesley and Fred Rothwell (New York: Macmillan, 1921). Bergsen's title translates as 'Laughter, an essay on the meaning of the comic.' Sourced at <http://babel.hathitrust.org/cgi/pt?id=mdp.39015083253750;view=1up;seq=11> [accessed 17 March 2016].

17. Judy Simmons, 'The Mask Beneath the Mask: Katherine Mansfield' in *Diaries and Journals of Literary Women* (Hampshire; Macmillan, 1990), p. 159.

18. Oates, p. 36.

19. Grosz, Introduction, p. 7.

20. Royle, p. 12.

21. George du Maurier, *Trilby* (London: The Pilot Press, 1947).

22. Bergson, sourced at <gutenberg.org> [accessed 29.6.2022], p. 29.

23. Oates, p. 37.

24. Du Maurier letter to Maud Waddell, 2 March 1925. EUL MS 207/6/4/1, courtesy of Special Collections.

25. Arendt, p. 19.

26. Oates, p. 37, p. 126, pp. 35–36.

27. Calder, p. 52.

28. Oates, p. 143.

29. Dunn, p. 247.

30. Du Maurier, *The Birds and Other Stories* (London; Virago, 2004), p. 134.

31. Perry, p. 57.

32. Ina Habermann, *Myth, Memory and the Middlebrow: Priestley, du Maurier and the Symbolic Form of Englishness* (London: Palgrave Macmillan, 2010), p. 172.

33. Habermann: pp. 172–85.

34. Royle, p. 142.

35. Oates, p. 78.

36. Heeley, p. 83.

37. Du Maurier letter to Victor Gollancz, 14 November 1955. MSS.157/3/I/DM/12 courtesy of Modern Records Centre.

38. Royle, p. 24.

39. Du Maurier, *Myself When Young,* p. 71.

40. Dunn, p. 76.

41. Du Maurier letter to Victor Gollancz, 14 November 1955. MSS.157/3/I/DM/12 courtesy of The Modern Records Centre, p. 2.

42. Roehberger, p. 11.

43. Winston Churchill 'The Few' speech to the House of Commons, 20 August 1940. Sourced at <http://www.churchill-society-london.org.uk/thefew.html> [accessed 15 March 2016].

Chapter Eight

'The Little Photographer' [feet] (1952)

Du Maurier's novels and short stories were often serialised in magazines to advertise publication as seen with 'The Alibi' in the earlier chapter. *The Daily Mirror* ran a full-page advert for *Woman's Own* magazine under the byline 'YOU . . . and your BODY' including this puff for the upcoming serial 'The Little Photographer.' 'Ever since *WOMAN'S OWN* published "My Cousin Rachel" readers have been clamouring for another Daphne du Maurier serial, and here it is, an exciting new story with a modern Riviera setting, from the pen of this brilliant novelist.'[1] This joyful blurb shows how little the subversive content of du Maurier's stories was recognised despite reviews summing them up as tales of 'sin and retribution.' Reviews of *The Apple Tree* in the *Times Literary Supplement* cite 'The Little Photographer' as a well-told tale' (19 August 1952), and *The Liverpool Daily Post* comments: 'Miss du Maurier achieves brilliant success in a couple of short novels and four short stories, all of which exude the very breath of thrilling malevolence' (1 September 1952).[2] In 'The Little Photographer' subjects with anatomical perfection, and others with impairment, highlight cultural desires for physical and moral symmetry in a coupling that transgresses the unspoken but culturally dominant laws of class and economics. The move from balance to disharmony and disproportion suggests ugliness as Aristotle's golden ratio is upset and moral virtue is no longer balanced between the opposing extremes of aestheticism and 'uncontrollable impulses.'[3] As in the previous chapter on 'The Alibi' the inclusion of death in this narrative represents the movement from life to 'non-life' as desire invites violence to disrupt stasis.[4]

In common with many other stories in du Maurier's corpus this complex narrative has a dialogic relation to classical texts. Although critics like Gretlund argue '[i]f they are embedded in a well-written short story, submerged texts are invisible to the inexperienced eye,' here, the unlikely pairing of beauty and ugliness is a definite nod to the Greek myth of the marriage of Aphrodite and Hephaistus.[5] The artisan Hephaistus and his children are notable exceptions to the commonly seductive Olympian gods. The divine, but lame, smith forges Zeus' thunderbolts and crafts a net of metal to publicly ensnare Aphrodite and her lover Ares while the other gods look on and laugh. Similarly, M. Paul threatens to destroy the Marquise's life with the exposure of their liaison. Yet, in du Maurier's revisioning it is the Hephaistus figure who is doomed, and Aphrodite/ the Marquise is not caught by her husband but rather latently snared in a net of her own fashioning. Du Maurier's mismatched couple enjoy a cross-class, adulterous liaison that threatens primogeniture and the patriarchal status quo with the pregnancy of a disabled, illegitimate child. The attraction to difference, in this case physical and social, illustrates the truth of Scarry's surmise that 'beauty, sooner or later, brings us into contact with our own capacity for making errors.'[6] Though du Maurier is not known for her feminism it is notable that she engages in the revisioning of classical texts so prevalent among modernist women authors in which male dominated versions are reworked to include a primary female perspective. Early examples include H.D. [Hilda Doolittle], Katherine Mansfield, Virginia Woolf, and Elizabeth Bowen, while later twentieth-century instances are Margaret Atwood, Natalie Haynes and Pat Barker.

In an undated letter from the early 1950s du Maurier summarises the plot of this story to Oriel Malet as follows: 'my next story [. . .] is one you will hate. Not macabre really, about a sensual rather foolish woman, who, through idleness, lets a honky man from a shop make love to her, and then when he begins to get serious she gets frightened—she only means it as a pastime – but I shan't tell you how it ends.'[7] Malet subsequently cited 'The Little Photographer' as the best story in the collection. It is another du Maurier variant on the relationship between fatal desire and the grotesque body, a story that foregrounds the carnal encounter between Madame la Marquise, a beautiful but restless aristocrat, and Monsieur Paul, a crippled photographer. The text is situated between 'The Apple Tree' and 'Kiss Me Again, Stranger,' two stories in a collection of six that explore the complexities of thwarted desire where, '[t]he freak and the grotesque overlap as bodily categories.'[8] The backdrop of French nobility lends the story a period feel and the Marquise's desire for the material body of the socially inferior photographer illustrates how in society 'the top includes the low symbolically, as a primarily eroticised constituent of its own fantasy life.' Stallybrass and White indicate just how social transgressions are illustrated by depiction of the human body: 'we have plumbed the depths of social classification, the lower bodily stratum, the sewers, the underworld—what one might call the rock bottom of symbolic form.'[9] Du

Maurier's corpus of short fiction interrogates the dichotomies of image versus reality, perception versus truth, artifice versus innocence, and, in 'The Little Photographer' the Marquise and her eponymous lover dramatize the tragi-comic consequences of consummated desire on the human body.

The union between the aristocratic and the artisan body is a fertile one as the photographer replicates the Marquise's beauty in the paper facsimiles of his craft and the human flesh of the baby to come. Scarry makes this clear in her study of beauty which 'brings copies of itself into being. It makes us draw it, take photographs of it, or describe it to other people.'[10] In 'The Little Photographer' M. Paul is in danger through the sense of sight as 'the perceiver who is imperilled, overpowered, by crossing paths with someone beautiful,' while Madame la Marquise is threatened by touch which 'brings immediacy to ugliness.' The farthest connotation of touch is injury which philosopher Scarry defines as the true opposite of beauty: 'Ugly touch can stain, infect, abuse or violate.' Her research also outlines how accounts of beauty from earlier centuries include the aspect of mortal danger for ordinary people when encountering outstanding beauty, something that rings true in this particular tale.[11] In this text the boundaries of the body are aligned with social borders, which when crossed, erupt in a Bakhtinian carnival of fertile disorder. Thus, M. Paul's high-booted disfigured foot acts metonymically in that, for the Marquise, it is a titillating corporal invitation to engage in illicit sexual activity with a crippled, lower-class male. It is useful to consider the medical aspects and the definitions. *Blacks Medical Dictionary* defines clubfoot as a condition also known as Talipes, 'a deformity in which the foot is permanently twisted at the ankle-joint,' so that the sole of the foot no longer rests on the ground when the body is standing. The cause is due to 'some arrest of development resulting in a congenital deformity' and is twice as common in boys,' both pieces of information that have a bearing on the denouement. The gender of the baby will influence the destiny of the mother, the Marquise, and the author again invites the reader to consider the body as fate.

Du Maurier specialises in the fractured family and this Cinderella story gone awry has an unhappy-ever-after with a suitor's foot that fits a cripple's boot. The daughter of a hardworking surgeon and an ailing mother is elevated into the French aristocracy into a life of chateaux and servants where she is the beautiful princess awakened to fairy-tale connubial bliss. A succession of appreciative audiences watch the Marquise enact her dance of performative femininity, their admiration elicits the 'sense of happiness that she felt must only come to a prima donna after the clamour of long applause' (186).[12] With echoes of Jane Austen's well-known dictum on bachelor fortunes and marriage, 'It is a truth universally acknowledged, that a single man in possession of a good fortune, must be in want of a wife,' the Marquise-to-be conflates the man with his fortune and asks, 'what could be better in life than a Marquis who was also *un homme sérieux*? What more lovely than that château and those vast estates?' (162).[13] Later, she too has become a piece of property, to be posed and placed, delivered, and fetched, when the Marquis is not attending to business.

The world of fairy tale, however, becomes mundane when the Marquise finds herself neglected by her husband's work commitments which leave him no time for her 'in spite of his devotion' (163). This heroine is now trapped by luxurious circumstances and not, 'free to come and go' as she pleases (165). The Marquise's restricted life is contrasted with that of the American visitors to the resort whose loud enjoyment is satirised by du Maurier, who often singles out American characters for mockery, in for example, 'Not After Midnight,' 'Leading Lady,' and her novel *Rule Britannia* [1972]. The Marquise's married best friend has taken a lover, and the increasingly sexually aware Marquise intuits that this is a common occurrence among the nobility. Stallybrass and White describe how as the social classes became more physically separated, and their bodies more strictly controlled in clothes and behaviour, the attraction of difference also increased dramatically. 'As the bourgeoisie produced new forms of regulation and prohibition governing their one bodies, they wrote ever more loquaciously of the body of the other—of the city's "scum."'[14] The bodies of the Marquise and M. Paul are the space where du Maurier enacts the conflict between power and desire, and the ensuing violence, with the focus on happiness, marital harmony, and femininity as all fundamentally performative acts.

The story works dialogically as the untold perspective of the late wife in Robert Browning's dramatic monologue 'My Last Duchess.' In that poem the aristocratic husband's 'gift of a nine-hundred years old name' (LL 43–47) leads to his disappointment and her death: here it leads to another restricted, lonely life in a gilded cage where the Marquise is morbidly static in her perfect reflection. 'Now as the Madame la Marquise, she had no one with whom to share confidences, laughter. Everyone about her was middle-aged, dull, rooted to a life long-lived that never changed [. . .] Never a new face, never the arrival of a stranger.' (163) Du Maurier's revised version of Browning's text swaps the gender of the characters making the female protagonist the murderer. She exploits Browning's plot of high-status discontent by both following and subverting the original power dynamics. The Marquise is also a literary relative to the second Mrs de Winter in *Rebecca* and, as is traditional in most European culture, on marriage her identity is subsumed into her husband's: his aristocratic title is the only name she bears in the narrative. Like the photographer she, too, is known by her profession: that of aristocratic wife and the mother of legitimate heirs. Dissatisfied with her marriage and her lifestyle, the Marquise holidays alone with the children and their English governess. Out of boredom she seduces M. Paul, a humble worker from the nearby town whose profession makes him the perfect audience for her display of feminised bodily perfection. Du Maurier's short stories exemplify Mitchell and Snyder's dictum that: 'Difference demands display. Display demands difference.'[15]

The juxtaposition of sublime and grotesque bodies continues when the Marquise's ennui leads her to walk during siesta time to the deserted town, where she pauses at the cool basement of the photographer's shop and sees him as a man for the first time. M. Paul, an artisan lensman, has a face 'so unusual, so gentle, that it might have come straight from a stained-glass saint in a cathedral' (169), but he has equally diabolic associations in that his deformity is his grotesquely 'misshapen foot' (173). The first description of him slips into the free indirect thoughts of the Marquise and she is more titillated than pitying, more mesmerised than repulsed by her lame admirer who paradoxically embodies sublime art and conspicuous disfigurement. 'Her eyes fell to the boot. [. . .] His step was slow, more dragging, and the Marquise felt a kind of compassion for his deformity, for surely the misshapen foot beneath the boot must pain him constantly, and the high boot, especially in hot weather, crush and sear his flesh.' (173) The verbs are potent and unusually sensual for a description of hurt, a detached examination of a creature's state unexpectedly encountered rather than an empathetic acknowledgement of a fellow human's condition.

As with classicist Robert Graves' one-shoed heroes of myth, M. Paul's 'satirically' deformed foot renders his mismatched limbs asymmetrical and like Marina Warner's description of the Devil, he limps: 'walking *pede claudio*, listing to the left.'[16] Warner continues, describing the lame Caribbean figure of 'La Diablesse' whereby '[a]symmetry often intensifies the presence of unofficial, even forbidden knowledge: the Devil wears motley, his limbs are mismatched, and he limps.'[17] Like Oedipus, M. Paul is a catalyst for change, and in common with Tiresias the Prophet or one-shoed Jason of the Argonauts: he is a man to be feared. For the Marquise his mystery centres on his disability: 'His right foot was encased in a high-fitted boot. Yet, curiously, the sight of this did not repel her or bring her to nervous laughter, as it had done the night before when she had seen the sister. His high boot had a fascination, strange, unknown.' (172) The Marquise's 'stifled hysteria' on first seeing the crippled sibling evokes Mary Russo's work on the Female Grotesque which she defines as a 'constitutive aspect of [. . .] the sublime,' as represented by the Marquise's physical perfection. She is aroused by M. Paul's difference to the men of her rank, yet although she enjoys his bare arms and chest, her paraphilia centres on his deformed foot with its special high-fitting boot. Russo's definition is useful: '[t]he grotesque body is open, protruding, irregular, secreting, multiple and changing; it is identified with "low" culture or the carnivalesque, and with social transformation.'[18] The eroticisation of feet has a long history and Warner surmises this may be because, 'they are the lowest part of the body and in touch with the earth as opposed to the heavens.'[19] Disability is at the core of the plot and is the reason for the attraction, and this unusual combination renders this story a captivating addition to the corporeal model of analysis. Du Maurier takes the reader into the darker areas of desire where it is the disfigurement itself which arouses the Marquise and proves irresistible in combination with the thrill of social transgression.

The blunt and dated terminology is of its time and shocking to contemporary readers, Mitchell and Snyder offer their careful definition of the cripple as defined within their theory of narrative prosthesis:

> We use the term *cripple* to stress its historical associations with essentialist notions of malignancy and incapacity. The term constructs individuals and groups violating social fictions of symmetry, health, and normalcy, as embodying a marked deviance. Buried in the term is much more than a descriptive designation of individual limitation; it is an evaluative term that qualitatively differentiates between bodies in terms of aesthetics and abilities. Cripples are those who inspire pity and pathos while also evoking fears of divine retribution and an illogic in nature.[20]

In contrast, the little photographer's desire is predicated upon the attractive image and the fantasy of the idealised normative body that the Marquise is careful to present. There is sardonic and irreverent humour in that M. Paul is reading a 'tender romance' while about to throw himself into a real-life thriller of fatal desire. He satiates himself on what Angela Carter views as the 'soft pornography' of the romance in which a 'male-dominated society produces a pornography of universal female acquiescence.'[21] However, in her work on the writings of the Marquis de Sade, Carter goes on to note that, 'for Sade, all tenderness is false, a deceit, a trap; all pleasure contains within itself the seeds of atrocities; all beds are minefields.' There are significant parallels as in that narrative the Marquise is fixated on power, not affection, and although her lover speaks the language of passion, he is only interested in capturing her body, in actuality and on film.

The Marquise takes pains to create a portrayal of perfection because of 'the glance of admiration, swiftly suppressed—she wanted that' (163). Her attraction to the cripple is apposite in that together they represent the physical extremities of perfection and imperfection. They are a foil for each other as the Marquise's excessive beauty also renders her a freak of nature. While dressing she considers the adoration generally caused by her charming appearance, as always, 'many people turned to look at her, or even stepped aside to let her pass, in unconscious homage to her beauty' (184). It is clear that without other people's admiration reflected back at her, the Marquise does not exist to herself, and this explains her desperate narcissism. She only ever sees herself from the perspective of others; fellow diners at the hotel, strangers in the town, the maître d'hotel, the governess, the photographer. All her actions are performative, 'she made a tableau, ready set, for him to gaze upon' but designed to look so artlessly natural that even the experienced photographer whose life's work is the creation of poses, is deceived: '[i]t is quite beautiful.' He says, '[s]o very natural, so full of grace.' (173) That the scene is entirely unnatural is missed even by the experienced and professional artificer of the status and eternal image.

Like the photographer the Marquise is also an artist, but her body is her canvas. We first encounter her 'adorning' her nails (161). She takes care to choose the perfect shade of nail polish, and chooses her clothes and hair ribbon around the peony pink, enjoying the synergy between the hauteur of the flower and her social position. The peony rose is tall in the flower bed and looks down upon the humble grass, much as the Marquise disregards ordinary people as necessary, but unimportant. She lies in peaceful contentment, but '[t]he spell' is 'broken' by a bee entering a flower, ceasing to hum, and leaving newly 'intoxicated' (161–62). This vision of erotic union leaves her feeling dissatisfied, and like the peony, she metaphorically, and with sexual invitation, 'opens her petals' to the sun at high noon when she lies with M. Paul in the long grass.

The language of oriental religious rituals frames the dressing scene and foregrounds M. Paul's subsequent slavish adoration and the exercise of her newfound power over another. She adorns herself 'like a priestess' crouching 'eastern fashion,' and the language is rich with exotic terms that position him as an acolyte at the shrine of her beauty: 'his large eyes, humble and devoted, were fixed upon her with all the deep abasement of a slave' (182). 'The Marquise repressed a desire to laugh. It was quite absurd, his admiration. Yet, funny . . . it gave her a sense of power' (171). He has the 'dumb brown eyes' of a servile animal, wears a 'rapturous expression' when he sees her, and begs to take photographs of her (172, 179, 186). To the Marquise's ears his voice is 'cultivated, liquid, a voice that matched the eyes of the gazelle,' an ironically fleet and agile animal totem for a cripple incapable of speed or grace (169). Like the sacrificial doe used symbolically in 'The Blue Lenses,' and the chamois employed literally as the hunted creature in 'The Chamois,' the gazelle is prey for predators. This foreshadowing is heightened by the

Marquise's sense of personal power which renders her 'conscious of an inner triumph that she was in such command of the situation' (181).

When M. Paul first photographs her and the children he is left exhausted, 'dragging his boot more heavily than before,' while the Marquise, who is often wearied by her idle life, is invigorated and 'full of a new energy' (176). She tells him of her need for photographic instruction and he responds by describing his secret walks to snap scenery on the cliff top, which occur during the siesta when the place is deserted. To get to the hollow in the grass involves following a path 'so close to the cliff's edge that a false step, bringing a stumble, would spell danger' but the Marquise is excited by the risk as she is by the other risks she is taking (179). McKee's comments on character signify what makes a plot a knife-edge of possibility: '[w]e give the ultimate values to those things that demand the ultimate risks—our freedom, our lives, our souls. [. . .] to live meaningfully is to be at perpetual risk.'[22] In this instance the catalyst for the risk-taking is desire, the desire for change, for freedom, for power.

Without her rank and her beauty the Marquise is a cipher whose life has no meaning. By enjoying her visually and sexually M. Paul brings her from stasis into action, into life, not to life. Sitting '[b]efore the mirror,' she worships at an altar where the divine is replaced by her reflection, and she is judged by the laws of beauty in a mirror that cannot lie (163). In 'The Blue Lenses' Marda West is faced by her reflection as a doe, prey for carnivores, and a metaphor for the dangers of feminine passivity in marriage. Here the image translates into power not powerlessness and female beauty is a lure for the unwary. The Marquise's dialogue with her double/ image is like that of Narcissus, whose adored watery reflection drowned him, likewise, her vanity is her undoing. The lines of the myth of 'Narcissus and Echo' in Ovid's original text resonate with the Marquise's self-regard.[23] Her experience of things external to her is always mediated, first by the relationship she has with herself, and secondly by her experience of herself as an attractive object that only exists when viewed through the male gaze.[24] This is supported by Russo's argument that '[f]emininity is a mask which masks non-identity.'

The Marquise enjoys the power of 'passion between strangers' and for her it is a physical act minus emotional content. She epitomises Luce Irigaray's concept of the masquerade where the female only experiences desire through the males desire for them.[25] For M. Paul it is true love and all the lovers need in order to be together forever is courage. As the formal properties of genre are disrupted the characters express confusion: M. Paul considers himself the hero of high romance, but his beloved seeks excitement, not love. 'The Little Photographer' parallels the plot of 'Kiss Me Again, Stranger' as once again the characters' motivations diverge to dramatic and comic effect. She describes his touch as the featherlight of a bird's wing and the brushing of a dragonfly's wings. The lovers are positioned as dichotomous: he is animal, she is human, he is natural, she is cultivated, in a reversal of the common gender binaries. In 'The Blue Lenses' the mirror's reflection of the deer indicates Marda's vulnerability and a sacrifice that happens outside the scope of the story, here, the 'gazelle eyes,' the 'gentle eyes, mirroring his nature,' bely the determination of M. Paul's character, a trait that will cost him his life (170, 175) .

It is the professional task of a photographer to capture beauty in a fixed and timeless image and M. Paul ensures the Marquise's immortality in photographs, some sanctioned and some illicit. She considers them the best taken of her, and they re-present the Marquise to herself: eternally beautiful, static and sterile, framed and captured. On the photographic paper the Marquise as subject is the image of perfection and she has a substance which is only commonly there when admiration occurs. Thus, her 'sense of secret pleasure that [comes] with admiration' is the manner in which she objectifies herself (170). Thomson's observations about the image of the freak resonate with both the ostensible freak, M. Paul, and the freak he desires: the Marquise. By forcibly 'ejecting' M. Paul from her life, and indeed his life too, the Marquise swaps places and becomes integrally monstrous by her actions.

> The freak illustrates our so-called normal pleasure and fascination with our mirror-images, a fascination with the limits of our own identities as they are witnessed from the outside. This is a narcissistic delight at the shape of our own externality, which is always inaccessible to us by direct means and is achievable only if we can occupy the perspective others have on us.[26]

At the core of their story is a concern with entrapment and escape and the body is highlighted as the ultimate prison, or channel to oblivion, that humans can know.

Du Maurier's abiding concern with behavioural artifice and authenticity is present in many other stories from throughout her writing career, among which 'Leading Lady' is a notable example. As with the protagonist of that story, the Marquise is a consummate actress whose every movement is a pose and whose every utterance is scripted. Her apparent naturalness is strategic and unnatural and it is a mode that led her from the haute bourgeoisie to an existence where she is a bought, and paid for, decorative object. She is a living doll without affection for the Marquis, her children, or her lover. Concurrent with her adultery is 'the curiously satisfying knowledge that what she did was without emotion of any sort. Her mind and affections were quite untouched.' (186) The Marquise swiftly becomes bored with the 'daily ritual' of love-making that first excited her. Now, she 'would get through the business quickly, with an ill grace' (187–88). The excitement of the illicit has palled and now greater stimulation is required for the same heights of emotion. After three long weeks, 'to recapture her enjoyment she was obliged to treat the photographer no longer as a lay-figure [. . .] but as a person whose feelings she could wound' (187). This defies McKee's argument that '[t]hose in power never want us to feel. Thought can be controlled and manipulated, but emotion is wilful and unpredictable.'[27] The Marquise wants M. Paul to feel hurt and she has the power to elicit that emotion from him, in this she epitomises concerns over female power and emotional control over males. In the gender wars manipulation is a key component and as Grosz points out: '[a]t the end of the nineteenth century, satirical drawings of women pulling the strings of tiny puppet men reflected anxieties about the increasingly independent New Woman.'[28] The Marquise plays with Paul's feelings like a puppeteer, one of du Maurier's recurring images of control and violence directed upon the human form, repeated in 'The Alibi' and 'The Doll.'

The Marquise is unpleasantly surprised when M. Paul relates his plan to follow her to the family home when the holiday ends, intending to join her Parisian household as footman, to enable the continuance of their liaison. Du Maurier's wit is apparent in the wordplay involved in a cripple aspiring to be a footman. The Marquise is horrified at his plan to live with her noble family in the centre of Paris. Her thoughts are expressed in staccato bursts that indicate her panic, which escalates when he will not be paid off, or subscribe to her version of their relationship which firmly excludes romantic love. 'The degradation of this—this creature, there really was no other word for him—in the house, always waiting, always hoping' (191). The affair is positioned as sexually transgressive in that it allows the debased and the low access to cultural spaces that only the aristocractic occupy. M. Paul, a humble peasant, wants to be part of the chateaux with its ladies sipping tea in the salon and the 'solemn long avenue of trees' (164), and his blackmailing sister wants to be close to the Parisian household. Like the Marquis, who quickly turns into a frog once she marries him, her lover is no longer alluringly strange, and the Marquise finds that her actions have unexpected consequences which infect her body, and through her the entire body of society.

Her character is another exception to Žižek's theory of du Maurier's stable of female masochists, instead she sadistically torments M. Paul, revelling in her power to hurt him through mockery. She is pleased when 'anxiety and pain come into his eyes,' when a 'look of dejection fall[s] upon his whole person' and in whatever makes him realise 'how unworthy he was of her, how inferior in every way' (187). After these satisfying moments she cheerfully imagines him 'limping back, tired and unhappy, to the shop in the little town' (188). Having escaped the 'tyranny of home,' the Marquise experimentally adopts the behaviour of a tyrant towards a man who treats her 'with humility, with reverence,' much as she herself is called upon to obey the whims of her inconstant husband (170). '[I]t was a stimulation to the Marquise to witness his distress,' although when he cries she reflects that, '[a] man who gave way to emotion was pitiable' (189–92). A view with which du Maurier doubtless sympathised. The author expressed her dissatisfaction regarding her husband's behaviour in a letter to a friend: 'We have all got to cope in the future but so must Moper, eventually too, and not just be the man who takes and takes and takes.' Moper was du Maurier's unflattering nickname for her husband, whose emotional well-being was often a drain, and which belied the implied strength imbued in his public roles of war hero and Lieutenant-General.[29]

Suddenly, the Marquise is disaffected, and the grassy bower 'took on a sordid, shameful appearance, which had once seemed so secret and so warm' (192). To the Marquise M. Paul is a menial and when he protests at his role and her pay-off, it is as if her hairdresser is refusing payment. Her attitude is reminiscent of the Marquise de Merteuil in *Dangerous Liaisons*, a powerful woman who plays a man's game (seduction and betrayal) for self-satisfaction and the power kick. The Marquise de Merteuil is like a general before battle stating that 'One must conquer or die' yet it is not warfare but love at issue. Unlike 'silly' women of 'feeling,' she will not 'creep along [. . .] between recklessness and timidity.' She understands that '[t]here is no one without a secret which it is in his interest never to reveal' and she is an independent thinker who is 'indignant if anyone tries to wrest [her] ideas' from her, or 'surprise her against her will.' There is no sense that she will change her ways, only the trace of a thought that with her excellent wits, she will certainly do better than survive.[30] According to Thompson the hyper-visual physical text of the freak (M. Paul), enables the viewer's body (the Marquise), to become a 'seemingly neutral, tractable, and invulnerable instrument of the autonomous will, suitable to the uniform abstract citizenry democracy institutes.' Thomson describes how modernisation 'reimagined and reshaped the body' in addition to relocating it, discussing how the way the body looked, and worked, became an ever more vital social resource.

> All these dislocations created anonymity, forcing people to rely upon bodily appearance rather than kinship or local memberships as indices of identity and social position. In addition, secularisation deemphasised the condition of one's soul, while an intensifying market system spawned the anxious display of status, and technologies such as portraiture photography located identity in one's exterior image.[31]

In the act of pushing M. Paul off the cliff to his death the Marquise kills the threat to the prevailing social order. She has enjoyed her dalliance with exoticism as represented by his physical and social deformity. This perversion means the Marquise (the subject), excludes Monsieur Paul (the abject) but she cannot ignore him, and she resumes her proper position within the symbolic patriarchal order. Unable to withstand her detachment and cruelty he obligingly suffers until his world starts to collapse, he is 'abject' (189), more animal than man, a model of Julia Kristeva's theory of abjection where meaning collapses.[32]

His corpse is a signifier that provides a 'contained and stable arena in which to explore horrors occurring off the page'—illicit sexual activity, illegitimacy, and the disruption of primogeniture.[33] Du Maurier's stories revisit and destabilise normative power structures in the manner of the fairy tale, where the 'gap between the behaviour expected of children and the conduct expected of wives is not [. . .] as great as one might expect.' Maria Tatar states that in these familiar childhood tales '[w]oman is by nature a transgressor' whose attractiveness is a dangerous lure. This story ventures into this realm when M. Paul calls the Marquise '*La belle au bois dormant,*' as she dozes in the grassy hollow he has prepared (181). This is the French title of 'Sleeping Beauty' which translates into English as 'The Beauty Sleeping in the Wood,' a title that implicitly references the mother ogress character from the original tale who kills children, and kisses no-one. It is significant that the Marquise has had two daughters and as yet she has failed to fulfil the primary duty of an aristocratic wife: there is no son to inherit the title and the estates.

The Marquise is both enchanted princess, asleep for one hundred years in a dull marriage and about to awaken to desire, and Snow White's disaffected stepmother whose demand of 'Mirror, mirror on the wall, who is the fairest of them all?' requires endless affirmation and human sacrifice. The Marquise's knowledge of her own beauty leads to a narcissistic superiority and Tatar isolates this as typical of folklore heroines, among whom 'vanity and pride—traits that breed a wilful self-sufficiency—figure especially prominently.'[34] The 'demon' of dissatisfaction breaks the Marquise's sleeping beauty spell: she is a girl from the lycée who escapes one mundane existence only to find herself in another. 'She was pretending now; not to be a lady, as then, but to be—what? She was not sure. But something other than the self who now, for so long, was in truth a real lady [. . .] surrounded by so many ancient things and people that each one of them had the mustiness of death.' (181) Du Maurier revises the oral formula of the tale into a grim latter-day plot where awakening to bitter truths is not fairy tale, but fatal.

Her experiment with real-life drama leads to the death of M. Paul. The Marquise is one of several female killers in du Maurier's corpus of shorter fiction, and these include the characters of the usherette in 'Kiss Me Again Stranger,' Anna in 'The Alibi,' and Midge in 'The Apple Tree.' These plots invert the traditional male-on-female violence of the psycho-drama and dramatic monologue and here it is the Marquise who murders M. Paul, but not until he threatens her with exposure.

> 'Stop that noise,' she said in sudden fury. 'For God's sake pull yourself together.'
> The crying ceased. He took his hands away from his ravaged face. He stared at her, trembling, his brown eyes blind with pain. 'I have been mistaken in you,' he said. 'I know you now for what you are. You are a wicked woman and you go about ruining the lives of innocent men like myself. I shall tell your husband everything.'
> The Marquise said nothing. He was unbalanced, mad . . . (192)

M. Paul is an artisan whose hands, we learn, are 'deft and efficient' as those 'of an artist' (173). This, and his clubfoot suggests the myth of malformed Hephaestus, the smith of the Greek Gods, whose stormy relations with his wife Aphrodite, rocked Mount Olympus. Hephaestus is powerful but he is 'crook-footed' and supplanted in his wife's affections by the more martial and attractive Ares. Hephaestus, the 'shrivelled of foot,' now sees his beloved, goddess of love and beauty—clearly. His vengeance involves ensnaring the couple in a metal net of his own devising and exhibiting them publicly to the rest of the gods. Having invested heavily in the myth of beauty and virtue combined, M. Paul is also brutally disillusioned and, perceiving the Marquise accurately for the first time, he is unwisely candid about his intended vengeance. Then, the Marquise suddenly reveals her other self—the crone of Fate—who cuts the thread of his life in a joyous impulse that evokes Mikhail Bakhtin's jeering hag.[35] 'He stooped, by the opening at the cliff's edge, to pick up his stick, and as he did so the terrible impulse was born in her, and flooded her whole being, and would not be denied. Leaning forward, her hands outstretched, she pushed his stooping body. He did not utter a single cry. He fell and was gone.' (193) Having taken her pleasure the Marquise eliminates M. Paul and thus the evidence of her perfidy. She prepares for her next role as innocent bystander, by touching up her macquillage with rouge. It looks theatrical like 'the painted spots on a clown's face' in a mocking echo of her habitually successful artifice (194). After murdering M. Paul she bathes in the sea in an act of ritual cleansing and catharsis. She does this knowingly as wet hair from a swim will 'seem natural' as she plays 'the part' of a relaxed holidaymaker (194). In this baptism she is symbolically reborn and du Maurier's character illustrates the gender politics shown in Carter's warning from 1979, two decades after publication: 'A free woman in an unfree society will be a monster. Her freedom will be a condition of personal privilege that deprives those on which she exercises it of her own freedom. The most extreme kind of this deprivation is murder. These women murder.'[36] If du Maurier is a feminist: she is a murderous one.

At the start of the story the reader learns that '[t]he spell was broken' (162), the fairy-tale prince is away on business, again, and the Marquise is free to pursue her fatal desires. Du Maurier plays both presenter and critic of illicit desire as the story illustrates both pleasure and punishment: her characters are always responsible for their own downfalls and the Marquise's cardinal, and original, sin is curiosity. If, as McKee states, '[t]he protagonist seeks an object of desire beyond his reach,' then the Marquise easily obtains her object of desire by seducing M. Paul, this is however only her conscious desire. In truth, she wants to retain the status of her aristocratic position and enjoy illicit sexual diversions to demonstrate her power.[37] Tatar says that for fairy tales the pattern shows how: 'Curiosity goes hand in hand with defiance' and although the stories appear to follow a patriarchally sanctioned cautionary model—prohibition, transgression, punishment—they give voice to cultural anxieties about the 'proper' place for women.[38] Du Maurier's version of the fairy tale does exactly that and she writes it long before Carter, Donaghue, and others take up the challenge and revisit the genre.

By embarking upon an affair with a manual worker the Marquise allows a liminal space to open in which social stratifications are flouted and class miscegenation is possible. It is a structure du Maurier used previously in *Rebecca* [1938] and it ties into post-war paranoia over the blurring of social conventions. Douane's comment on the film adaptation of *Rebecca* [1940], directed by Alfred Hitchcock and starring Laurence Olivier and Joan Fontaine, is that 'the mixture effected by a marriage between two different classes produces horror and paranoia.'[39] The character of the Marquise risks all in this cross-class experiment, succeeding in her primary conscious aim, but failing to control consequences which unexpectedly expose her to threats, blackmail, and a pregnancy that will prove her marital perfidy. Bakhtin's theory of carnival and the grotesque details the challenge to class boundaries where the physical union of beauty and deformity is unpalatable outside of the realm of fantasy. He argues that the stain of crossing boundaries is ineradicable, and this is played out in the ramifications of Madame la Marquise's desire for 'passion between strangers' (166). This places her in the power of her lover's sister, the blackmailer who personifies what she most fears: the 'ugly, shuffling, crippled woman,' the personification of Bakhtin's theoretical hag and as a beautiful woman, her most dreaded and probable, fate (170).

Russo furthers Bakhtin's concept of grotesque realism in which the 'open, extended, secreting body, the body of becoming, process and change' opposes what she labels the '[c]lassical body which is monumental, static, closed and sleek, corresponding to the aspirations of bourgeois individualism.' M. Paul and Madame la Marquise are respective representatives of each category, and the possibility of a child from their union is a direct example of Russo's definition of carnival as a 'site of insurgency.' This concept suggests that the debased enters the site of high culture to 'resist, exaggerate, and destabilise the distinctions and boundaries that mark and maintain high culture and organised society.' Cast out from the chateau, the Marquise will be the 'laughing pregnant hag' that offers 'death that gives birth,' the figure of the Female Grotesque which Bakhtin originates, and Russo elaborates.[40]

There are three crisis points in close succession in the final pages, each of which feels like the final event. The Marquise pushes M. Paul off the cliff, his sister initiates blackmail, and the returning Marquis unwittingly introduces his wife to the idea of a possible pregnancy with a congenitally deformed issue. As the Marquis deplores congenital defects to his wife who is probably pregnant with a crippled child, readers remember that for feminism 'the body is typically regarded as passive and reproductive but largely unproductive, an object which struggles between its "inhabitant" and others/ exploiters.'[41] Du Maurier is always asking 'who is exploiting who?' This signposts the probability that the Marquise has conceived from her liaison with M. Paul. In Derek Hoddencott's play, which is adapted from the story, it is made explicit that having infiltrated the aristocracy, the Marquise indulges the licentious behaviour of her low origins and thus invites the physical and moral degeneration of the aristocracy.[42] It is worth noting that in the novel of *Rebecca* Maxim de Winter murders his first wife for threatening the act the Marquise commits: disrupting the law of primogeniture with an illegitimate child from an adulterous liaison. Hoddinott's adaptation of the story clearly infers that the Marquise is pregnant and will have a disabled child.

As Tatar wryly comments, '[i]t is one of the lesser-known facts of folkloric life that women are rarely as virtuous as they are beautiful.' Since '[n]o condition is better designed to put a woman in her "proper" place than pregnancy,' the Marquise's exercise in power is short lived as she moves inexorably from the role of murderer to mother.[43] The story ends with the Marquise's punishment for her transgressions yet to happen, if it happens at all. Du Maurier crafts chillingly appropriate punishments for her perpetrators in a letter to her publisher: '[Murderers are] possessed of an unnatural sort of greed that made them become murderers, and so a menace to society. They chose their weapon to destroy, therefore it seems to me just that same weapon should be used by them to create.'[44] Like Eve, the first woman of Judaeo-Christian culture, the Marquise's carnal curiosity is punished through the mortification of childbirth. That this happens off the page is a convenient means of rendering it unreal for the reader.

The Marquise's circumscribed existence is mirrored in the constraints of M. Paul's disability that necessitate the physical support of permanent encasement, in this case a boot. From the outset she is fixated by his deformity, imagining the hidden limb, the pain, and the necessary rituals of care in thoughts framed in language that becomes steadily more eroticised before she 'guiltily raises her eyes from the boot' (172). In M. Paul's family lameness is normal as his sister, also 'limped wretchedly' (185). To the Marquise it presents something 'counter, original, spare, strange,' his bodily contrast to her physical perfection is exciting, and monstrous, and rare.[45]

> Her eyes fell to the boot. His limp was not so pronounced as the sister's, he did not walk with that lurching, jerky step that produced stifled hysteria in the watcher. His step was slow, more dragging, and the Marquise felt a kind of compassion for his deformity, for surely the misshapen foot beneath the boot must pain him constantly, and the high boot, especially in hot weather, crush and sear his flesh. (173)

The Marquise indulges in sadistic fantasies about the photographer's disability; there is a lingering violence in the verb 'sear,' more commonly associated with animal meat than human tissue. This free indirect description indicates a sense of superiority, and pleasure in the man's disfigurement and pain and precisely subverts the meaning of the word 'compassion' which means, in its most common usage, 'to suffer with.'[46] M. Paul's threat to the prevailing order, is a continuation of the tradition in which '[i]n the classical period, cripples served as the sign and function of a social disorder writ large—a symbolic function that continues across all historical epochs.'[47] He is objectified, desired, and possessed, then discarded after a struggle by the exploiter, in this case a more powerful, and more beautiful, woman.

This echoes the core theme of Michel de Montaigne's essay 'Of Cripples' (1577), in which he argues for the close association between the miraculous and the monstrous, using them as facilitators for—and to show the limits of—self-knowledge: 'I have never seen greater monster or miracle in the world than myself: [. . .] but the more I frequent and the better I know myself, the more does my own deformity astonish me, the less I understand myself.'[48] To de Montaigne we are all deformed until we know ourselves yet cripples are 'liminal cases—de Montaigne leaves them as the extreme evidence of the soul impinging upon the shape of the "shoe" it wears.' While the Marquise bears no physical indicators of her amorality, M. Paul wears his imperfection on his outer casing, his body. For Nietzsche, 'cripples stand for that which is definitionally undesirable, for they are locked into a predicament of eternal, unchanging, and absolute deviancy.' This underscores the 'physiognomic circus' du Maurier engages in by using body parts for broader symbolic purposes, and the sharp contrast between these interpretations of the 'corporeally deviant' is summarised by Mitchell and Snyder: 'Montaigne's pragmatic approach to deformed bodies presages the emergence of Enlightenment science and a refusal to interpret bodies as conveyances for hypersocial meanings. In stark contrast Nietzsche ironically champions the value of disability as extreme devalued difference.'[49]

The notion that one's thinking can itself be crooked is furthered in the arguments of Lawrence D. Kritzman. To share the mental space of the Marquise is to share her blurring of what Kritzman refers to as 'the boundary between representation and reality' and the deformed reasoning that results. In his analysis: 'Montaigne uses the figure of deformity to describe the monstrous representations that the imagination is capable of engendering through the power of unbridled speculation. The desire to create something out of nothing produces an effect that is the result of reason's error.' In Kritzman's study of de Montaigne he explains that 'the monstrous stems from the perception of deviation from the normative; difference, portrayed as a visual "effect," attests to the rarity attributed to the object of the gaze.'[50] M. Paul is a tempting mixture of the sexually potent and the physically repellent, he offers an incomplete male body to the Marquise's curious gaze, which nonetheless hints at the potential for overcompensation in other areas. In his essay, 'Of Cripples,' Montaigne is clear: 'tis a common proverb in Italy, that he knows not Venus in her perfect sweetness who has never lain with a lame mistress. Fortune, or some particular incident, long ago put this saying into the mouths of the people; and the same is said of men as well as of women; for the queen of the Amazons answered the Scythian who courted her to love, "Lame men perform best."' The passage from 'The Little Photographer' is sensually redolent with the lexicon of power and fetishism.

> she [. . .] noticed that as he knelt he kept his weight upon one knee only, thrusting the deformed foot in the high boot to one side. Idly, she wondered if it hurt to lean upon it. The boot was highly polished, much brighter than the leather shoe upon the left foot, and she had a sudden vision of him taking great pains with the boot every morning when he dressed, polishing it, rubbing it, perhaps, with a wash-leather cloth. (182)

The attractively asymmetrical photographer is an essential counterpart to the Marquise's symmetrical perfection: the imbalance is reflected in their relationship. Mitchell and Snyder state that '[v]isible degeneracy, impotency, congenital deformity, festering ulcerations, and bleeding wounds [. . .] provide the contrastive bodily coordinates to the muscular, aesthetic, and symmetrical bodies of the healthy citizenry.' They are foils for each other as, 'the "healthy" corporeal surface fails to achieve its symbolic effect without its disabled counterpart,' and his physical aberration is the outward manifestation of her moral turpitude. Mitchell and Snyder trace the changes in historical attitudes towards the human body detailing how: 'Physiognomy became the paradigm of access to the ephemeral and intangible workings of the interior body. Speculative qualities such as moral integrity, honesty, trustworthiness, criminality, fortitude, cynicism, sanity [. . .] suddenly became available for scrutiny by virtue of the "irregularities" of the body that enveloped them.'[51]

This cultural hangover has its roots in our history of circus freaks and is an instance of what Kritzman calls de Montaigne's 'epistemological equation between "looking" and "lacking,"' a connection he develops from *monstrare* and its etymological roots in 'demonstrate.'[52] While du Maurier does write into the tradition of de Sade, and Carter, creating a 'museum of woman-monsters,' her clear gaze ensures that every other character also shows their monstrous side.[53] Leonard Kriegal's comments on physical disability also serve for the Marquise who is an emotional cripple: 'The cripple is threat and recipient of compassion, both to be damned and pitied—and frequently to be damned as well as pitied.'[54] Du Maurier was born in the Edwardian era and her stories present sinister manipulation by both genders, illustrating fears over the increasing trend towards social and political power for women.

This chapter illustrates how each story adds to the picture of du Maurier's re-member-ing the dis-membered body invoking some of its 'myriad symbolic associations.' Carter's summation of de Sade's writing has important applications to du Maurier's 'macabre' short stories which examine attempts to 'exterminat[e] the deviant as a purification of the *social* body' (my italics).[55] 'Sade's work [. . .] has been instrumental in shaping aspects of the modern sensibility; its paranoia, its despair, its sexual terrors, its omnivorous egocentricity, its tolerance of massacre, holocaust, annihilation.'[56] These comments are equally true of this corpus of short stories. Within this dark summation of society's malaise, we must remind ourselves that du Maurier is a mistress of mockery, and this tale of fetishism, congenital deformity, moral corruption, and artifice combines the horrific with the ludic, embodying Bergson's insights on laughter. 'Laughter is, above all, a corrective. Being intended to humiliate, it must make a painful impression on the person against whom it is directed. By laughter, society avenges itself for the liberties taken with it. It would fail in its object if it bore the stamp of sympathy or kindness.'[57]

This text symbolises the foot of du Maurier's corpus of short story material. Here, reflecting upon the beautiful and the impaired human form brings both into sharp relief, illuminating the contrasts and suggesting the sterility of separation in both corporeal and social categories. The asymmetrical is privileged, questioning cultural 'predilections towards symmetry in evolutionary biology that led asymmetry to be associated with infection, disease and poor mate selection.'[58] It is impossible to separate the diseased, the deformed, the impaired, just as we cannot cut off a limb from the organism that is human society. As Stallybrass and White indicate, our 'disgust always bears the imprint of desire. These low domains, apparently expelled as "Other," return as the object of nostalgia, longing and fascination.'[59]

There is a growing interest culturally in how our bodies work, how far they can be pushed to extremes (of beauty, or fitness, or ill-health), and this is partly a reflection of our terror of being subject to what Hamlet calls, 'the thousand natural shocks that flesh is heir to' (Act III, Sc. 1). Reyes work on Body Gothic outlines how '[e]ffective viscerality is more complicated to achieve than has thus far been conceded,' and that the form in itself both demarcates, and also destabilises, what is traditional and what is taboo.[60] In this model the mode both presents and polices the boundaries of what is considered acceptable and what is threatening to the status quo, for example, the links between disability and desire remain largely unacceptable in contemporary culture and noticeably absent from the political and social agenda. This is something du Maurier challenges in this text, and the open-endedness of 'The Little Photographer' further compels the reader to speculate and suggest 'futures unknown outside of the text,'[61] as 'all the weight of the short story is on the conclusion.'[62]

The Marquise is left not knowing whether or not she is pregnant at the denouement, and this is simply one instance of a woman whose beauty is tiresomely familiar to her, yet who dwells in a body of whose desires and processes she is fatally unaware. She is a stranger to her own physical self, which links to Reyes' comment that 'the body here is one that cannot be controlled, which ages and hurts, and which sometimes appears as the greatest and most feared stranger.'[63] These are stories which present characters at odds with their ageing bodies, their physical processes or desires, and the boundaries circumscribed by corporeal existence. The variety of physical changes in the characters includes desire, consummation, conception and death indicating the fragility of our belief in the corporeal stability of our bodies which are ever-changing. This fallacy is demonstrated by Scarry:

> This genre of error [. . .] has the peculiarity that when the beautiful person or thing ceases to be beautiful, it often incites the perceiver to repudiate, scorn, or even denounce the object as an invalid candidate or carrier of beauty. It is as though the person or thing had not merely been beautiful but had actually made a claim that it was beautiful, and further, a claim that it would be beautiful forever.[64]

The dangers of physical beauty is a theme continued in 'The Doll' where both genders project violence onto the object of their desire. 'The Little Photographer' presents another of du Maurier's female murderers whose moral punishment centres on her body even as her immoral pleasure is centred on the deformity of M. Paul. This symmetry contrasts with 'The Doll' where a fragmented narrative illustrates the distance between socially prescribed roles and human impulses. The subject of automata and dolls has a rich literary history, but the presentation of a male doll as partner, sexual and otherwise, is challengingly new. Decades before Angela Carter's interrogation of de Sade in *The Sadeian Woman* [1979], 'The Doll' presents a female sadist satisfying her desires on a male replicant. Just as the Marquise satisfied her lust for excitement on M. Paul before discarding him when no longer needed. In du Maurier's own words on authorship: 'The writer, more than any other artist, stands self-betrayed. The painter can catch a living scene on canvas, or a sitter's mood, and still stay hidden from his or her contemporaries, and from posterity too; but the writer, in the very choice of words and subjects, admits and indeed confesses, the problem within.'[65] For du Maurier the entire body is the canvas and the somatic is the best means through which to challenge sterile conformity.

NOTES

1. Advertisement for *Woman's Own* in *Daily Express* Thursday 13 November 1952, p. 10. *The Daily Express* Online Archive <http://www.ukpressonline.co.uk/ukpressonline/?sf=express> [accessed 5 February 2016].
2. MSS.157 courtesy of The Modern Records Centre.
3. Howatson, p. 59.
4. Winther, 'Closure and Pre-Closure as Narrative Grid in Short Story Analysis' in *The Art of Brevity:* p. 59–69 (p. 60).
5. Gretlund, 'Architecture in Short Stories by Flannery O'Connor and Eudora Welty' in *The Art of Brevity,* p. 138–51 (p. 151).
6. Scarry, *On Beauty and Being Just,* p. 31.
7. Malet, p. 28.
8. Mary Russo, *The Female Grotesque: Risk, Excess and Modernity* (London: Routledge, 1995), p. 79.
9. Stallybrass and White, p. 3–5.
10. Scarry, *On Beauty and Being Just*, p. 3.
11. Scarry, 'Part Two: On Beauty and Being Fair,' *On Beauty and Being Just.* p. 73.
12. Du Maurier, *The Birds and Other Stories* (London: Virago, 2004). All further references will be to this edition.
13. Jane Austen, chapter 1, *Pride and Prejudice* (London: Penguin, 1972), p. 51.
14. Stallybrass and White, p. 126.

15. Mitchell and Snyder, p. 55.

16. Robert Graves, *The White Goddess: A Historical Grammar of Poetic Myth*, ed. by Grevel Lindop, General and Patrick J. M. Quinn, fourth edn. (London: Faber and Faber, 1997).

17. Warner, p. 121.

18. Russo, p. 8.

19. Warner, p. 115.

20. Mitchell and Snyder, p. 185.

21. Carter, *The Sadeian Woman* (London: Virago, 1979), p. 20–25.

22. McKee, p. 149.

23. Ovid, pp. 61–66. LL III. 301–429.

24. Laura Mulvey, 'Visual Pleasure and Narrative Cinema,' sourced at <Laura Mulvey, Visual Pleasure.pdf (amherst.edu)> [accessed 29.6.2022].

25. Russo, p. 69.

26. Thomson, p. 65.

27. McKee, p. 130.

28. Grosz, p. 108.

29. Du Maurier letter to Maureen Baker-Munton, 4 July 1957 quoted in Forster p. 425.

30. Choderlos de Laclos, *Dangerous Liaisons* [1782] (London: Penguin, 2007). pp. 185–87.

31. Thomson, p. 10–12.

32. Julia Kristeva, *Powers of Horror: An Essay on Abjection* (Guildford: Columbia University Press, 1982).

33. J. C. Bernthal, 'If Not Yourself, Who Would You Be?': Writing the Female Body in Agatha Christie's Second World War Detective Fiction' in *Women: A Cultural Review*, 26: 1–2 (2015), 40–56. Sourced at <http://dx.doi.org/10.1080/09574042.2015.1035023> [accessed 29.6 2022], p. 43.

34. Tatar, p. 96, p. 104, p. 98.

35. Russo, chapter 2, 'Carnival and Theory,' p. 73.

36. Carter, p. 27.

37. Mckee, p. 147.

38. Tatar, p. 30.

39. Douane, p. 173. *Rebecca* (Selznick International Pictures, 1940).

40. Russo, p. 62–63, p. 69.

41. Grosz, p. 9.

42. Derek Hoddinott, *The Little Photographer* (London: Samuel French, 1979).

43. Tatar, p. 98.

44. Du Maurier letter to Gollancz, 14 November 1955. MSS.157/3/I/DM/12 courtesy of The Modern Records Centre, p. 2.

45. Gerard Manley Hopkins, 'Pied Beauty,' *Poems of Gerard Manley Hopkins* ed. by Robert Bridges (London: Humphrey Milford, 1918).

46. (a derivation from the Latin *com + pati*). cf. compassion *n*, *OED* 2.

47. Mitchell and Snyder, p. 65.

48. Michel de Montaigne, Chapter X1 'Of Cripples' in *Les Essais of Michel de Montaigne* [1577], Sourced at <Essays of Michel de Montaigne (gutenberg.org)> [accessed 29.6.2022].

49. Mitchell and Snyder, p. 83, p. 59, p. 66–67.

50. Lawrence D. Kritzman, 'Representing the Monster: Cognition, Cripples, and Other Limp Parts in Montaigne's "Des Boyteux" in *Monster Theory: Reading Culture,* ed. by Jeffrey Jerome Cohen (London; University of Minnesota Press, 1996), p. 151, p. 173.

51. Mitchell and Snyder, p. 58–64.

52. Kritzman, p. 174.

53. Carter, p. 25.

54. Kriegal quoted in Mitchell and Snyder, p. 7, p. 18.

55. Mitchell and Snyder, p. 54, p. 62.

56. Carter, p. 32.

57. Bergson, p. 29.

58. Umberto Eco, 'On the History of Ugliness.' Quoted in Henderson, p. 128.

59. Stallybrass and White, p. 191.

60. Reyes, p. 2.

61. Winther, p. 62.

62. Boris Ejxenbaum quoted in May, p. xvii.

63. Reyes, 18–19.

64. Scarry, p. 49.

65. Du Maurier, Preface, *Best Stories of Phyllis Bottome,* p. 9.

Chapter Nine

'The Doll' [body] (1937, 2011)

Having examined du Maurier's use of corporeal symbolism it is time to bring together the disassembled anatomy of this analysis of her shorter fiction. The divided parts of the body are brought together in this chapter on the earliest story in the study, 'The Doll' which was written in 1928. Among the most disconcerting of the texts, 'The Doll' enacts a 'destabilising place' for consideration of embodiment, gender relations, and the use and abuse of power. In the introduction to her analysis of primates, humans, and cyborgs, Haraway comments that she is writing a 'cautionary tale about the evolution of bodies, politics, and stories' and it is that sense of the cautionary tale that tracks so much of the somatic in this collection of narratives.[1] Though there are no records for du Maurier's reading list apart from hints in her correspondence, 'The Doll' was written in the year Radcliffe Hall published *The Well of Loneliness*, D. H. Lawrence published *Lady Chatterley's Lover* (in France), and women received the vote on the same terms as men as a result of the 'Representation of the People Act' (over 21). These are a few explanatory factors positioning 'The Doll' as a literary challenge to the normative gender roles of the period.

This story has a dialogic subtext with the myths of both Pygmalion and Ate the 'personification of blind folly who leads her victims astray.'[2] In the story of 'Pygmalion' the King of Cyprus falls in love with a beautiful statue of Venus, and here the myth is updated and re-gendered by du Maurier as a male simulacra with a female lover and another, jealous male admirer. Melville comments that one of Ovid's favourite ideas is 'the power of art to equal or indeed outdo nature' and this is one facet of this multifaceted text.[3] As has been illustrated in previous chapters, when characters in du Maurier's stories are infatuated and their feelings are unreciprocated the result is often violence. As Paul Lee explains, 'Ate is the cognate in the word "inf-atu-ation." Ate goes to atu. Ate is the blinding that leads to rash acts that eventuate in self-destruction.'[4] In this narrative both central characters appear infatuated but only Rebecca has a partner for life in Julio, the doll who cannot abandon her. Much of the text concerns male impotence at female caprice. In her book on robotic simulacra Julie Wosk asserts that '[r]obot women have often been envisioned by men as both nurturing and alluring.' This is a unique story centralising female desire for a male automata and foreshadows postmodern anxieties about technology and gender years before the cyborg was invented.[5] The binaries of machine/ person, human/ other, mind/ body are questioned in a text that suggests, but does not yet give voice to, the perspective of the ultimate outsider: the doll Julio.

Du Maurier may have been aware of stories such as 'The Doll' by Vernon Lee, first published as 'The Image' [1896], where the female narrator finds the 'unnerving presence of a huge, lifelike doll dressed in the clothes of a beautiful countess who died in childbirth early in her marriage.' The doll seems to come to life only when finally put to rest through immolation in the flames of a funeral pyre.[6] 'The Doll' by du Maurier likewise refigures bodies into uncanny alignments and the late twentieth-century advent of cyberfiction seems to reify the paradigm of 'women are aligned with the body, men are aligned with the mind—even when the body is a mechanical one.'[7] However, on investigation it becomes clear that the cyborg is composed of human and other and thus draws attention to the apparent 'impermeability of the boundary between them.' This 'uncertainty or ambiguity about whether a being is animate or inanimate—or whether an entity that appears lifeless is actually alive' is a feature of the *unheimliche*, the concept of the 'uncanny' that encapsulates human unease over accurate-seeming imitations. Freud comments that 'Jentsch has as an example Hoffmann's story "The Sandman" and described the uncanny as a condition of uncertainty or ambiguity about whether a being is animate or inanimate—or whether an entity that appears lifeless is actually alive.' For Jentsch, uneasiness is the production of imitation and in this category he includes life-size dolls with eyes that open and close (like Julio). For Freud the anxiety is more about fears of castration and while in 'The Sandman' this centers on losing one's eyes, in du Maurier's texts the fear is what one will see when they open, or how one is seen.[8] At page 24 of 'The Doll' Julio looks straight at the narrator who is immediately consumed with violent rage. Although du Maurier's 'The Doll' is not a definitive cyberfiction text it is prescient and postmodernist in form and theme.

There is no escape from embodiment as one of the characters is pure body, and one—the narrator—is a disembodied voice in a journal. There is no physical description of him, the doctor who finds the text has never seen him, and his clothes are discarded in a presumed, though not confirmed, suicide attempt. His physical absence is notable in a text that centralises corporeal presence and his mental degeneration results in increasingly fragmented entries that finally dwindle into nothing. The narrator lacks an integrated stable identity and is consequently no competition for the female protagonist's affection for a non-sentient male. The framing device of a letter is a self-reflexive inclusion that appears to ground the narrative in realism but rather foregrounds the unreliability of *both* narrators, another structural feature that aligns du Maurier with the modernist writers. A feature Head presents in a discussion of the way that technical devices apparently distance the narrative from reality, encouraging 'self-reflexivity and an awareness of artifice actually demystifies literature and reinforces the genre's capability to reflect the realities of modern life.'[9]

The nameless narrator as disembodied commentator and the eponymous 'doll' epitomise Henri Bergson's concept of 'man as a jointed puppet,' an apparently living being with hidden interior mechanical workings. In Bergson's essay 'Laughter: An Essay on the Meaning of the Comic,' he identifies our uneasy relationship with our physicality and the propensity to release that tension through laughter. A life-size human doll is both horrific and funny, sexual desire for that doll in preference to a living human is fascinating for the reader and humiliating for the rejected narrator. Bergson's comments work as an analysis of du Maurier's subtlety in revealing forbidden desires. In the story the narrator is ridiculed for his juvenile crush and subsequent failure to attract Rebecca, yet her desire for the doll is not ridiculed, raising the question of whether her preference is justified by the text. Bergsen states that '[i]n this sense, laughter cannot be absolutely just. Nor should it be kind-hearted either. Its function is to intimidate by humiliating.' He adds that 'we had better not investigate this point too closely, for we should not find anything very flattering to ourselves.'[10] Du Maurier uses her fiction to hold up an unflattering mirror to our darkest selves and encourages unkind laughter usually at the expense of the self-deluded. 'The Doll' invites consideration of the body in the broadest and the narrowest sense, an entire body without a mind to create desire, a mind without a body to enact desire, and a female character whose monstrousness is that, as a free woman, she can choose between them.

The story exemplifies the statement that, '[o]ur best literature seeks to articulate the vantage point of the socially devalued.'[11] Julio the life-size doll, represents the automatons and robots that have swiftly begun to inhabit our world, those who are the least valued and least represented 'citizens' of the twenty-first century. This is in line with du Maurier's privileging of the marginalised perspective in stories already discussed whose focalizers include; the elderly, a blind patient, a child, a cripple, and the asexual. The story introduces the themes of violence, desire, possession, reality, and representation that unify and dominate the corpus. But in this text the themes are brought home to the human form in its entirety and its entire absence as the mechanical is preferred to the flesh.

Perhaps unsurprisingly considering the subject matter and the period, 'The Doll' first appeared in 1937 and was republished as a rediscovered du Maurier gem by Virago in 2011.[12] The discovery of the story is as tantalising as its subject matter and it was unearthed by Ann Willmore, proprietor of Bookends of Fowey, a specialist bookshop in sourcing texts by du Maurier. After noticing a mention of the story in du Maurier's literary memoir *Myself When Young,* Willmore found 'The Doll' in an out-of-print collection of editorial rejections called *The Editor Regrets* [1937]. The collection also includes stories from Dorothy Whipple, C. S. Forester and H. E. Bates. It is a radical work, ground-breaking in that it centralises female desire yet tricksterish because the frame narrative guides readers to expect the opposite. Nearly one hundred years after 'The Doll' was written, 'the idea of creating an artificial human has been and remains a captivating goal,' and du Maurier's emphasis on corporeality takes the form of substituting the entire human body with a replicant.[13]

In addition, there is a family link to the topic of human facsimiles which goes back to du Maurier's grandfather's painting days in Paris, a time when life-size puppets were often used as cheap alternatives to paying human models to sit for artists. 'The Real Thing' [1892], is a story by Henry James inspired by a conversation with George du Maurier, in which the 'real thing' of the title are aristocrats who pose as artists models but who fail to sit well for the painter and have to be replaced by his dressed up servants.[14] As an anti-aristocratic satire it can be compared to du Maurier's story 'The Little Photographer' and it has clear parallels with 'The Doll.' The framing device for this text is a foreword penned by one Dr E. Strongman who discovers a journal on a beach detailing the author's obsession with the peripatetic violinist, Rebecca. He hears her performing at a party, is immediately captivated and determined to possess her. He attempts to initiate a liaison but is astounded when instead she 'introduces' him to her doll, Julio. Now fully obsessed, the narrator threatens violence, Rebecca disappears with Julio and the narrative trails off into silence. Unhelpfully, and despite frequent editorial interpolations, Dr E. Strongman offers no explanatory afterword although he does hint at the denouement in his foreword. 'Either the wretched man drowned himself near the spot where he hid his pocket-book, and his body has been lost at sea; or he is still wandering about the world trying to forget himself and his tragedy.' (13) The device of the ellipses is a regular feature of this text and it is always employed at moments of drama or where sexual content might be expected to appear.

The text is initially destabilised by Dr E. Strongman who claims to be indulging 'the entreaties of many friends' by publishing fifteen pages of the 'shabby' pocketbook that is filled with what he diagnoses as the 'hysterical product of a diseased mind' (13). There are no clues as to what he is a doctor of although he confidently exposes the author of the tale as mentally ill and the text as being as broken as its supposed author. '[S]odden' and 'discoloured by salt water,' the pages are 'damaged by exposure' there are 'many gaps,' the narrative is 'without sequence,' rendering it 'abrupt' and 'unsatisfactory' (13). In fact it may be the doctor-as-editor who is selectively excising those parts he considers unacceptable for the reader and the nested narrative has the effect of unsettling the reader although it may be swiftly forgotten as du Maurier's customary heightened tension takes over in another gripping yarn. Dr E. Strongman's purported reluctance to tell the story recalls Henry James' character Douglas, the first narrator in 'The Turn of the Screw' who is beseeched by guests to send for the manuscript of a first-hand account of a true ghost story written by a governess. She has been dead for twenty years and the manuscript is kept in a locked drawer. Douglas is subsequently replaced by an unnamed narrator who actually relates the story. This destabilising of textual provenance is in line with both gothic and modernist literary traits, yet, du Maurier's choice of editor is typically paradoxical. As Sceats and Cunningham argue, 'the master and the professor are at one with tradition and culture, part of the academic or literary mainstream,' and Dr Strongman's professional status gives credibility to his diagnosis of a melodrama of jealous desire. The doctor re-presents the text as a medical treatise and his unchallenged authority invites a resistant reading predicated on a search for lacunae within the text. This device is used in another (unpublished) du Maurier story, 'Last Pages of a Diary,' which again features a frustrated psychopath (a recurrent motif, as in 'The Alibi'). There is a foreword by the doctor, a description of the man, his life and the apparent absence of any previous trouble. There follows a description of how he was found on the evening of 16 July having lost his reason. The Doctor is unable to account for anything except that the man's brain was failing. 'Was there anything behind it? No one will ever be able to say. Here is the diary, the only evidence that remains.'[15] According to Sceats and Cunningham's premise Dr E Strongman's 'I' is 'a universal subject, which [. . .] transcend[s] all cultural and historical specifics "translating" into any language—and one which can unquestioningly assert itself as both the "writer" and the "man."'[16] However, the 'strong man' may also be the 'wrong man' to present and interpret the material. Dr Strongman's patriarchal reassurance is a contrast to the overwrought narrator and his justification for publication, as detailed in the foreword, feels suspiciously overdone.

Each time the narrative trajectory approaches climax the pages are missing or discoloured requiring Dr Strongman's editorial intervention in parenthesis: 'you have not kissed Rebecca, you cannot know. You are a fool asleep. You have never begun to imagine . . . (*Note*. Much of this seems completely unintelligible, and the quarter page that follows consists of nothing but broken sentences and half formed ideas. Then the narrative continues.)' (27) This glimpse of off-stage events trailing off into ellipses always occurs at critical moments such as the narrator's discussion with Rebecca about love, and when he bursts in on Rebecca and Julio together obscuring the reader's opportunity to 'see,' or rather have accurately described what the narrator sees. The story combines first-person narration, the letter and the editorial interlocutions, all of which serve as reminders of the unreliability of the account. The frame narrative destabilises the facts and the story 'problematises definition, rationalisation, finding and demonstrating 'proof' or truth, essentially epistemic questions.' In 'The Alibi,' 'The Doll' and 'Kiss Me Again, Stranger,' female voices are mediated by a male narrator. While female characters are central their speech is related and interpreted by male characters who are more or less well disposed to them. These female voices are 'adjacent and adjunct,' but their inclusion undermines patriarchal narrative authority even as the doctor undermines the narrator and his interpretation of the events.[17]

The story focuses on the complex navigations of jealousy and sexual violence in a heteronormative arena, yet, the text begins with a potentially homoerotic statement: 'For I am poisoned, I cannot sleep, I cannot close my eyes without seeing his damned face . . . ' (14). Despite the narrator's focus on Rebecca as the catalyst for his despair, Julio dominates his thoughts. He speaks of tender love without practising it and Julio represents his unspoken, unnatural desires: it is the doll who is the true object of his obsession and indifference that fuels his desire. His rages concern Rebecca: 'What did I love in you but your indifference, and the suggestions that lay beneath your indifference?' yet these words could as easily be about Julio (15). The implication is that indifference is the catalyst for Rebecca's desire too, as is obliquely referenced in their later conversation about sadism. Julio is a lifeless, lifelike, human simulacra, the mirror for human desires, a cadaver in whose visage the narrator sees the reflection of his own mortality. There is a history of artificial human replacements in art and literature dating back to Ovid and beyond. One of the more notorious is Oskar Kokoschka's three-year affair with Alma Mahler, wife of the composer Gustav Mahler. On her death Kokoschka commissioned Munich-based doll maker Hermione Moos to create a life size doll of his inamorata.[18] This mannequin, man-akin-to-a-doll, is Freud's double made manifest—the 'uncanny harbinger of death,' a life-size momento mori.[19]

This is a story comparing the power dynamics of male desire and female desire. In *The Sadeian Woman* Carter asserts that, '[t]o be the *object* of desire is to be defined in the passive case. To exist in the passive case is to die in the passive case—that is, to be killed. This is the moral of the fairy tale about the perfect woman.'[20] Julio is inanimate and non-living, hence desired, and thus he epitomises Carter's summation. Rebecca, has agency and is proactive, much to the fury of her human lover who resents her objectification of Julio because it enacts a resistance to his objectification of her. This model, proposed by de Sade and reified by Carter, is one in which desire imposes passivity which transforms the person into simulacra, and thus renders them desirable. In 'The Doll' the narrator expresses his passion as an impulse to kill.

Du Maurier's interest lies in the anatomy of control and the autonomy of desire, and in these texts the influence of Robert Browning's dramatic monologues is often apparent. The narrator has a reverie about strangling Rebecca when they first meet at Vorki's party, and the language clearly evokes Browning's murderous suitors. 'Her throat was very long and thin, like a swan's. I remember thinking how easy it would be to tighten the scarf and strangle her. I imagined her face when dying—her lips parted, and the enquiring look in her eyes—they would show white, but she would not be afraid.' (17) The unidentified narrator of Browning's 'Porphyria's Lover' [1842] kills his lover to keep her, likewise, explaining to his listeners how he knows that death is in her best interest. Lines 53–56 show the narrator describing Porphyria's putative emotions in chilling terms: 'So glad it has its utmost will/ That all it scorned at once is fled/ Porphyria's love, she guessed not how/ Her darling one wish would be heard.'[21] The homicidal narrator, and his plan to achieve freedom for females through murdering them, is transformed and updated in 'The Doll.' Both texts are studies in jealousy. However, unlike Browning's poem 'The Doll' has a protagonist and an antagonist, whereas Porphyria is a passive victim who makes a pretty, doll-like corpse. At least Rebecca's character is present through reported speech in this story. Yet, du Maurier's narrator always describes Rebecca in terms of her physical position as if she is merely a doll to be posed, and an early verbal slip reveals that he has positioned her as the audience to his tale of woe. 'The room was full, a lot of people were talking by the piano—Vorki was there, they were trying to make him sing, and Olga was screaming with laughter. I always hated the hard thin reed of her laugh. *You were sitting*—Rebecca was sitting on a stool by the fire. Her legs were twisted under her, and she looked like an elf, a sort of boy.' (16, italics mine). This early verbal slip indicates Rebecca as the listener to the tale and not the reader, though the slip is swiftly corrected. The slippage suggests an uncomfortable literary cousinship with Browning's murderer.

As if living under a curse the narrator is compelled to repeat his tale: 'I'm forgetting days and weeks as I write this, it's like rising from the dead, it's like being reincarnated from dust and ashes to live it again, to live my whole cursed life again—for what was my life before I loved Rebecca, where was I, who was I?' (22). The extremes of his self-pity and frustrated rage are couched in hyperbolic language: 'I have never been so unutterably alone. Why should it help me to write this?,' and the comical quasi-Shakespearean drama of, 'Vomit forth the poison in my brain' (14). As previously stated, 'Last Pages of a Diary' is an unpublished early story (the notebook is dated 1926 when du Maurier was only 19) that has direct connections to the structure and subject of 'The Doll.' The draft covers a ten-day period and the central character is a self-important, self-pitying man called Stephen Willis (Willis is also the name of the gardener in 'The Apple Tree'). As the isolated narrator degenerates into full madness the final line of text reads: 'I have suddenly become aware that . . .'[22] Without self-knowledge this narrator cannot grasp the fact that the Rebecca he desired was a dream figure, while the violinist is a real woman with desires that do not match his. Only when she is 'restrained, breathless' and her 'little voice' is finally silenced, will she be controllable (19). The sexual content is implicit. Framed by unpublished stories, letters, and earlier texts the narrator's story in 'The Doll' is haunted by another text hidden in the ellipses, tangents and lacunae: Julio and Rebecca's story.[23]

In later years du Maurier expressed irritation with the mores of her time and expressed her view that reticence about sexual matters was unhealthy. In her correspondence with Maud Waddell she argues for greater freedom of information for people in general. 'If only they were brought up to know about sex like they know the rain falls from the sky, half the battle would be over. It's all the mystery and giggle-behind-the-hand that causes the trouble. As DH Lawrence said, one is brought up in the belief that sex is "natures dirty little secret" and I fear that is how most people regard it.' Despite this lengthy comment she herself kept the ellipses in her stories while delicately circling the topic of sexual attraction. She portrays the descent into sexual obsession with unnerving accuracy. The narrator, of course, would know Rebecca's mind were they to be together. 'Her eyes would be transfigured as if by a shaft of silver' and should he kill her, 'the enquiring look in her eyes—they would show white, but she would not be afraid' (17). Again, the correlations with Porphyria's unloving lover are plain:

No pain felt she;
I am quite sure she felt no pain,
As a shut bud that holds a bee,
I warily oped her lids
Laughed the blue eyes without a stain (LL 41–5).

In common with Browning's protagonist, the narrator of 'The Doll' adopts the traditionally feminised stance of unfairly rejected lover and victim. Du Maurier's stories present female murderers but males who only fantasise about committing murder. Here the narrative style occludes and direct interpolations halt any suspension of disbelief or narrative empathy, the narrator is certain readers will empathise with his views though empathy is a quality he definitely lacks. Curiously, the quality of empathy is a recurring one within literature on the relations of, and the differences between, replicants and humans and it is a coinage by May Sinclair, an author from the early part of the twentieth century.[24] In Philip K. Dick's seminal science fiction novel, *Do Androids Dream of Electric Sheep?* protagonist Rick Deckard opines: 'Empathy evidently existed only within the human community [. . .] ultimately, the empathic gift blurred the boundaries between hunter and victim, between the successful and the defeated.'[25] Stefan Hawlin comments that the murderer's 'mindset is an exaggeration of feelings or tendencies that we may all have experienced,' but despite the lack of female fear in 'The Doll' or female pain in the poem, these are not 'tender' murderers.[26]

The title focuses on the simulacra and not the humans in the text. The word 'doll' is one that is culturally gendered as female, and it is perhaps the centrality of the male doll, Julio, that indicates why the story was neglected by publishers for nearly a century. Although there is not much data on the first sex dolls, the 1980s Realdoll American brand have charged $7,000 and above for several female options, with just one male doll called 'Charlie.' Meredith G. F. Worthen comments that the male sex doll is depicted in non-eroticised poses in contrast to female dolls and according to her study the inclusion of male dolls is a 'relatively new phenomenon.'[27] Du Maurier's gender inversion plays upon the denotation of the toy as a 'female pet, a mistress,' a 'plaything' and 'a pretty, but silly or frivolous woman.'[28] The character of Rebecca is described in a paradoxical melange of appellations incorporating religious iconography, the childlike and the fairy tale. She is a saint and a devil, an 'elf, a sort of boy' and has a 'slim body like a boy' (16). She has animalistic characteristics such as 'teeth, sharp and white as ivory' and 'savage hair, electric, dark, uncontrolled' that indicate depravity not refinement (15). Richardson comments that 'Terms like "primitive," "savage," "uncivilized," and "erotic"' characterise Otherness, and that skin is, 'a marker of cultural difference that purportedly distinguishe[s] refinement from depravity.'[29] Rebecca's beauty, her 'skin, pale coffee, and clear, clear as water,' is as much a threat to convention as are her actions (17). The description is reminiscent of Edward Rochester's image of a bestial and sexualised Bertha Mason in *Jane Eyre*, and passages on the contradictory nature of women purportedly written by male writers in *A Room of One's Own* (1927).[30] 'Have they souls or have they not souls? Some savages say they have none. Others, on the contrary, maintain that women are half divine and worship them on that account. Some sages hold that they are shallower in the brain; others that they are deeper in the consciousness.' Woolf's polemical essay was published a year after 'The Doll' was written and her irony is itself, savage.[31]

The protagonist Rebecca does not engage with, or respond to, the narrator. When he speaks, her smile is 'apart, unearthly, it had no relation to anything one said' (17). Her smile has no relation to anything *he* says as she is not listening to him and she seems 'strange, detached [. . .] bored' (20). The narrator is a zealot in his quest to possess what he sees as divinely pure, her. Her bedroom is 'furnished like a nun's cell, quite plain and bare,' her eyes are as 'pure as water' and he believes her to be virginal and 'untouched' (21). Rebecca has never kissed a man but the narrator doubts 'the truth' (28). The first time that he listens to her play, the prose is purple with tension and excitement, mirroring an orgasm in heightened language and pace.

> I don't know what she played but it was shattering—stupendous. I was not aware of anything but that I and Rebecca were together—out of this world, away, lost—lost in unutterable bliss. We were climbing, then flying higher—higher. At one time the violin seemed to protest, and it was as if she were refusing me, and I were pursuing her—then there came a torrent of sound, a medley of acceptance and denial, a confusion of notes in which were mingled desire and sweetness, and intolerable pleasure. I could feel my heart beating like the throb of some mighty vessel, and the blood pounded in my temples. (18)

To the narrator her 'dangerous' musical talent is seductive, its frenzied passion contrasts with what he perceives as her resistance. He vouchsafes: '[h]er words bewildered me, they seemed utterly inexplicable. She was not lying, her eyes looked straight into mine, and she was smiling' (19). This second sentence operates almost syllogistically, the double meaning of the word 'lying' radically alters the sense of the final two clauses. If we take lying to mean deceitful, the sentence can be understood to mean that Rebecca is seated, honest, and making smiling eye contact with the narrator. Equally, if lying refers to a prone position, as would be expected from the sexual fervour and climax of her performance, then we know that she is deceiving, for she could not look 'straight into his eyes,' or 'smile.' Either way, his words reveal that he is not in control: 'I must wait until she wanted me again' (26). The indifference shown by Rebecca and the fanatical desire of the narrator have their counterpart in Monte Verità where another heroine abandons her male partner for a non-heterosexual alternative.

To date, du Maurier has not been regarded as a feminist writer, but this story is like all challenging artistic (re)presentation, like a doll to be repositioned as the reader desires. The plot has parallels with the 'The Alibi' in that there is an eastern European Jewish woman with a peripatetic life-style, a young male that she can position as she wishes, and a psychopathic male fantasist frustrated by his inability to control others. The story can be read as an early fictional experiment with the 'female gaze' long before John Berger and Laura Mulvey's ground-breaking work on the 'male gaze' in the 1970s, here it is the male form that is a passive object to be posed and used. Despite the narrator's efforts to constrain Rebecca to a puppet role for his gratification, her wilful and active behaviour challenges Berger's analysis that in art, 'men act and women appear.'[32]

By applying Mulvey and Berger's theories on representation in art, the female protagonist in this story can be seen to inhabit the same space of power that would conventionally be occupied by a male. The 'male gaze' is radically disrupted by female occupation of the position of viewer, something Wosk considers in her comments on male designers of female simulacra: 'men's idealisation of the artificial female, their longing for a woman who will validate and complement them, and the problematic nature of the male gaze—their ways of projecting onto these artificial women awoke their most deeply felt longings, which could distort their vision and point of view.'[33]

Wosk investigates how, historically, dolls are 'pretty, manipulable playthings for men's delectation and desire' By swapping the gender of the doll and its owner, du Maurier allows for female desire and female pleasure in a context that excludes all but the semblance of a living man. No wonder the narrator is frustrated by his exclusion. It is not that Rebecca does not feel desire, it is that she has more pleasure from the fake than the real. And since she has embraced and kissed Julio, and perhaps more than this, she is in an informed position from which to compare and choose. The narrator's fury arises not only from a frustration of his role as a dominant, desiring actor in the relationship, but also because he is unable to dominate since he is not reciprocally desired by Rebecca. Further than this, he is supplanted by an inanimate and totally passive *object*, which is, in his own and only his own judgement, inferior to him.

Wosk identifies the paradox that while '[i]n men's fantasies about ultra-realistic female robots, the artificial woman often trumps the real woman,' yet, '[f]ictional female robots often help men feel comfortable with their own gender identity.'[34] Julio and the narrator are both playthings and pets, while Rebecca's words are ventriloquised twice over, once by the editorial decisions of the unstable narrator and once by the omniscient editor Dr E. Strongman. There is an ellipsis immediately after an interruption by Dr Strongman and Rebecca's explanation jerks into 'not really cold' she insisted, 'I've tried to explain to you that I'm odd in some ways, I've never met anyone to care for, I've never been in love. I've always disliked people rather than been attracted by them."' (21). As mentioned previously Katherine Mansfield was an inspiration for du Maurier and this passage begins with intimations of sexual frigidity that are reminiscent of Mansfield's short story 'Bliss' and her character Bertha Young's uneasy justification of a passionless marriage to the socially outgoing, and unfaithful, Henry.[35] This serves to position du Maurier as the storyteller and her ventriloquist narrator Strongman/ wrong man, as a teller of tall stories. Du Maurier evidently wanted to experiment with the borders of acceptability, and the fact that this tale languished for so long is testament to a readership that was not ready.

Rebecca pointedly asks: '[i]s it possible to love someone so much, that it gives one a pleasure, an unaccountable pleasure to hurt them?' and she then opens the door into the room in which Julio sits (22). This behaviour is reminiscent of Madame la Marquise in 'The little Photographer,' another one of du Maurier's sadistic female characters. Two thirds of the way into the story, Julio is revealed to be a life-sized male doll that can be made to move by screws and wires—an automaton. A contemporary advert for a life-sized human doll indicates the current use of such items and the description reads as follows: 'The body in action moves like a living being, pressing, embracing, changing position at will by simple pressure. The mechanism which gives life to the apparatus is very substantial and cannot get out of order. The complete apparatus, guaranteed against breakage, man or woman, 3000 francs.'[36] In his study on the proliferation of robots in the twenty-first century, David Levy sums up our 'quasi-human relationship with the machine as helpmate, as true friend, as permissive parent, as sex object, and as sex partner.' The benefits of having an endlessly compliant and attractive lover are obvious, as Iwan Bloch surmises in his comments on *La Femme Endormie* [1899] a story by Madame B: 'the love heroine is an artificial doll, which [. . .] can be employed for all possible sexual artificialities, without, like a living woman, resisting them in any way.'[37] Wosk agrees, stating that a robot is a perfect woman because 'she does what she is told, she can't talk, can't eat.'[38] Like his descendant the robot, Julio is impervious to Rebecca's exploration of the limits of 'an equal mingling of pleasure and pain,' just as he is incapable of being hurt by her 'experiment, a rare sensation' (22).

In her short stories du Maurier swaps gender roles from normative societal patterns and this generates unpredictable results. 'The Doll' operates intertextually in several ways that illustrate male fear of female sexuality. One of which is with the Bluebeard fairy tale, here, the narrator is let into Rebecca's darkened red curtained room which is the location for an inert male body. Julio is the successful rival for Rebecca's affection, and the nemesis for the narrator's psyche. Notably his speech demonstrates obsession with the doll rather than with the woman he apparently desires. There are parallels with 'The Rendezvous' [1980] another plot in which an older dominant man is outwitted by the room-swapping reversals of a younger woman. That Rebecca and the narrator share necrophiliac tendencies is intimated in the conflation of sex and violence in their initial meeting. Their thoughts and dialogue are saturated with the twin impetus of desire and death (Eros and Thanatos). Du Maurier's arch humour is easily missed, as when the psychopathic narrator carefully explains sadism to the 'thoughtfully' nodding Rebecca: 'She puzzled me, but I tried to explain to her what was meant by sadism. She seemed to understand, and nodded her head thoughtfully once or twice.' (22) It is directly after this exchange that Rebecca reveals her womb-like inner sanctum, in 'half-darkness' and velvet draped 'as if to deaden any sound,' the right place for a girl dressed in scarlet (22). Lest the reader disregard the clues of manipulation and seduction, the demon Mephistopheles from the renaissance play *Dr Faustus* is used as a comparison to Rebecca and the reiteration of 'savage' intimates her dark impulses.

Wosk's summary of female automata works just as well for Julio: '[t]ales about artificial women so often circle around issues of control.'[39] However, it is the 'soul-less' doll who has the attributes of a 'satyr'; 'evil,' 'cruel,' 'depraved,' with the 'eyes of a hawk' that 'stare right though one' (23). The convincing description of Julio's physical aspect parallels a 1909 advertisement for a *hommes* or *dames de voyage* doll: 'There's the inner framework which is carefully articulated, there's the hair on the head, the body hair, the teeth, the nails! There's the skin, which has to be given a certain tint, certain contours, a particular pattern of veins. There are the eyes, which need to be given some expressions, there's the tongue [. . .] the only thing *these* haven't got is the power of speech!' These dolls were used for fornicatory purposes on long voyages and are now an increasingly common substitute for human-to-human sexual congress.

Regarded by the narrator as a 'loathsome toy' (24), Julio is the only character who, as a non-sentient, cannot object, cannot fantasise about sexual violence, inflict pain, or kill, yet it is he who bears the brunt of the narrator's rage and frustration from start of story to finish. On the second page it is

Julio's 'filthy battered body' the narrator imagines throwing from the window, a murderous action to a readership as yet unaware that this is a built-to-scale human doll and not a human (14). The narrator is looking into a mirror of distorted behaviour that gives an accurate reflection of his own desires.

Perhaps the most shocking aspect of the story is not that there is a male doll that satisfies the sexual desires of a young woman, but that she prefers the doll to a relationship with a man of flesh and blood. This centralises female desire and female sexual preference, a topic that was a relatively recent phenomena at the time of writing and which emerged in the texts of New Woman writers such as George Egerton and Kate Chopin (*Keynotes* [1893] and *The Awakening* [1899]). It is worth noting that Chopin's celebrated texts foregrounds a woman's desire to have freedom *from* sex as much as her right to have sexual freedom. Wosk states: '[o]ne of the reasons people pursue sexual relations with prostitutes is so they have access to sexual practices denied them with their partners who may be unwilling, or unable, to accommodate their desires.' Julio can neither resist nor respond, and Rebecca is spared what the narrator represents, and what Levy cites, as 'the responsibilities or emotional attachments of a conventional relationship.'[40] In Levy's view robots are now so lifelike humans relate to them without any qualms and the more convincingly human the replicant, the more authentic the human response. For this to work the replicant must be 'almost completely indistinguishable from a human being,' and must have the ability to make 'meaningful eye contact' and be 'physically convincing.' One example of this is Orient Industries, the most successful manufacturers of sex dolls in Japan where sexual replicants are commonly called Dutch Wives. According to the manufacturers: '[a] Dutch wife is not merely a doll, or an object. She can be an irreplaceable lover, who provides a sense of emotional healing.' They were made from rubber and plastic, and were constructed and purchased for use during long voyages. Today, the business is increasingly lucrative and the company makes human facsimiles that are virtually indistinguishable from the real thing. Du Maurier's unpublishable story from 1928 has become a reality in the new millennium, albeit largely for male heterosexuals who comprise the market of consumers. Thus, if the plot is transposed into real life the narrator gets a choice of replicant 'Julias' while Rebecca is limited to one version of Julio, a male doll that remains largely unsold.

Levy identifies how '[t]he commodity thus becomes increasingly personalised to its owner through repeated use and interaction, and as it does so, it takes on, within the owner's mind, an aura of uniqueness.' 'Most humans attribute others with having minds—that is, feelings, beliefs, and intentions different from their own. [. . .] Anything that bears some similarities to a human being, and with which a person has repeated interactions, is treated as if it has a mind.'[41] Rebecca introduces Julio to the narrator, the doll has his own room in her flat, a fire to keep him warm, and when she is gone he goes with her too. She treats him as a person and so he has personhood for the narrator too who also responds to the facsimile as a loathed rival despite his lack of sentience, and life.

Teresa Peterson describes the character of Rebecca as being 'imprisoned in a weird, bizarre relationship' yet this observation misapprehends the purpose and dynamic of Rebecca and Julio's 'unholy rapture' (29).[42] Does Rebecca recognise the inherently murderous impulses of the narrator and share a similar predilection? She chooses a human replicant who cannot be killed for a paramour. Julio straddles the boundaries of life and death in that he is described as being 'human enough, damnably lifelike, with a foul distinctive personality, but a doll' (24). Rebecca has found a vessel to contain her overlapping sexual and violent fantasies—a non-destructive outlet. By misunderstanding her intentions the narrator removes himself forever from the intimacy he claims to crave. Rebecca's point is that it is the 'hurt' that they have in common rather than the 'love.' It is just as well that she wishes to commune in violence rather than in passion and, even if the narrator was correct in his mistaken thought that she had feelings for him, this is as likely to lead to his death at her hands, as her death at his. As previously indicated, Du Maurier's short fiction illustrates her gallery of violent female characters and Rebecca's brief comments suggest that she is one of them.

In this grimly witty story, du Maurier plays with our expectations of the romance genre as the narrator constantly misinterprets the evidence before him. Wosk cites the comic aspects in 'mistaking reality for artifice,' and this is usually done the other way round but here it is the fake that is treated as the real.[43] It is not Rebecca who is 'restrained and soul-less' but the doll which she restrains and uses as a man-toy, and by inference anyone else who fatally embarks upon an intimacy with her (15). In the same way as Rebecca the eponymous heroine of du Maurier's 1938 novel, this Rebecca is misrepresented by everyone and labelled savage and uncontrolled, yet restraint appears to be her modus operandi. The narrator bathetically whines: 'What have I not done with you in dreams, Rebecca?' but it is her indifference that excites him (15). What he sees as Rebecca's 'tight repression that suggests a hidden fire,' is an indifference to him as partner that his immature ego cannot accept (15). The text is framed by his rage, which leads to self-destruction when violence towards Rebecca and Julio is thwarted. Although the text is open ended Rebecca seems to escape her obsessive stalker and her independence is rewarded by freedom, sexual and otherwise. 'The Happy Valley' is another early story in this collection, which is suggestive of the themes that dominate *Rebecca* [1938], marital danger, dream-visions, untimely death. The violinist's eponymous literary 'twin' is the self-motivated architect of her own, and almost her husband's, death. In his failure to physically possess her, or to destroy Julio the doll, the narrator disintegrates psychologically and apparently destroys his own body by drowning.

The reader sees Julio through the eyes of the jaundiced narrator, as such the lurid description of his evil mouth, 'sensual and depraved,' 'cruel, gleaming, and narrow' eyes, and 'ashen' face should be sceptically received. Yet like Pygmalion's Galatea, this 'boy of about sixteen, dressed in a dinner-jacket, shirt and waistcoat, and long Spanish trousers' is attractive (23). Julio is 'a machine—something worked by screws—he was not alive, not human,' and the narrator is hopeful that Rebecca will discard Julio for a real man, dismissively calling 'it' a 'toy' (24). The *OED* definition for 'automaton' includes: '1) Something which has the power of spontaneous motion or movement; 2) A human being viewed materially; 3) A piece of mechanism having its motive power so concealed that it appears to move spontaneously.' Wendy Beth Hyman clarifies definitions of 'automata' by stating that: 'to take the inanimate and infuse it with motion and apparent life [. . .] this is what we think of as an automaton. But to take a human being and see it reductively as inanimate: this too is an automaton.'[44]

In the introduction to her study of the automata in Renaissance literature she posits that '[u]nlike every other animal in Eden, Adam has been handcrafted, or "formed," in the likeness of a pre-existing model.' 'Humans are the one artificial animal, the Creator's image and likeness upon earth . . . our essential and defining characteristic—the sine qua non of our existence—is the fact that we are living images, flesh and blood imitations.'[45] In common with Levy's perspective on developments in robotics, Hyman challenges our attachment to what were previously the solely human characteristics of speech and movement, relegating the quality of humanness to the category of 'diminishing residuum.'[46] She argues that personhood is becoming a matter of perspective and the text supports this view in that the narrator is just as determined to label Rebecca as Other: '[i]ntense, restrained and soulless; for you must be soulless to do what you have done' (15). As the reader does not get to know what this is the mystery remains and the horror is all the worse for remaining unknowable.

The Jamesian chiasmus of artist's models and true aristocrats illustrated in his short story 'The Real Thing,' is relevant. 'They had accepted their failure, but they couldn't accept their fate. They had bowed their heads in bewilderment to the perverse and cruel law in virtue of which the real thing could be so much less precious than the unreal; but they didn't want to starve. If my servants were my models, my models might be my servants.'[47] By the end of the narrative Julio and Rebecca have become a couple, a 'them,' and the lifeless doll is permanently invested with the envied role of the 'other man' who successfully won the girl. 'And I am deceiving myself when I say that she would have come to me. She would never have loved me—she will never love any man. [. . .] I pity her. she misses so much—so much—and no one will ever know the truth.' (14–15). A wooden Frankenstein's monster, Julio is patriarchal science creating its own superior replacement but as Rebecca defiantly cries: 'I don't want you. I don't need you' (30). Jean Baudrillard states that signs mask the absence of a basic reality and cannot present it other than under the sign of (re)production. He cites the automaton as a counterfeit that plays with reality, 'questions humanness, soul, mortality. An obvious but theatrical fake.'[48] Julio is, moreover, a man with whom the narrator cannot compete even as he himself becomes mannequin-ised, sleeping fully dressed and 'wash[ing] . . . *mechanically*' (26, italics mine).

Levy explores the notion that one day soon androids and gynods will exist in a limbo state of 'almost alive,' and be 'in many ways superior to mere mortals,' capable of inspiring romantic love and perhaps being better at it than their human makers.[49] This comment feeds straight into the unnamed narrator's insecurities regarding the wet-mouthed Julio who is preferred by Rebecca. Feminism and science have successfully challenged Freud's paradigm of the active sperm and the passive egg, supposedly mirrored in female receptivity and male dominance in sexual relations. In fiction the woman pursuing her own desire has traditionally been punished, but du Maurier allows her female characters agency. Rebecca does not, and cannot, subordinate her desires to Julio's as traditional gender conventions dictate: he has no desires. The narrator cannot conceive of such a pattern and so rejects the notion in favour of what he does understand—Julio as Other, as rival, as repellent, grotesque, and an insane, reductive choice. Thus, Rebecca's sexuality is not passive or benign, indeed her actions refute the 'men crave power and orgasm, while women seek reciprocity and intimacy' pattern. Any reciprocal intimacy with a wooden doll must perforce be imaginary while orgasmic power is paramount and satisfied by the self.

Du Maurier makes use of uncanny, transgressive material from literary and real-life appropriations including puppets and the mannequins used by painters in her grandfather's time. One example Munro mentions is the dolls of Hans Bellmer, made by him and captured on film in an anonymously published series entitled 'La Poupée' or 'The Doll' [1934].[50] The techniques used in 'The Doll' are also found in her work more broadly, and not only display a distinctive modernist sensibility but also anticipate postmodernist writers such as Angela Carter. This story is not shocking compared to Carter's heady blend of violent sensuality, but 'The Doll' was written fifty years before *The*

Bloody Chamber (1979). With its Baudrillardian male simulacra 'The Doll' was a challenging text for 1928 and remains so today. If, '[p]ower and sexual desire are deeply, perhaps intrinsically connected in ways we do not fully understand,' then stories such as 'The Doll' surely aid explication.[51]

The reification of the corporeal in the stories indicates the truth of the statement that, 'narratives turn signs of cultural deviance into textually marked bodies.'[52] The doll is a glimpse of the end of sentience, the end of our individual awareness of being-in-the-world which we have yet to fully comprehend. Humans wilfully create their own robotic replacements and tellingly, Julio's mouth 'leer[s] foolishly' at the narrator as if to mock his redundancy, and ours (24). Dr E. Strongman's interruptions remind the reader of the vulnerability of the mind, and the doll conveys the fragility of the human body that is our truest home.

The short stories of Guy de Maupassant were an early inspiration for du Maurier and his story, 'The Ruse,' has clear parallels with 'The Doll,' with its doll-like corpse, dressing up and scheming doctor who oversees the deception. Commenting on the intertextual relations in her biography of du Maurier, Forster says there is 'no sign of this influence in Daphne's own stories' but this is refuted by the obvious connection between these two texts.[53] 'It was a terrible business. I took his limbs one by one, like those of an enormous doll, and held them out to the clothes the women brought. Like that we put on his socks, underpants, trousers and waistcoat, although we had a great deal of trouble getting his arms into the sleeves.'[54] The reader only encounters the lover in the story as a dead human doll yet he/it remains the subject of female desire despite the altered state:

> Her kisses fell like blows on the closed lips, on the dead eyes, on the temples and the forehead. And then, putting her lips to his ear, as if he could still hear her and she were about to whisper something to make their embraces still more ardent, she repeated several times in a heartrending voice: "Good-bye darling."

This is the imagined behaviour that torments the narrator in 'The Doll' as he dwells on Rebecca and Julio entwined forever while he is cast out and excluded from her company, never to be the object or the subject of her desire. Nicholas Royles states: '[a]t the heart of desire, of the desire to write, of the desire to remember and of the desire to appropriate, to have as one's own, to have as one's own thing, is the otherness of a foreign body, a mechanical and deathly power of repetition.'[55] 'The Doll' is an open-ended text and as such an example of du Maurier's tendency to rework fairy-tale elements into ambiguous, modernist fiction and the narrator's failure to possess Rebecca's body is played out in a Sisyphean repetition couched in his compulsive need to retell the experience.

This physical and verbal play upon the presence and absence of sentient life centres upon the figure of the mannequin, a thing that illustrates the final joke—the kiss of death is already on us. Our bodies are *where we live* and Julio illustrates the image we cannot see—how we will look when we die. He is the final full stop of unpalatable truths. Together, he and the narrator serve as the exemplar of Cartesian dualism. Namely, that '[t]he body is a self-moving machine, a mechanical device, functioning according to causal laws and the laws of nature.'[56] The emasculated narrator cries out an aggressively defensive justification from the depths of his rejected ego: 'I should have taught her what it is to be loved by a man,—yes—a man, and I would have thrown his filthy battered body from the window, watched him disappear forever, his evil scarlet mouth distorted' (14). He imagines Julio's 'battered body' with satisfaction, as if the doll is, in fact, sensate.

In the Judeo-Christian tradition humans are a simulacrum of God, so the automaton in human form is a copy of a copy of the divine. Julio is a filthy distorted type, a copy of a copy whose existence collapses the real and the imaginary.[57] He is Baudrillard's 'counterfeit who plays with reality,' a corpse who questions what comprises humanity, a soulless wooden repository for multiple fantasies, an unwanted reminder that, 'human beings are essentially machines.'[58] Wosk elaborates the point further by stating: 'That's why dolls haunt us. They are modelled on humans [. . .] They make us face the terror of being reduced to simple mechanisms. This theological aspect is part of a larger debate about quality and consistency of manufacturing. Wosk comments that 'British critics like John Ruskin [. . .] fretted that the copies were debasements of the much-superior originals, while manufacturers not surprisingly insisted that reproductions were superior to the originals. The play ['Pygmalion'] becomes a gloss on creating reproductions, in this case, a lovely Galatea who comes to life from stone.'[59]

In 'The Doll' du Maurier uses the entire body to show the uncanny, the freak and the monster, as embodied by Julio and personified by Rebecca and the narrator. Julio is handsome, easily controlled, and always sexually available. He is a non-consumer, has no biological or emotional needs, and could not convey them even if he had. His literary precursors are female automata such as Olympia, Amelia or the statue Galatea who can do everything 'but think,' and can thus be controlled, cannot be offended, are never ill, only speak when spoken to, and are obedient servants. These replicants are more beautiful than living women, the life-size mechanical dolls are 'childlike, naive, asexual—far safer, in the men's eyes, than real women.'[60] The character of Harry Burton in Ernest Edward Kellett's 'The Lady Automaton' strongly expresses his preference for Amelia over living women: 'What are all these painted dolls to her. *They* have nothing to say for themselves, *they* are mere bundles of conventionality, but *she*—she is all soul.'[61] By the end of what Wosk calls a 'cautionary tale about belief in artifice,' Amelia is broken and her suitors dead or destroyed. Here, the narrator is broken, and the lovers are gone.

'The Doll' is a satire on early twentieth-century gender relations, and like other stories centralising female automata, du Maurier uses Julio to depict 'men's fears of increasingly independent women, fears suggested by contemporary caricatures of men as puppets being manipulated by women.'[62] The reason that Hoffmann's and du Maurier's stories have strong parallels is the idea that individual perspective can, and does, alter reality, thus Nathaniel thinks Clara is an 'automaton.'[63] The story also works as a skit presenting female dissatisfactions with the realities of the male body, and as a literary response to the considerable amount of fiction traditionally using female simulacra to depict the ideal woman. Grosz relates how 'misogynist thought confines women to the biological requirements of reproduction on the assumption that because of particular biological, physiological, and endocrinological transformations, women are somehow *more* biological, *more* corporeal, and *more* natural than men.'[64]

'The Doll' imbricates sentient and non-sentient human forms and destabilises the differences between them. Du Maurier uses the familiar trope of boy meets girl as a vehicle for the transgressive, the disturbing, the macabre, a mode that establishes her work as the forerunner of writers such as Carter and Winterson. This early story is part of twentieth-century debates over the relationship between humans and technology, the desire and fear of 'alternate visions of self' that is expressed here in 'disgust at difference, at the body, at the Other.'[65] Just as Grosz states that 'bodies, individualities, are historical, social, cultural weavings of biology,' 'The Doll' continues the theme of the entire replacement of a human with a facsimile, a transgressive act that threatens the sanctity of person-on-person relations.[66]

The threat is made more potent by the speed at which we are becoming ever more dependent upon technology, but the story also considers the perspective of the objectified. Julio is the abject, the 'not I' of Kristevan theory, which escapes destruction by the irate narrator, and the text itself. We are left with the gibbering utterances of the unhinged narrator in another story where du Maurier 'refuses to restore order and normality.'[67] In the field of Body Gothic, Reyes definition of corporeal transgression is pertinent, 'I understand [it] to be a fictional representation of the body exceeding itself or falling apart, either opening up or being altered past the point where it would be recognised by normative understandings of human corporeality.'[68] The key word here is 'normative.' In her short stories du Maurier uses corporeal dissection to highlight the pathology of the essential freakishness of us all.

She then uses it to enact punishment upon the normal citizenry of her fiction. Thompson's comments on freakishness are significant when considering du Maurier's representations of corporeal difference:

> Although extraordinary bodily forms have always been acknowledged as atypical, the cultural resonances accorded them arise from the historical and intellectual moments in which those bodies are embedded. Because such bodies are rare, unique, material, and confounding of cultural categories, they function as magnets to which culture secures its anxieties, questions, and needs at any given moment. Like the bodies of females and slaves, the monstrous body exists in societies to be exploited for someone else's purposes. Under the extreme pressures of modernity [. . .] the significances imposed upon such bodies intensified.[69]

The texts emphasise that the deformed Other cannot be excluded, a view congruent with Ralph Waldo Emerson's views on the catalogue of body parts, or 'walking monsters' that comprise society: a feature he frames in corporeal terminology.[70] Emerson warns that '[t]he state of society is one in which the members have suffered amputation from the trunk, and strut about so many walking monsters—a good finger, a neck, a stomach, an elbow, but never a man.' This follows the social model of the ancient Greek tradition in which the individual is a part of the whole organism and their well-being affects the entire body of society. Du Maurier's pathology of desire dissects the human anatomy into sections that each symbolise a facet of culture and community. The dismembered parts can be found in her stories but, as Emerson says, 'you must take the whole society to find the whole man.' This chapter illustrates how: '[b]odies show up in stories as dynamic entities that resist or refuse the cultural scripts assigned to them.' 'The corporeal metaphor offers narrative the one thing it cannot possess—an anchor in materiality.'[71]

NOTES

1. Haraway, p. 1–2.
2. Howatson, entry for 'Ate,' p. 69.
3. Melville, 'Notes to 232–37 (p. 434). pp. 232–34 (p. 232).
4. Lee, 'Socrates and the Rise of Rational Self-consciousness in Ancient Greece.' Sourced at <ectopia.org> [accessed 29.6.22].
5. Wosk, p. 153.
6. Vernon Lee, 'The Doll,' *Hauntings and Other Fantastic Tales* (Peterborough, Canada: Broadview Press, 2006), p. 62.
7. Austin Booth, 'Women's Cyberfiction: an Introduction' in *Reload: Rethinking Women + Cyberculture,* ed. by Austin Booth and Mary Flannagan (Massachusetts: Massachusetts Institute of Technology, 2002), p. 32–33.

8. See Freud, 'Das Unheimliche,' 'The Uncanny,' [1919], and Ernest Jentsch 'On the Psychology of the Uncanny,' [1906], p. 56.

9. Head, p. 185.

10. Bergson, p. 29.

11. Mitchell and Snyder, p. 178.

12. *The Doll: Short Stories* (London: Virago, 2011). All further references are to this edition.

13. Wosk, p. 72.

14. Henry James, *The Turn of the Screw and Other Stories*, ed. by T. J. Lustig (Oxford: Oxford University Press, 2008), p. 113–236.

15. Notebook, EUL MS 144/1/1/1, courtesy of Special Collections.

16. Sceats and Cunningham, p. 31–32.

17. Sceats and Cunningham, p. 31, p. 39.

18. Jane Larson, 'The Artist's Inspiration: Alma Mahler's Influence on Oskar Kokoschka's Work,' 3 February 2006, pp. 1–15. Sourced at <www.carleton.edu/departments/gmrs/vienna/Kokoschka-Mahler.doc> [Accessed 17 November 2021].

19. Royle, p. 190.

20. Carter, p. 76–77.

21. Browning, 'Porphyria's Lover,' *The Poems of Browning,* Vol.1 1826–1840, ed. by John Woolford and Daniel Karlin (London: Longman, 1991), p. 329–31.

22. EUL MS 144/1/1/1, courtesy of Special Collections.

23. Du Maurier letter to Maud Waddell, 30 November 1931. EUL MS 207/6/4/1, courtesy of Special Collections.

24. Nicole Fluhr, 'Empathy and Identity in Vernon Lee's Hauntings' in *Victorian Studies* 48.2 (2006): 287–94.

25. Philip K. Dick, *Do Androids Dream of Electric Sheep?* (New York: Del Rey Books, 1968), p. 30–31.

26. Stefan Hawlin, *The Complete Critical Guide to Robert Browning* (London: Routledge, 2002), p. 74.

27. Merideth G. F. Worthen, *Sexual Deviance and Society: A Sociological Examination* (London: Routledge, 2016), p. 45.

28. 'Doll' *n* 2a and 3, *OED* 2.

29. Richardson, p. 90.

30. Charlotte Bronte, *Jane Eyre* [1837], ed. by Margaret Smith (Oxford: Oxford University Press, 2008).

31. Virginia Woolf, *A Room of One's Own and Three Guineas* (Oxford: Oxford University Press, 2015). p. 23.

32. John Berger, *Ways of Seeing* (London: Penguin, 1972), and Mulvey [1975].

33. Wosk, p. 56.

34. Wosk, p. 80, p. 165, p. 109.

35. Mansfield, *Bliss and Other Stories*, pp. 64–95.

36. David Levy, *Love + Sex With Robots* (London: Duckworth Overlook, 2008). p. 239, p. 192.

37. Iwan Bloch quoted in Levy, p. 180.

38. Wosk, p. 135.

39. Wosk, p. 108.
40. Levy, p. 211.
41. Levy, p. 118–19, pp. 247–53 (p. 179), p. 29, p. 48.
42. Teresa Peterson, 'Daphne du Maurier's Short Stories: Horror, the Macabre and the Bizarre' in *Journal of the Australasian Universities Modern Language Association* 118 (2009), 51–72 (68).
43. Wosk, p. 138.
44. Wendy Beth Hyman, 'Introduction, *The Automaton in English Renaissance Literature* (Farnham: Ashgate, 2011), p. 6.
45. Scott Maisano, chapter 2, 'Descartes avec Milton: The Automata in the Garden' in Hyman, p. 30.
46. Hyman, p. 6.
47. James. Henry James 'The Real Thing.' Sourced at <The Real Thing and Other Tales, by Henry James (gutenberg.org)> [accessed 17 November 2021].
48. Chris Horrocks and Zoran Jevtic, *Baudrillard: A Graphic Guide* (Malta: Gutenburg Press, 1996), p. 109.
49. Levy, pp. 304–5.
50. Jane Munro, *Silent Partners: Artist and Mannequin from Function to Fetish* (London: Yale University Press). p. 213.
51. Sceats and Cunningham, p. 42.
52. Mitchell and Snyder, p. 54.
53. Forster p. 32, p. 55.
54. Maupassant, 'The Ruse,' p. 123–29, p. 127.
55. Royle, p. 193.
56. Grosz, p. 6.
57. Wosk, p. 15.
58. Horrocks and Jevtic, p. 109.
59. Wosk, p. 134–35.
60. Wosk, p. 19–20.
61. Kellett, cited in Wosk, p. 22.
62. Wosk, p. 19–22.
63. Hoffmann, p. 128.
64. Grosz, p. 14.
65. Wisker, '"Don't Look Now"! The Compulsions and Revelations of Daphne du Maurier's Horror Writing,' p. 19–33.
66. Grosz, p. 12.
67. Wisker, p. 26.
68. Reyes, p. 11.
69. Thomson, p. 2.
70. Ralph Waldo Emerson, 'The American Scholar,' August 31, 1837. Sourced at <http://www.rwe.org/the-american-scholar.html> [accessed 8 December 2021].
71. Mitchell and Snyder, p. 49, p. 63.

III

A Pathology of Desire

Chapter Ten

Reconstructive Surgery

The popularity of du Maurier's novels has distracted attention from the short stories and undermined the author's reputation as a serious writer engaging with the issues of her day. Until the centenary of her birth in 2007 there was a distinct and pervasive attitude of dismissal towards her work, as indicated in Clare Tomalin's passing reference to her in a biography of Jane Austen.

> In her teens [Jane Austen] enthused about Charlotte Smith, the Daphne du Maurier of the 1780s and 1790s [. . .] with her *thrilling* heroes and *gorgeously picturesque* scenery [. . .] and her *rambling* narratives.[1] (italics mine)

This gushing and inaccurate view has been dismantled by re-considering the short fiction in summary and in detail, referencing both published and archival material in demonstrating the conceptual framework of corporeality that pervades du Maurier's fiction. The author has been repositioned as a twentieth-century artist, thinker, and moral philosopher whose works wrestle with the issues facing British society in the aftermath of the Second World War. The reductive image of her as a middlebrow romance novelist or Cornish hermit is rejected as du Maurier is a thoroughly cosmopolitan and radical writer whose stories re-present desire and blur the conventions of genre.[2] As Wisker accurately observes, du Maurier's 'mixing of genres might have made her difficult to shelve.' The research was provoked by the absence of critical material on du Maurier in general and proves that the stories are not juvenilia, nor are they preparatory sketches for the better-known novels. This work presents a vital contribution to the field by discussing and outlining the concerns of eight of the sixty-eight stories that constitute du Maurier's output as a writer of short fiction over a forty-year period.

The chapters of close commentary reveal the stories to be intellectual as well as entertaining illustrations of the zeitgeist of Britain in the post-war period. The stories have been considered in the context of modernist influence and elements of an avant-garde literary influence have been substantiated. Du Maurier's short fiction recognisably prefigures the mythic appropriations and foregrounding of the body in the work of post-modern women writers, especially Angela Carter and Jeanette Winterson. In fact, Winterson describes *Oranges Are Not The Only Fruit* as 'experimental' and 'anti-linear,' with a 'complicated narrative structure disguised as a simple one.'[3] These remarks can just as easily apply to du Maurier's short stories, which offer the reader a surface charm that belies the complexities and ambiguous ethical questions posed by the work.

The corporeality that is identified here as unifying du Maurier's short stories is used as the central governing concept and binds the multiple theoretical viewpoints together, revealing how the writer's persistent highlighting of the human form addresses the contradictions of twentieth-century reality. The body is the site of dramatic and psychological investigation, argument, the locus of desire and discussion in the short stories—recurrent devices are the transfiguration of the human body into the realm of the animal kingdom, or the disfiguration of the human form into disability or hideousness. Du Maurier presents desire as a tendency as likely to involve the pleasures in committing violent acts or escaping societal stuctures than those concomittant in the sexual act. This research reveals the stories as more violent in content than the novels, with characters who seem to achieve their desire(s) only to find they have been tricked. Sexual desire, the lust for power, physical domination and punitive violence are exposed as dangerous chimeras that bring disaster to those who single-mindedly pursue them.

Du Maurier's aesthetic of disfigurement is most pronounced in her post-war collections and her stories place human ugliness under the spotlight, where it becomes a catalyst for change and a quality with infinite variety. The stories covered here were predominantly written after the two world wars of the last century and they illustrate the ugly aftermath of ideological attempts to perfect and unify humankind in a forcefully homogenised society. As Henderson concludes, it is ugliness, disproportion, and deformity that lends itself to humanity's need for identification, not godlike beauty and symmetry. As human beings we identify with, and are fascinated by, that which is incomplete, broken, damaged or lost. And, by centralising moral obstacles in her stories du Maurier implicitly encourages the reader to avoid them, as Reyes work on what he refers to as 'Carnographic nightmares' suggests, they serve a 'creative as well as a cautionary purpose.' He writes of 'corporeal intelligibility,' that is to say the empathetic response by readers to the pain exhibited by characters, the depiction of which serves as a reminder of their own physicality from which there is no escape, save by death.[4] Texts that centralise this 'vicarious nature of pain' bring us back to the physical self and are increasingly part of an unfolding response to the underlying spiritual crisis in western societies. It follows that without spiritual sustenance and avenues to access divine reassurance, humans are more reliant upon their somatic selfhood than ever. This is an uncomfortable fact in the current intellect-driven culture that must be faced if humans are to move closer to unified harmony with their physical, animal selves.

This research presents the theme of corporeality and bodily dismemberment as a paradigmatic and exemplary reading of du Maurier's work. The evidence illustrates how this writer utilises the myriad facets of our bodily experience to craft fiction that foregrounds key aspects of her literary art and avoids the reductive tendencies evident in established approaches. The diminishing and muffling effects of labels such as romance, historical, gothic, Cornish, middlebrow and woman writer is challenged here in readings that emphasise the variety and scope of a small percentage of the texts under one overarching theme. To a significant extent the conceptual paradigm helps uncover the topics of disability, freakishness, the grotesque, the abject, hybridity, human facsimiles, psychological repression, the uncanny, androgyny, beauty and ugliness. Each story within this study represents one aspect of the physical human form, foregrounded within the text as significant to the plot, intimating arguments and ideas well beyond the limits of the narrative. This work defines the stories as multi-valent: it is the breadth of the locations, the variety of the characters and the unusual events which make it hard to generalise or dismiss fiction that disturbs the reader long after the story has ended.

Du Maurier's employment of the corporeal framework incorporates presentations of the human form in physical states ranging from the extremes of perfection and beauty to impairment and disability. Each time a body part is referenced it is used symbolically to draw attention to a broader issue which may be common or singular, as in for example collective anxiety about technology in 'The Doll.' This oblique and subtle practice necessitates a close reading of individual stories together with group comparison in order to ascertain where corporeality is present, and to what ends it is being employed. This ground-breaking study of du Maurier's short fiction highlights avenues for further research. The paradoxical, ambivalent, and open-ended form of the texts indicates modernist traits from which this research clearly identifies the influence of Katherine Mansfield and others. Consideration of how Mansfield's reputation has been affected by not producing a novel is germane to du Maurier's eclipse as a short story writer. The stories incorporate aspects of modernism that have not yet been examined in detail and it would be fruitful to compare du Maurier with other short story writers such as Mansfield, Elizabeth Bowen, H.D., Virginia Woolf and Rebecca West to offer a more nuanced location for her work within the canon.

Future directions for research may include a continuation of this thematic approach to other stories, as it enables multiple theoretical avenues and connections within the corpus and to other works by other writers. This thesis analyses eight of the forty-nine published stories but there are other texts for which corporeality is a significant metaphor that are outside the scope of this research. The eight chapters of close reading go some way towards addressing the lack of research on the stories but only for those texts analysed here: this thesis highlights the fact that the other published and unpublished stories demand equal attention. There are hints at other stories that may lie in unpublished correspondence which need to be addressed, and archival embargoes on crucial data whose duration ends within the decade. The hitherto inaccessible letters between du Maurier and Gollancz and Forster's biographical source material may be pivotal to understanding the editorial process and personal context of this great short story writer.

After presenting a long-overdue narrative and bibliographical account of the short story collections, this thematic study of bodily dismemberment has mapped the subject territory of the Daphne du Maurier short story for the first time. In this process the works have been resituated within a comprehensive critical overview of du Maurier studies from the timing of the first reception of her work in the press through to her current reputation in the academy.

NOTES

1. Clare Tomalin, *Jane Austen: A Life* (London: Virago, 1997), p. 68.
2. Wisker, 'Dangerous Borders,' p. 86.
3. Winterson, preface, *Oranges Are Not The Only Fruit* [1985] (London: Vintage, 1991), p. xiii.
4. Reyes, p. 27, p. 8, p.17.

The Bare Bones

This appendix sets out the sixty-eight published short stories by collection except for *Happy Christmas* which was a sole publication, and includes a brief synopsis, the number of pages of text, the setting, and an indication as to whether each story incorporates the theme of corporeality. The end of one collection and the start of another is indicated by a series of three asterisks.

At the end of the listing there is the most comprehensive listing currently available of some of the stories and the magazines or collections in which they were first published, and the unpublished stories at Special Collections, University of Exeter.

COLLECTIONS

1942 *Happy Christmas* (London: Century Publishing, 1942)
1942 *Come Wind, Come Weather*
1952 *The Apple Tree* (London; Gollancz)
1953 *Happy Christmas* (London: Todd)
1955 *Early Stories* (London: Todd)
[republished by Bantam Books 1959?]
1959 *The Breaking Point and Other Stories* (London; Gollancz)
1960 *The Treasury of du Maurier Short Stories* (London: Gollancz)
[A one-volume reissue of 'The Apple Tree' and 'The Breaking Point']
1961 *The Lover: And Other Stories* (Ace Books)
1971 *Not After Midnight* (London: Gollancz)
1980 *The Rendezvous and Other Stories* (London: Gollancz)
1987 *Classics From the Macabre* (London: Gollancz)
2011 *The Doll: Short Stories* (London: Virago)

Happy Christmas (London: Century Publishing, 1942) 25 pp.

The Lawrence family are preparing to celebrate Christmas when they get the unwelcome news they are to be billeted with a Jewish couple who are refugees. They grudgingly install the couple in the garage and return to their sumptuous festivities. Much to their resentment the next morning the refugees are gone and they learn that the woman was pregnant and ill.

Come Wind, Come Weather (London: Heinemann, 1942) 53 pp. [11 stories]

Daphne du Maurier wrote these eleven stories as morale-boosting propaganda during the Second World War. Based on true events, they are aimed at encouraging people to cheerfully endure the struggles of wartime life, as detailed in the 'Epilogue.' Individual stories were published in local newspapers all over the country and in this booklet sold to raise money for the Soldiers', Sailors' and Airmens' Families Association. Different editions contain slightly different stories and the stories published in the newspapers sometimes vary slightly from the versions published in the booklet. The collection is an inroad into polemical non-fiction that is unusual in du Maurier's oeuvre and is a departure from the process of intellectual fermentation she commonly favoured.

'Come Wind, Come Weather' 4 pp.
'The Admiralty Regrets' 4 pp.
'George and Jimmy' 4 pp.
'Over the Ration Books' 4 pp.
'A Nation's Strength' 5 pp.
'A Miner's Tale' 5 pp.
"Physician, Heal Thyself" 5pp.
'Spitfire Megan' 3pp.
'London, 1940?' 4 pp.
'Mrs. Hill and the Soldiers' 6 pp.
'In a London Air-raid Shelter' 6 pp.

Early Stories (London: Todd, 1955) [18 stories]
'Adieu Sagesse' is set in a British seaside town and centres on escape from convention to freedom at sea. 20 pp.

Old Ferguson is a dull banker with a wife and three children. He finally escapes his bourgeois existence by renovating an old boat and embarking on a sea voyage with the man who repaired the boat, for destinations unknown. The name of their vessel is the story's title: '*Farewell Wisdom.*'

'Angels and Archangels' charts the hypocrisy of the corrupt Anglican vicar of St Swithin's Church in London. 10 pp

The Reverend James Holloway takes a holiday in Dorset with an aristocratic friend who the reader suspects may be his mistress. While absent his curate's sermons harangue the worldly congregation who leave only to be replaced by the poor and needy. Informed by letter, Reverend Holloway returns.

'The Closing Door' is a story in an urban setting that follows a man just diagnosed with a fatal disease. 11 pp.

A young man receives the news that he has a terminal illness, soon to be fatal. His fiancée's joy in life strikes a discordant note and the figure of a paralysed beggar shows him what lies ahead. This story accords with the framework concept of corporeality.

'A Difference in Temperament' depicts marital disharmony. 10 pp.

The dissection of a marital tiff between unnamed characters. Honest communication is notably absent and the continuous nature of the spats is indicated by the ambiguous ending where nothing is resolved.

'Fairy Tale' focuses on the dreams of economic stability of an ailing gambler's wife. 10pp.

In a garret a sick woman awaits her gambler husband's return. After threats from the landlord the man returns having won this time. He makes a fantasy of comfort in the cheerless space having first ascertained that his wife forgives him. The fairy tale of the title is her fantasy of him as a stable provider.

'Frustration' centres on the contrast between the dream and the reality of wedded life. 10 pp.

A newlywed couple embark on their honeymoon and their hopes of romantic bliss are shattered by thunderstorms, collapsed tents, a lost wedding ring, and jobs that exclude time together.

'And Now to God the Father' returns to the location of St Swithins Church in London and religious corruption (see above). 26 pp.

The Reverend James Holloway appears in an earlier story in this collection called 'Angels and Archangels.' He is a social climber whose religious hypocrisy fits in well with the values of his rich and worldly congregation. His advice to an unmarried, pregnant girl leads directly to her suicide by drowning. This story accords with the framework concept of corporeality.

'Indiscretion' is a story set in London that deals with deception and consequence. 10 pp

A cynical employee relates the story of being robbed after being duped by a woman in apparently tragic circumstances. In response his boss invites him to meet his perfect fiancée. She is the thief and an indiscreet allusion to her encounter with the employee fatally betrays her identity.

'La Sainte-Vierge' is set in Brittany and foregrounds romantic love as an illusion. 9 pp.

Marie is a young Breton housewife who idealises her faithless fisherman husband, Jean. While praying for Jean's safe return from sea, to the village icon of the Virgin and Child, she sees what she thinks is a holy vision. It is Jean making love to another woman. This plot aligns with the framework concept of corporeality.

'Leading Lady' has an urban location and continues the theme of artifice as a means of control. 15 pp.

An ageing actress uses her professional skills to ensure the patronage of a rich sponsor and the infatuation of a rising actor. Her lies eliminate the young actor from the cast of the upcoming play.

'The Lover' positions romance as a charade from the male perspective. 10 pp.

'The Lover' is the obverse story to 'Leading Lady.' The reader is compelled to see women from a gigolo's perspective. Clingy and pathetic, a series of women are mercilessly exploited for financial benefit.

'Mazie' is set in London, highlighting the contrast between male 'johns' and female prostitutes where physical desire equates to sexual versus subsistence. 14 pp.

A prostitute encounters another working girl (Dolly) who has fallen on hard times after a termination and sees a crone begging outside the restaurant where she is eating with a client. Both episodes indicate her future life, and she yearns for escape on a boat down the Thames to the scene on a poster of the seaside. This plot aligns with the framework concept of corporeality.

'Nothing Hurts For Long' is an ironic take on the frustrated desires of a young wife. 16 pp.

A young wife's excitement over her husband's return from a three-month business trip abroad is dampened by the marital crisis of her friend. His disappointing return, fat and indifferent to her, destroys her girlish illusions of married life.

'Panic' is set in Montmartre, Paris. Desire has fatal consequences for both lovers. 9 pp.
An illicit weekend in Paris results in the dramatic escape of the man after the girl dies during their night together. His missing wallet shows there will be no escape after all. This plot aligns with the framework concept of corporeality.

'Piccadilly' underground station, London, symbolises one girl's fall into immorality. 14 pp.
A prostitute tells how her respectable existence in service was transformed into the precarious existence of a thief and a sex worker. Jim, a professional pickpocket, trains Mazie and leaves her when she is arrested and imprisoned. This story stands independently but also serves as a prequel story to 'Mazie' (see above). This plot aligns with the framework concept of corporeality.

'The Supreme Artist' is set in London's theatre-land where artifice is a professional skill. 8 pp.
For an ageing, but still successful actor, the surprise visit of a matronly fan to his dressing-room stirs an unwelcome sense of age and lost youth. She is a long-forgotten inamorata from his youth whose identity he cannot recall. The woman is twice forgotten as his insecurity escalates showing his inauthentic emotions to be the acting skills his profession demands.

'Tame Cat' uses locations in London and Paris to present adult perfidy and youthful disillusionment. 16 pp.
The final return from boarding school to home as a grown-up young woman is marred by a daughter's realisation that the man she thought was her 'Uncle Jim' has been her mother's consort for years, and he is now keen to start a parallel relationship with her. The mother's jealousy ensures that her daughter is regarded as a scheming jezebel and accordingly ousted from maternal affection. This plot aligns with the framework concept of corporeality.

'Week- End' illustrates the dangers of romantic pretence. 10 pp.
A couple go away for the weekend only to discover that their romance is based upon errors of judgement and that both of them are too unattractively selfish to succeed in a sincere relationship. A satire on image versus reality.

***The Apple Tree* (London: Gollancz, 1952) [6 stories]**
'The Birds' is set in Cornwall and centres on animal violence against the human body. 39 pp.
Nat Hocken and his wife are trapped after their Cornish community is attacked by birds intent on killing humans. There is no help, local or official,

and the story ends with them barricaded in the cottage and running out of food. This story accords with the framework concept of corporeality.

'Monte Verità' is set in Switzerland and southern England. with a focus on escape from materialist values and body-centred pleasures. 73 pp.
Victor and Anna are married but she leaves him after discovering an enclosed community on Monte Verità (the 'mountain of truth'). He moves to live nearby and dying, he is discovered by a friend who delivers a message to Anna. Allowed into the community of androgynous women, his epiphanic experience is broken by seeing Anna's advanced leprosy. The colony is attacked and razed by irate villagers, bereft of their young women. This story accords with the framework concept of corporeality

'The Apple Tree' is set in southern England where marital disharmony is found in the garden rather than the home, and haunts the psyche when the body dies. 45 pp.
'Buzz' and 'Midge' are a middle-aged married couple and when she suddenly dies, his newfound enthusiasm for life is blighted by neurotic guilt over marital neglect and a romantic wartime liaison. His behaviour becomes ever more erratic and he dies by the eponymous, and to him murderous, apple tree which personifies the deceased Midge. This story accords with the concept framework of corporeality.

'The Little Photographer' is a story of murder and blackmail set in a coastal resort in France. 45 pp.
The beautiful and privileged Marquise, mother of two daughters, is bored. Her holiday association with a lame photographer ends when he threatens her with exposure and she pushes him off a cliff. His sister blackmails her and the story ends with a life of boredom exchanged for one of tension. This story accords with the concept framework of corporeality.

'Kiss Me Again, Stranger' is the story of a female serial killer in north London. 25 pp.
In post-war London, a mechanic goes to the cinema and meets an usherette whom he escorts home on the bus. An orphaned, feral child, she grew up on the bomb sites and now murders RAF pilots in revenge for the tragedies brought about by war. She is caught and the mechanic is left with the heart-shaped brooch he bought but did not get the chance to give her. This story accords with the concept framework of corporeality.

'The Old Man' is a story of familial abuse set in a coastal location in England. 11 pp.
A description of an abusive and violent family life ends with the murder of a son by his father. The twist is that these are swans, not humans. This story accords with the concept framework of corporeality.

***The Breaking Point* (London: Gollancz, 1959) [8 stories]**
The Alibi is set near London's Embankment and centres on the consequences of murder, real or fantasy. 43 pp.
James Fenton randomly rents a room from poor Jewish immigrant Anna Kaufman intent on murdering her and her three-year-old son Johnny. The front of being a painter soon becomes a consuming passion, and when Anna hands him a packaged foetus for disposal he unwittingly becomes a police suspect. Returned to her house for questioning, Anna and Johnny are found gassed in the basement and Fenton is denounced as a terrible painter by his wife. He confesses to the murders. This story accords with the concept framework of corporeality.

'The Blue Lenses' is set in southern England where materialistic and sexual desire motivate apparently certain animalistic violence. 38 pp.
Marda West is recovering from an eye operation and when the bandages are removed everyone around her has animal heads in keeping with their personalities. The snake and vulture are reserved for her sinister night nurse and controlling husband while she has a doe's head 'ready for sacrifice.' This story accords with the concept framework of corporeality.

'Ganymede' is set in Venice where desire leads to accidental death. 40 pp.
A classical scholar becomes embroiled with a Venetian family when he has a crush on a beautiful teenage waiter. When 'Ganymede' dies in a waterskiing accident for which he as 'Zeus' is responsible, he has to leave his job, support the boy's family, and move to 'Little Venice' in London. There he finds an Italian restaurant with a young waiter. This story accords with the concept framework of corporeality.

'The Pool' is set in southern England where childhood fantasy leads to near-death and the brutal physical realities of puberty. 31 pp.
Roger and Deborah are children visiting their grandparents where Deborah has a fascination with the pool in their garden. Desperate to be alone she invents ruses to be rid of Roger and visits the pool by moonlight. Escaping to another world she immerses herself and wakes in her own bed to find that menstruation has started and the 'hidden world' is lost to her forever. This story accords with the concept framework of corporeality.

'The Archduchess' is set in the fictional country of Ronda in Europe and relates how revolution and economic progress fatally disrupts a fairy-tale kingdom. 43 pp.
Ronda is mythically beautiful but has greedy and dissatisfied inhabitants whose actions lead to revolution and environmentally damaging consumerism. The royal family are symbols of societal changes that leave the final member, the Archduchess, humbly dancing for tourists in the royal square.

'The Menace' is set in Hollywood, Los Angeles and traces the effect of new media forms on an existing star. 39 pp.
Barry Jeans is a movie star in America when the 'feelies' are introduced revealing his power to emote on screen worryingly low. Attempts to rectify this fail, until he bumps into a childhood sweetheart, now a grandmother, whose familiar kindness unlocks his feelings enabling him to respond to excel in the new medium.

'The Chamois' is set in Greece and centres on the desire for power and control through hunting, sexual and animal. The result in both cases is death. 32 pp.
Another unstable marriage, the perfectionistic husband hunts the elusive chamois to nullify his own feelings of inadequacy and fear. At the denouement it is unclear whether he has killed the deer, or their goatherd guide, and the wife's attitude indicates the latter. They leave the mountain in harmony. This story accords with the concept framework of corporeality.

'The Lordly Ones' is set on Exmoor and explores violence towards children and animals. 16 pp.
Ben, a mute boy, is thought to be 'backward,' and his miserable existence causes his parents to move to a more isolated home on the moors. Once there, Ben steals food for the 'moors' whom he understands to be hungry and homeless families living rough. After a severe beating, he escapes to be with them, and is succoured by their warmth and kindness. The families of horses flee from the men with sticks who come to rescue Ben. This story accords with the concept framework of corporeality.

***Not After Midnight—and Other Stories* (London: Gollancz, 1971) [5 stories]**
***Don't Look Now* is set in Venice where untimely death links child and parent, accident and murder to psychic prediction. 50 pp.**
John and Laura are on holiday trying to forget the death by drowning of their six-year-old daughter. They encounter two old ladies, one a psychic, who tells them their daughter is smiling and sitting with them. John's scepti-

cism leads him to ignore the comforting vision and subsequent more disturbing portents. He is murdered by a red-cloaked dwarf after dismissing what turn out to be accurate warnings from his own talent for second sight. This story accords with the conceptual framework of corporeality.

'Not After Midnight' is set on the Greek island of Crete and uses mythical referents in a story of drunkenness and lechery. 45 pp.
A disgraced teacher of classics leaves his boys' school to recover on a painting holiday. He encounters a boorish couple illicitly diving for historical artefacts and becomes drawn into their world, discovering that the previous inhabitant of his chalet mysteriously drowned. He is given a drinking amphora by the couple decorated with the faces of Dionysus and Silenus. He finds the bloated body of the drunkard husband before facing his own alcoholism. This story accords with the concept framework of corporeality.

'A Borderline Case' centres on incest set against a backdrop of terrorism in Ireland. 62 pp.
Fledgling actress Shelagh Money watches her father die with a look of horror on his face after seeing an old photograph of his old friend. Her search for the reason takes her to a remote island where Irish resistance to English domination takes the form of violent reprisals. After a fling with one of the group she returns to take up the role of Viola in Twelfth Night, only to be sent a photograph of her father's friend in the same role. She knows her father died of shock as it is obvious that the man is her biological father. This story accords with the concept framework of corporeality.

'The Way of the Cross' is a Chaucerian tale of scatological and bawdy misfortunes that befall a package tour of pilgrims en route to Jerusalem. 65 pp.
A diverse group of pilgrims travel from their village to the Holy Land where each of them suffers physical or emotional trauma leading to epiphanies that destroy self-delusions. The only one spared is Robin, a precocious child whose innocent remarks are the catalyst for many of the comi-tragic moments. This story accords with the concept framework of corporeality.

'The Breakthrough' is set in coastal East Anglia where scientific experiments are in process to contain the spirit after death, each person using a name from Greek myth. 42 pp.
An unwelcome secondment takes Stephen Saunders, 'a chap who won't talk,' to Saxmere where James Maclean is conducting illicit experiments on a dying man and a psychic child to isolate and contain what he calls 'Force Six'—the

human soul. Stephen is seduced by the team's strength of belief and agrees to act as technical support. The hypothesis appears to have been proven but the child's pain halts the process and the solution to the 'meaning of death' is lost. Despite the failure Maclean vows to continue the project. This story accords with the concept framework of corporeality.

***The Rendezvous and Other Stories* (London: Gollancz, 1980)**
[fourteen stories, ten already published in *Early Stories*, with four additional stories and a preface by Daphne du Maurier. The republished stories are: 'Panic,' 'The Supreme Artist,' 'Adieu Sagesse,' 'Fairy Tale,' 'La Sainte-Vierge,' 'Leading Lady,' 'The Lover,' 'The Closing Door,' 'Indiscretion,' 'Angels and Archangels']. The plots of the new stories are summarised below.

'No Motive' is set in southern England and Switzerland. The human capacity to forget trauma is shown as fallible and the result is self-destruction. 45 pp.
Happily married and newly pregnant, Lady Mary Farren shoots herself one morning at the family home. Detective Black is commissioned to find the motive by her husband, Sir John. He discovers that the teenage Mary birthed a red-haired baby boy suffering permanent amnesia after the adoption. The reappearance of her son and a chance comment on 'carrot' haired people cause the memory to resurface and motivate her suicide. This story accords with the concept framework of corporeality.

'The Rendezvous' is set in London and Switzerland. A writer disregards physical and emotional needs, only to find the repercussions are professional as well as personal, and the situation is too late to rectify. 32 pp.
Robert Scrivener, a well-known English novelist, corresponds with a young Swiss fan named Annette Limoges. On a lecture trip to Geneva they meet but the infatuated Scrivener is forced to accept Annette's preference for a young, fit, handsome partner in Alberto. On seeing a film adaptation of a rival's novel he recognises his snobbery over his life's work as pointlessly hollow and weeps. This story accords with the concept framework of corporeality.

'Escort' is a maritime story set during the Second World War where a merchant ship is hunted by a U-boat and subsequently protected by a ghostly vessel. 18 pp.
Ravenswing is a tramp steamer bearing cargo from Scandinavia to Hull in the early days of the Second World War. William Blunt is first officer and assumes command when the captain becomes sick. A U-boat is spotted and Blunt hides the boat in a fog bank where *Ravenswing* nearly collides with a sailing ship. Blunt visits the ship and realises it is a man o'war with a crew

in antique uniforms. The captain offers to escort *Ravenswing*, Blunt accepts, and the escort vanishes with the dawn.

'Split Second' is set in London and centres on the psychological trauma of dislocation as a catalyst for physical violence. 53 pp.
Mrs Ellis is a widow with one daughter, Susan, by her late husband, Wilfred. She leaves her cosy home for a walk and returns to find the house filled with bedsitters, the neighbourhood drastically altered from wartime bombings, and no record of her existence anywhere. This story accords with the concept framework of corporeality.

***The Doll: Short Stories* (London: Virago, 2011)**
[13 stories, all written between 1926 and1932 and first published in journals and magazines between 1927 and 1930, except for 'The Limpet.' 'And Now to God the Father,' 'A Difference in Temperament,' 'Frustration,' 'Piccadilly,' 'Tame Cat,' 'Mazie,' 'Nothing Hurts for Long' and 'Week-End' were first published in *Early Stories* (London, Todd, 1955)].

'East Wind' is set on St Hilda's- island in the Atlantic where foreign sailors are blown in by strong winds evoking desire and violence in the islanders. 12 pp.
A change in wind direction becalms a ship whose undisciplined crew disrupt the monotonous lives of the St Hildeans. The dull existence of fisherman Guthrie explodes when he discovers his wife Jane has been seduced by one of the sailors and, enraged, he takes an axe to her. This story accords with the concept framework of corporeality.

'The Doll' is set in Bloomsbury, London where an immigrant violinist is the locus of unrequited passion for the male narrator whose obsession she ultimately escapes. 18 pp.
An abandoned and unfinished journal seems to be the suicide note of a despairing lover, published by the man who found it on a beach, Dr Strongman. The narrator meets Rebecca at a party, hears her play and is captivated. His pursuit is abruptly curtailed when he 'meets' Julio, her life-size male doll. Now paranoid, his neurosis alters from violence to others to self-destruction when he finds Rebecca and Julio are gone.

'The Happy Valley' is set in the fictional county of Ryeshire in southern England where a young woman sees visions of a future in which she is absent through death. 12 pp.
The name links to the Manderley estate, the setting for *Rebecca*, and is a prequel in that this is the story of an unnamed wife haunted by visions of her own

ghost. From the outset she has prescient awareness of future events including her marriage, motherhood, everything except the manner of her death.

'And His Letters Grew Colder' is a story in the epistolary form between a married woman 'Mrs. AB' and her brother's friend, 'XYZ.' The plot dissects the development of the romance from infatuation to heartbreak. 19 pp.
'XYZ' has recently arrived in the UK from his plantation in China with an introduction to 'Mrs AB.' Their acquaintance develops into a passionate liaison and rapidly passes through the stages of attraction, consummation, and detachment, before ending in alienation and rejection.

'The Limpet' is set in London and employs the form of a dramatic monologue to showcase a woman with a destructively parasitic nature. 28 pp.
This truncated bildungsroman has a protagonist who brings doubt, disaster, and death, to anyone unfortunate enoughto become proximate. Dilly Sawbones manipulates others for her own benefit, enjoys her sense of always being cleverer than them but is finally found in self-pitying loneliness, haunted by the shades of those she exploited.

EUL MS 144/1/1/1, Courtesy of Special Collections, University of Exeter [Notebook, black leather, inscribed May 1923 on flyleaf, signed Daphne du Maurier]

1. 'Tea-time'
2. 'South Kensington'
3. 'A Modern'
4. 'Noon'
5. 'Lundy'
6. 'The Old Woman'
7. 'The Terror'
8. 'The Top of a Bus'
9. The Old Man' [published]
10. 'In The Name of the Father' [published]
11. 'The Azalea'
12. 'East Wind' [published]
13. 'The Story of a Weak Man'
14. 'Peace'
15. 'Salle D'attente
16. 'Mazie' [published]
17. 'Adieu Sagesse' [published]

PUBLISHING HISTORY OF THE STORIES

1929 'And Now to God the Father' *The Bystander,* 8 May
'Consider the Lilies' was an earlier title under which the story was published in a small paperback leaflet.
1929 'A Difference in Temperament' *The Bystander,* June
1930 'Adieu Sagesse' *Cassell's Magazine of Fiction* October
1932 'The Happy Valley' *The Illustrated London News* Christmas
1931 'And His Letters Grew Colder' *Hearst's International Combined with Cosmopolitan,* September
1931 'Panic' *Saturday Review* February 28
Avon Monthly Short Story No.15, 1944
1932 'The Happy Valley' *Illustrated London News,* Christmas
1934 'Leading Lady' *Brittania and Eve* July
1935 'Mousie and Hoosie' *Modern Story* October
1937 'The Doll' *The Editor Regrets* (Michael Joseph) ed. by George Joseph
1940 'Escort' *Saturday Evening Post, Argosy* October, *Magpie* October1951
1942 *Come Wind, Come Weather* (London: Heinemann)
1942 *Happy Christmas* (London: Century Publishing)
1944 'Spring Picture' was published as a single story in a slim hardback book. It was never published again under that title but was included in *Early Stories* (London: Todd) and The Rendezvous and Other Stories with the title
'The Closing Door'
1952 'The Birds' *Good Housekeeping* October
Alfred Hitchcock's Mystery Magazine August 1982
Good Housekeeping May 1985
1952 'Lover for the Marquise' *Cosmopolitan*, November
1953 'The Old Man' *Ellery Queen's Mystery Magazine*, February
The Australian Journal, 2 November
1955 *Early Stories* (London: Todd). The collection includes 'Frustration,' 'Piccadilly,' 'Tame Cat,' 'Mazie,' 'Nothing Hurts For Long,' 'The Weekend,' all first published in journals and magazines between 1927 and 1930
1956 'The Alibi' novelette *Ladies Home Journal,* April, *John Bull* 30 May
1959 'The Limpet' *Ladies Home Journal,* August, also US edition of *The Breaking Point* (New York: Doubleday, 1959)
1959 'The Blue Lenses' *Ladies Home Journal,* 25 May, *Alfred Hitchcock's Mystery Magazine* September 1995
1959 'The Rendezvous' *Cosmopolitan*, June
1959 'The Chamois' *Ladies Home Journal,* September
1966 'Don't Look Now' *Ladies Home Journal* 1970 *Ellery Queen's*

Anthology, 59, 1988

1986 'East Wind' *Ellery Queen's Mystery Magazine*, mid-December
1966 'The Breakthrough'
1970 'Don't look Now'
1971 'The Way of The Cross'
1971 'A Border-Line case'
1971 'Shock of Recognition' *Ladies Home Journal* August
1971 'Not After Midnight'
1980 'East Wind' (Exeter archives notebook 1926) first published in US edition of *The Rebecca Notebook* Doubleday and Co., 1980. (The original story can be located in du Maurier's 1926 notebook in Special Collections, University of Exeter)
1980 'The Rendezvous,' first published as the title story in the collection.

NB:

> 'London and Paris' was also published in a small paperback leaflet containing two stories, one called 'London' and the other called 'Paris.' 'London' changed its name to 'Mazie' and appears in *Early Stories* and *The Doll: Short Stories*. 'Paris' changed its name to 'Panic' and it appears in *Early Stories* and *The Rendezvous and Other Stories*.

NOTE

1. For more on the contents of *Illustrated London News* see <iln.org.uk> [accessed 7 June 2016].

Bibliography

For ease of reference, recent Virago editions have been used for page references throughout. Other works by du Maurier are listed by genre in chronological order of first publication date, this is indicated in square brackets where a first edition is not cited. All other editions are currently out of print and only available in archives or through specialist booksellers.

Annotations to archival material is per the catalogue description; additional material is indicated by square brackets.

Abi-Ezzi, Nathalie, 'An Analysis of the Treatment of the Double in the Works of Robert Louis Stevenson, Wilkie Collins and Daphne du Maurier,' (unpublished thesis, King's College, University of London, PhD, 2000).

Allen, Graham, *Intertextuality* (London: Routledge, 2011).

Arendt, Hannah, *The Human Condition* (Chicago: Cambridge University Press, 1958).

Aristotle, book four, Generation of Animals, quoted in Marie-Helene Huet, *Monstrous Imagination* (Cambridge, MA: Harvard University Press, 1993).

Arluke, Arnold, and Boria Sax, chapter 12, 'The Nazi Treatment of Animals and People' in *Reinventing Biology: Respect for Life and the Creation of Knowledge*, ed. by Lynda I. A. Birke and Ruth Hubbard (Bloomington: Indiana University Press, 1995).

Armitt, Lucie, *Contemporary Women's Fiction and the Fantastic* (London: Palgrave, 2000).

Armstrong, Isobel, *The Radical Aesthetic* (Massachusetts: Blackwell, 2000).

Auerbach, Nina, *Daphne du Maurier: Haunted Heiress* (Pennsylvania: University of Pennsylvania Press, 2000).

Austen, Jane, *Pride and Prejudice* ed. by Tony Tanner [1813]. (London: Penguin, 1972).

Bacchilega, Christina, *Postmodern Fairy Tales* (Philadelphia: University of Pennsylvania,1999).

Badsey, Stephen, *Arnhem 1944: Operation 'Market Garden'* (London: Praeger, 2004).

Bair, Dierdre, *Samuel Beckett: A Biography* (London: Vintage, 1990).

Bakhtin, Mikhail, *The Dialogic Imagination: Four Essays* (Austin: University of Texas Press, 1992).

———. 'Popular and Festive Forms' in *Rabelais and His World*, trans. by Helene Iswolsky (Bloomington: Indiana University Press, 1984).

Baugh, Albert C., '"The Middle English Period" 1100–1500' in *A Literary History of England,* second edn (London: Routledge, 1967).

Barthes, Roland, 'Theory of the Text' in *Untying the Text: A Post-Structuralist Reader*, ed. by Robert Young and Kegan Paul (London: Routledge, 1981), p. 31–47

Beauman, Nicola, *A Very Great Profession* (London: Virago, 1995).

———. Introduction, E. M. Delafield, *The Diary of a Provincial Lady* (London: Virago, 1984), p. vii–xvii.

Bellanca, Mary Ellen, 'The Monstrosity of Predation in Daphne du Maurier's "The Birds" in *Interdisciplinary Studies in Literature and Environment* 18:1 (Winter 2011), 26–46.

Berger, John, *Ways of Seeing* (London: Penguin, 1972).

Bergson, Henri, '*Le Rire. Essai sur la signification du comique'* trans. as 'Laughter, an essay on the meaning of the comic' trans. by Brereton Cloudesley and Fred Rothwell (New York: Macmillan, 1921). Sourced at <http://babel.hathitrust.org/cgi/pt?id=mdp.39015083253750;view=1up;seq=11> [accessed 17 March 2016].

Bernthal, J. C., 'If Not Yourself, Who Would You Be?': Writing the Female Body in Agatha Christie's Second World War Detective Fiction' in *Women: A Cultural Review*, 26: 1–2 (2015), 40–56. Sourced at <http://dx.doi.org/10.1080/09574042.2015.1035023> [accessed 29.6.22].

Beveridge, William, 'The Beveridge Report,' government report entitled 'Social Insurance and Allied Services,' (London: His Majesty's Stationery Office, 1942). Sourced at http://www.bl.uk/onlinegallery/takingliberties/staritems/712beveridgereport.html [accessed 2.11.21].

Bloch, Iwan, in David Levy, *Love + Sex With Robots* (London: Duckworth Overlook, 2008).

Booth, Austin, 'Women's Cyberfiction: An Introduction' in *Reload: Rethinking Women + Cyberculture*, ed. by Austin Booth and Mary Flannagan (Massachusetts: MIT Press, 2002).

Bordo, Susan, *Unbearable Weight: Feminism, Western Culture, and the Body* (London: University of California Press, 1993).

Brontë, Charlotte, *Jane Eyre* ed. by Margaret Smith, Introduction by Sally Shuttleworth [1837]. (Oxford: Oxford University Press, 2008).

Browning, Robert, 'Porphyria's Lover' in *The Poems of Browning,* Vol. 1, 1826–1840, ed. by John Woolford and Daniel Karlin (London: Longman, 1991), p. 329–31.

———. 'My Last Duchess' [1842]. *Norton Anthology of Poetry*, eds. Margaret Ferguson, MaryJo Salter and Jon Stallworthy, fifth edn, p. 1013.

Browning Christopher 'Kits,' *The Radio Times*, 28 April 2014, interviewer Ben Dowell. Sourced at <radiotimes.com> [accessed 15 July 2014].

Bryden, Ronald, 'Queen of the Wild Mullions' review in *The Spectator*, 20 April 1962, p. 22.

Carter, Angela, *The Bloody Chamber* (London: Vintage, 1979).

———. 'The Loves of Lady Purple' in *Wayward Girls, Wicked Women* (London: Virago, 1986), pp. 247–54.

Charques, R. D., review of *Rebecca* in the *Times Literary Supplement*, 6 August 1938. Sourced at http://www.the-tls.co.uk/articles/public/then-and-now-1938-2 / [accessed 25 April 2016].

Churchill, Winston, 'The Few' speech to the House of Commons, 20 August 1940. Sourced at <http://www.churchill-society-london.org.uk/thefew.html> [accessed 15.3.16].

Cohen, J. J. (ed.). *Monster Theory: Reading Culture* (Minneapolis: University of Minnesota Press, 1996).

Conrich, Ian, and Laura Sedgewick, *Gothic Dissections in Film and Literature: The Body in Parts* (London: Palgrave Macmillan, 2017

De Laclos, Choderlos, *Dangerous Liaisons* (London: Penguin, 2007).

De Maupassant, Guy, *Selected Short Stories* (London: Penguin, 1971).

Deleuze, Gilles, in David Farrell Krell, *Derrida and Our Animal Others: Derrida's Final Seminar, "The Beast and The Sovereign"* (Bloomington: Indiana University Press, 2013), p. 19

Derrida, Jaques, 'Introduction,' *The Animal That Therefore I Am,* quoted in David Farrell Krell, *Derrida and Our Animal Others: Derrida's Final Seminar, "The Beast and The Sovereign"* (Bloomington: Indiana University Press, 2013).

———. 'Memoirs of the Blind: The Self-portrait and Other Ruins' in section 2 'Blindness,' *A Companion to Derrida,* ed. by Zeynep Direk and Leonard Lawlor (Chichester: Wiley, Blackwell, 2014).

———. –in David Farrell Krell, *Derrida and Our Animal Others: Derrida's Final Seminar, "The Beast and The Sovereign"* (Bloomington: Indiana University Press, 2013).

Dick, Philip K., *Do Androids Dream of Electric Sheep?* (New York: Del Rey Books, Random House, 1975).

Dimbleby, Richard, report from Bergen-Belsen April 1945. Sourced at <https://www.youtube.com/watch?v=2hLYavpMSFs> [accessed 29.6.22].

Diprose, Rosalyn, and Jack Reynolds (eds.), *Merleau-Ponty, Key Concepts* (London: Routledge, 2014).

Direk, Zeynep, and Leonard Lawlor eds., *A Companion to Derrida* (Chichester: Blackwell, 2014).

Doolittle, Hilda, H.D., *H.D. Collected Poems 1912–1944*, ed. by Louis L. Martz (N.Y.: New directions Books, 1986).

Douane, Mary Anne, 'Female Spectatorship and Machines of Projection: *Caught* and *Rebecca*' in *The Desire to Desire: The Woman's Films of the 1940s* (Bloomington: Indiana University Press, 1987).

du Maurier, Daphne, 'The Doll,' *The Editor Regrets*, ed. by George Joseph (London: Michael Joseph, 1937).

Short Story Collections First Editions

———. *Come Wind, Come Weather* (London: Heinemann, 1940).
———. *Escort* (London: Todd Publishing, 1943).
———. *Consider the Lilies* (London: Todd, 1943).
———. *Spring Picture* (London: Todd Publishing, 1944).
———. *London and Paris* (Vallency Press, 1945).
———. *The Apple Tree: A Short Novel and Some Stories* (London, Gollancz, 1952).
———. *Happy Christmas* (London: Todd, 1953).
———. *Early Stories* (London: Todd, 1955).
———. *The Breaking Point and Other Stories* (London: Gollancz, 1959).
———. *The Treasury of du Maurier Short Stories* (London: Gollancz, 1960).
———. *Not After Midnight* (London: Gollancz, 1971).
———. *The Rendezvous and Other Stories* (London: Gollancz, 1980).
———. *Classics of the Macabre* (London: Gollancz, 1987).

Later Editions by Virago

———. *The Birds and Other Stories* (London: Virago, 2004).
———. *The Rendezvous and Other Stories* (London: Virago, 2005).
———. *The Breaking Point: Short Stories* (London: Virago, 2009).
———. *The Doll: Short Stories* (London: Virago, 2011).
———. *Don't Look Now and Other Stories* (London: Virago, 2015).

Novels

———. *The Loving Spirit* [1931]. (London: Penguin Books, 1965).
———. *I'll Never Be Young Again* [1932]. (New York: Penguin, 1966).
———. *The Progress of Julius* [Julius, 1933]. (London: Virago, 2004).
———. *Jamaica Inn* [1936]. (London: Virago, 2007).
———. *Rebecca* [1938]. (London: Virago, 2003).
———. *Frenchman's Creek* [1941]. (London: Virago, 2003).
———. *Hungry Hill* [1943]. (London: Penguin, 1969).
———. *The King's General* [1946]. (London: Gollancz, 1946).
———. *The Parasites* [1949]. (London: Gollancz, 1949).
———. *My Cousin Rachel* [1951]. (London: Virago, 2003).
———. *Mary Anne* [1954]. (London: Penguin, 1962).
———. *The Scapegoat* [1957]. (London: Virago, 2004).
———. *The Glass Blowers* [1963]. (London: Penguin, 1966).
———. *The Flight of the Falcon* [1965]. (London: Penguin, 1969).
———. *The House on the Strand* [1969]. (London: Gollancz, 1969).
———. *Rule Britannia* [1972]. (London: Pan, 1974).
———. *Don't Look Now and Other Stories* (London: Folio Society, 2007).

Plays

———. *Rebecca* (London: Gollancz, 1939).

———. *The Years Between: A Play* [London: Ryle, 1944]. (London: Gollancz, 1945).
———. *September Tide: A Play* (London: Samuel French, 1949).
———. in Malet, O., *Letters from Menabilly: Portrait of a Friendship* (London: Orion, 1993).
———. Introduction, Jane Austen, *Northanger Abbey* [1817]. (London: Williams and Norgate, 1949).
———. Preface to *Best Stories of Phyllis Bottome* (London: Faber and Faber, 1963), p. 9–12
———. Myself When Young: The Shaping of a Writer [1977]. (London: Virago, 2004). [first published as Growing Pains: The Shaping of a Writer].
———. *The Rebecca Notebook: And Other Memories* (Southampton: Camelot, 1981).
———. television interview, 'Modern Writers: Daphne du Maurier,' *Interviews with Remarkable Authors* series, 49 minutes, broadcast 8pm, BBC 2, 31 August 1971, producer Christopher Martin, interviewer Wilfred D'ath, BBC Times Life Production. Sourced at <http://www.bbc.co.uk/archive/writers/12222.shtml> [accessed 29.6.22].

Special Collections, University of Exeter
'Literary Papers of George du Maurier and Daphne du Maurier, c. 1893–1981'
EUL MS 144/1/1/1 Early manuscript notebooks 1923–1926
EUL MS 207/6/4/1 Letters to 'Tod' [Maud Whaddell].
EUL MS 207/6/1/6/1 Notebook of plot ideas and drafts of short stories
EUL MS 113/3/1/D Correspondence with A. L. Rowse 'Surnames D'
EUL MS 206 Daphne du Maurier MS, editorial papers of Sheila Hodges
EUL MS 207 Add. 5 Additional papers relating to Daphne du Maurier
EUL MS 307/2/4/1 1/7 2 *John Bull Everybody's Weekly*: Odhams Press Ltd, 1959, No. 2761, Vol. 105
Modern Records Centre, University of Warwick
MSS.157/3/LI/DL/1/1-316, 'From Darkness to Light, c.1956' Letter to Daphne du Maurier (31; filed as Lady Browning).
MSS.157/3/PAC/1/49-50; 'Pacifism, 1946–1964'
MSS.157/3/P/KN/1/89-90; 3/PUB/15/6,58;
MSS.157/3/I/DM/1-43 (http://mrc-catalogue.warwick.ac.uk/records/GLZ/C/53/DM). British Library
Add MS 113/ 3/ D. Daphne du Maurier letter to A. L. Rowse, 25 September 1967.
Vol. XXX. (ff. 201).1. ff 1–33 Du Maurier unpublished letter to Phyllis Bottome, 6 June 1959.
MS 890015/2/7/12 Correspondence with Daphne du Maurier; 1955–1964 [n.d.]. Partly typewritten and signed.

Duncker, Patricia, 'Re-Imagining the Fairy Tale: Angela Carter's Bloody Chambers, in *Literature and History* Vol.10 (1984), 3–14.
Dunn, Jane, *Virginia Woolf and Vanessa Bell: A Very Close Conspiracy* (London: Harper Press, 1993).
———., *Daphne du Maurier and Her Sisters* (London: Harper Press, 2013).

Eco, Umberto, 'On the History of Ugliness.' Sourced at <http://videolectures.net/cd07_eco_thu/> [accessed 29.6.22].

Edwards, Ruth Dudley, *Victor Gollancz: A Biography* (London: Gollancz, 1987).

Ehland, Christoph and Cornelia Wächter (eds). Introduction, *Middlebrow and Gender, 1890–1945* (Lieden: Brill, 2016).

Ejxenbaum, Boris, quoted in Charles E. May, *The New Short Story Theories* (Ohio: Ohio University Press, 1994).

Emerson, Ralph Waldo, 'The American Scholar' essay, sourced at <http://www.rwe.org/the-american-scholar.html> [accessed 30 July 2015].

Fawcett, Robert, *John Bull* magazine illustrations in edition week ending 30 May 1959.

Flanagan, Padraic, interview with Christopher 'Kits' Browning, *The Telegraph*, 'Daphne du Maurier "overlooked" by literary critics,' her son says.' Sourced at <http://www.telegraph.co.uk/culture/books/10766444/Daphne-du-Maurier-overlooked-by-literary-critics-her-son-says.html> [accessed 29.6.22].

Fluhr, Nicole, 'Empathy and Identity in Vernon Lee's Hauntings' in *Victorian Studies* 48.2 (2006).: 287–94.

Freud, Sigmund, 'The "Uncanny" [1919]. in *The Standard Edition of the Complete Psychological Works*, J. Strachey (ed. and trans.). vol. 17 (London: Penguin, 1953). Sourced at <https://web.mit.edu/allanmc/www/freud1.pdf> [accessed 29.6.22].

———. quoted in Phil Mollon, I*deas in Psychoanalysis: The Unconscious* ed. by Ivan Ward (Reading: Cox and Wyman, 2000).

Forster, Margaret, *Daphne du Maurier* (London: Arrow, 1993).

Graves, Robert, *The White Goddess: A Historical Grammar of Poetic Myth* 4th ed., ed. by Grevel Lindop, General ed. Patrick J. M. Quinn (London: Faber and Faber, 1997).

Gollancz, Victor, 'Papers of Sir Victor Gollancz (1893–1967), publisher and humanitarian campaigner,' MSS.157/3/I/DM/1-43 'Correspondence 1950–1970,' Modern Records Centre, University of Warwick.Thanks for, and comments on, books sent to Daphne du Maurier by Victor Gollancz. Reference to her writing processes. Family events; health; holidays abroad. Includes four-page letter, 14 November 1955, on capital punishment issue and alternatives to life imprisonment with letter from Gerald Gardiner to Victor Gollancz dealing with this point (12); poem in praise of Gaia and criticising the fatherhood of God (14); her reservations about a petition to release all political prisoners in South Africa, with Victor Gollancz's reply, urging the claims of Amnesty International, January 1964 (32–33).; her reaction to her husband's death, May 1965 (40), Modern Records Centre, University of Warwick MSS.157/3/LI/DR/2/1-173, Original file of correspondence in response to The Devil's repertoire, letter from Daphne du Maurier (34), Modern Records Centre, University of Warwick MSS.157/3/ASP/1/1-194 Anglo-Soviet Public Relations Committee, Modern Records Centre, University of Warwick.

Gretlund, Jan Norby, 'Architecture in Short Stories by Flannery O'Connor and Eudora Welty,' in *The Art of Brevity: Excursions in Short Fiction Theory and Analysis*, ed. by Per Winther, Jacob Lothe, Han H. Skei (Columbia: University of South Carolina Press, 2004), p. 138–51.

Grimm, Jacob and Wilhelm, *Grimm's Fairy Tales* [1812]. (London: Penguin, 1966).

Grosz, Elizabeth, *Volatile Bodies: Towards a Corporeal Feminism* (Bloomington: Indiana University Press, 1994).

———. 'Intolerable Ambiguity: Freaks as/ at the Limit' in *Freakery: Cultural Spectacles of the Extraordinary Body*, ed. by Rosemarie Garland Thomson (New York: New York University Press, 1996), p. 55–68.

Habermann, Ina, *Myth, Memory and the Middlebrow: Priestley, du Maurier and the Symbolic Form of Englishness* (London: Palgrave Macmillan, 2010), chapter 8 'Dreamtime in Cornwall,' p. 149–210.

Haggard, Henry Rider, *King Solomon's Mines* ed. by Dennis Butts (Oxford: Oxford University Press, 2008). [1885].

Hammill, Faye, Esme Miskimmin, Ashlie Sponenberg eds. *Encyclopaedia of Women's Writing 1900–1950* (London: Palgrave, 2006).

Haraway, Donna J., chapter 1, 'Animal Sociology and a Natural Economy of the Body Politic: A Political Physiology of Dominance' in *Simians, Cyborgs, and Women: The Reinvention of Nature* (London: Free Association Books, 1991), pp. 7–20.

Hardy, Thomas, *Tess of the d' Urbevilles*, chapter 19, 'Phase the Third: The Rally' (Oxford: Oxford University Press, 2005).

Havard, C. W. H. (ed.). *Black's Medical Dictionary,* 35th edn (London: A & C Black, 1987).

Hawlin, Stefan, *The Complete Critical Guide to Robert Browning,* series editors Richard Bradford and Jan Jedrzejezski (London: Routledge, 2002).

Head, Dominic, *The Modernist Short Story: A Study in Theory and Practice* (Cambridge: Cambridge University Press, 2009).

Heeley, Melanie Jane, 'Christianity Versus Paganism: Daphne du Maurier's Divided Mind' in *The Daphne du Maurier Companion*, ed. Helen Taylor (London: Virago, 2007), p. 122–32.

———. 'Resurrection, Renaissance and Rebirth: Religion, Psychology and Politics in the Life and Works of Daphne du Maurier' (unpublished thesis, University of Loughborough, PhD, 2007).

Hemingway, Ernest, 'The Cat in the Rain' in *The First Forty-One Stories* (London: Arrow, 2004).

Henderson, Gretchen E., *Ugliness: A Cultural History* (London: Reaktion Books, 2015).

Hitchcock, Alfred, dir. *Rebecca,* starring Laurence Olivier and Joan Fontaine (USA, Selznick International Pictures, 1940). [on DVD].

Hoddinott, Derek, *The Little Photographer* (London: Samuel French, 1979).

Hodges, Sheila, 'Editing Daphne du Maurier' in *Women's History Review*, 11:2 (2002), 293–306. Sourced at <http://dx.doi.org/10.1080/09612020200200322> 293–308 [accessed 29.6.22].

———. *Gollancz: The Story of a Publishing House 1928–1978* (London: Gollancz, 1978).

Hoffmann, E. T. A., 'The Sandman' in *Tales From Hoffmann* [1817]. (London: Penguin, 1982).

Holstein, Martha, *Women in Late Life: Critical Perspectives on Gender and Age* (London: Rowman and Littlefield, 2015).

Hopkins, Gerard Manley, 'Pied Beauty,' *Poems of Gerard Manley Hopkins* ed. by Robert Bridges [1918]. (London: Humphrey Milford, 1918).

Horner, Avril, and Sue Zlosnik, *Daphne du Maurier: Writing, Identity and the Gothic Imagination* (Basingstoke: Macmillan, 1998).

———. 'The Ghost and the Omnibus: The Gothic Virginia Woolf' in *Gothic Modernisms,* eds. Andrew Smith, Jeff Wallace (Hampshire: Palgrave, 2001), p. 62–77.

———. Daphne du Maurier entry in *Encyclopaedia of Women's Writing 1900–1950,* ed. by Faye Hammill, Esme Miskimmin, Ashlie Sponenberg (London: Palgrave, 2006), p. 76–77.

Horrocks, Chris, and Zoran Jevtic, *Baudrillard: A Graphic Guide* (Malta: Gutenburg Press, 1996).

Howatson, M. C. *The Oxford Companion to Classical Literature,* 2nd ed. (Oxford: Oxford University Press, 1989).

Huet, Marie-Hélène, *Monstrous Imagination* (Cambridge, MA: Harvard University Press, 1993).

Huysman, Joris-Karl, *En Route* ed. by W. Fleming, trans. by David Blow (Cambridge: Dedalus, 2002). [1895].

Jackson, Rosemary, *Fantasy: The Literature of Subversion* (London, Methuen, 1981).

Jacobus, Mary, Evelyn Fox Keller, Sally Shuttleworth eds., *Body Politics: Women and the Discourses of Science* (London: Routledge, 1990).

James, Henry, 'The Real Thing.' Sourced at <www.gutenberg.org> [accessed 29.6.22].

———. 'The Turn of the Screw,' *The Turn of the Screw and Other Stories*, ed. by T. J. Lustig (Oxford: Oxford University Press, 2008), p. 113–236.

Jentsch, Ernest, 'On the Psychology of the Uncanny' [originally published in two parts in Psychiatrisch-Neurologische Wochenschrift, 1906], trans. by Roy Sellars, *Angelaki: Journal of the Theoretical Humanities,* 2:1 (1996). 7–15.

Johnson, Samuel *The History of Rasselas, Prince of Abissinia*, ed. by Thomas Keymer (Oxford: Oxford University Press, 2009).

Joyce, James, letter to Grant Richards, 5 May 1906, *Selected Letters of James Joyce* [1966]., ed. by Richard Ellmann (London: Faber and Faber, 1975), Vol. 2, p. 134.

Kellet, Ernest Edward, 'The Lady Automaton' 1901, sourced at: <*Pearson's Magazine The Lady Automaton—By E.E. Kellett (forgottenfutures.com*> [accessed 29.6.22].

Kelly, Richard, *Daphne du Maurier* (Boston: Twayne, 1987).

———. *The Art of George du Maurier* (Hants: Scolar, 1996).

Kristeva, Julia, *Powers of Horror: An Essay on Abjection* (Guildford: Columbia University Press, 1982).

Kritzman, Lawrence D., 'Representing the Monster: Cognition, Cripples, and Other Limp Parts in Montaigne's 'Des Boyteux,'' *Monster Theory* (London: University of Minnesota Press, 1996).

Kynaston, David, *Austerity Britain 1945–51* (London; Bloomsbury, 2007).

Lacan, Jaques, in David Farrell Krell, *Derrida and Our Animal Others: Derrida's Final Seminar, "The Beast and The Sovereign"* (Bloomington: Indiana University Press, 2013), p. 16, p. 86, p. 169.

Larson, Jane, 'The Artist's Inspiration: Alma Mahler's Influence on Oskar Kokoschka's Work,' 3 February 2006, p. 1–15. Sourced at <www.carleton.edu/departments/gmrs/vienna/Kokoschka-Mahler.doc> [accessed 29.6.22].

Lawrence, D. H., 'The Blind Man,' *England My England and Other Stories* ([n.p]. Erik Publications, 2015), p. 53–73.

Lee, Paul, lecture 'Socrates and the Rise of Rational Self-consciousness in Ancient Greece.' Sourced at < ectopia.org> [accessed 29.6.22].

Lee, Vernon, 'The Doll' in *Hauntings and Other Fantastic Tales* (Peterborough, Canada: Broadview Press, 2006). [first published as 'The Image' in *The Cornhill Magazine*, 26, 1896].

Levy, David, *Love + Sex With Robots* (London: Duckworth Overlook, 2008).

Liggins, Emma, Andrew Maunder, Ruth Robbins (eds). *The British Short Story* (London: Palgrave Macmillan, 2011).

Macgrath, Patrick, Introduction, Daphne du Maurier, *Don't Look Now and Other Stories* (London: Folio Society, 2007).

———. 'Mistress of Menace,' *Guardian,* 5 May 2007

MacMillan, Harold, Prime Minister's speech, 20 July 1957. Sourced at <http://news.bbc.co.uk/onthisday/hi/dates/stories/july/20/newsid_3728000/3728225.stm> [accessed 29.6.22].

Maisano, Scott, 'Descartes avec Milton: The Automata in the Garden' in *The Automaton in English Renaissance Literature*, ed. by Wendy Beth Hyman (Farnham: Ashgate, 2011).

Malet, Oriel, *Daphne du Maurier: Letters from Menabilly* (London: Weidenfeld & Nicolson, 1993).

Mansfield, Katherine, *Bliss and Other Stories* [1918]. (London: Penguin, 1962).

———. *Selected Stories* [1920]. (London: W.W. Norton, 2006).

———. letter cited in Emmanouil Aretoulakis, 'Colonialism and the Need for Impurity: Katherine Mansfield, 'The Garden Party' and Postcolonial Feeling,' in *Katherine Mansfield and the (Post).colonial,* ed. by Janet Wilson, Gerri Kimber and Delia da Sousa Correa (Edinburgh: Edinburgh University Press, 2013), p. 45–62 (p. 45).

Marlowe, Christopher, *Dr Faustus*, ed. by David Scott Kaston (New York: Norton, 2005).

May, Charles E., *The New Short Story Theories* (Ohio: Ohio University Press, 1994).

———. *The Short Story: The Reality of Artifice* (London: Routledge, 2002).

———. 'Why Short Stories are Essential and Why They are Seldom Read' in *The Art of Brevity: Excursions in Short Fiction Theory and Analysis*, ed. by Per Winther, Jacob Lothe, Han H. Skei (Columbia: University of South Carolina Press, 2004). p. 14–24.

McClintock, Anne, *Imperial Leather: Race, Gender and Sexuality in the Colonial Contest* (London: Routledge, 1995).

McKee, Robert, *Story* (London: Methuen, 2014).

Midgley, Mary, 'Animals and the Problem of Evil,' in *Beast and Man* (London: Routledge, 1995).

Millay, Edna St. Vincent, *Norton Anthology of Poetry*, ed. by Margaret Ferguson, Mary Jo Salter, Jon Stallworthy (London: W.W. Norton, 2005), 5th ed., LL 1–8, p. 1383.

Mitchell, David T., and Sharon L. Snyder, Chapter 3: 'Montaigne's "Infinities of Formes" and Nietzsche's 'Higher Men"' in *Narrative Prosthesis: Disability and the Dependencies of Discourse* (Ann Arbor: The University of Michigan Press, 2002).

Mitchell, Margaret E., 'Beautiful Creatures': The Ethics of Female Beauty in Daphne du Maurier's Fiction' in *Women: A Cultural Review*, 20:1 (spring, 2000), 25–41.

Mollon, Phil, *Ideas in Psychoanalysis: The Unconscious*, series ed. Ivan Ward (Reading: Cox and Wyman, 2000).

Montaigne, Michel de, *Les Essais de Michel de Montaigne* (1877), Chapter 11 'Of Cripples,' sourced at Project Gutenberg: <gutenbery.org.> [accessed 29.6.22].

Mulvey, Laura. 'Visual Pleasure and Narrative Cinema'in *Film Theory and Criticism: Introductory Readings*. ed. by Leo Braudy and Marshall Cohen. (New York: OUP, 1999). pp. 833–44.

Munro, Jane, *Silent Partners: Artist and Mannequin from Function to Fetish* (New Haven and London: Yale University Press, Fitzwilliam Museum, Cambridge, 2014).

Newbolt, Henry, 'Vitaï Lampada' [1892]. Sourced at <http://www.gutenberg.org /cache/epub/13900/pg13900-images.html> [accessed 29.6.22].

Nietzsche, Friedrich, *Thus Spake Zarathustra*, quoted in chapter 3, 'Montaigne's "Infinities of Formes" and Nietzsche's "Higher Men"' in *Narrative Prosthesis: Disability and the Dependencies of Discourse* ed. by David T. Mitchell and Sharon L. Snyder (Ann Arbor: University of Michigan Press, 2002).

Oates, Jonathan, *John Christie of Rillington Place: Biography of a Serial Killer* (Barnsley: Pen & Sword Books Ltd, 2012).

Ovid, *Metamorphosis*, trans, by A. D. Melville, Introduction and notes by E. J. Kenney (Oxford: Oxford University Press, 1986).

Panter-Downes, Molly, *One Fine Day* (London: Virago Modern Classics, 2003), [1947].

Patmore, Coventry, 'The Angel in the House' [1854–1862]. Sourced at <http://www.gutenberg.org/files/4099/4099-h/4099-h.htm> [accessed 29.6.22].

Patterson, Don, *Reading Shakespeare's Sonnets: A New Commentary* (London: Faber, 2012).

Pender, Stephen, 'No Monsters at the resurrection: Inside some conjoined Twins' in J. J. Cohen, *Monster Theory: Reading Culture* (Minneapolis and London: University of Minnesota Press, 1996), p. 143–67.

Peterson, Teresa, 'Daphne du Maurier's Short Stories: Horror, the Macabre and the Bizarre,' in *Journal of the Australasian Universities Modern Language Association*, 118 (2009), 51–72.

———. 'Daphne du Maurier's *Rebecca:* The Shadow and the Substance' in *Journal of the Australasian Universities Modern Language Association*, 112 (2009), 53–66

Perry, Grayson, *Playing to the Gallery* (London: Penguin, 2014).

Pittard, Christopher, '"We are seeing the past through the wrong end of the telescope": Time, Space and Psychogeography in *Castle Dor*' in *Women: A Cultural Review* Special issue: Daphne du Maurier, 20:1 (2009), 57–73.

Pope, Alexander, 'Moral Essays Epistle IV' in *The Complete Poetical Works*, ed. by Henry W. Boynton (New York: Houghton, Mifflin, 1903), LL 149–50

Punter, David, *The Literature of Terror: A History of Gothic Fictions from 1765 to the Present Day* (London: Longman, 1980).

Quayson, Ato, 'Aesthetic Nervousness' in *The Disability Studies Reader*, ed. by Lennard J. Davis, 3rd edn. (New York: Routledge, 2010). p. 254–65.

Quiller-Couch, A., and Daphne du Maurier, *Castle D'or* (London: J. M. Dent, 1962).

Reid, Ian, *The Short Story: The Critical Idiom Series*, founder ed. John D. Jump. (Methuen: London, 1977).

Rawls, John, 'Fair Equality and Pure Procedure' in *A Theory of Justice* (Cambridge: Harvard University Press, 1971), pp. 83–83.

Reyes, Xavier Aldana, *Body Gothic: Corporeal Transgression in Contemporary Literature and Horror Film* (Cardiff, University of Wales Press, 2014).

Reynier, Christine, 'The Outrageousness of Outrage: Daphne du Maurier's "Monte Verità"' in *Études britanniques contemporaines*, 45 (20 October 2013), 2–11. Sourced at <http://ebc.revues.org/683> [accessed 29.6.22].

Richardson, Kristina L. *Difference and Disability in the Medieval Islamic World* (Edinburgh University Press: Edinburgh, 2012).

Roehberger, Mary, 'Origins, Development, Substance, and Design of the Short Story' p. 1–13, in *The Art of Brevity* (Columbia: University of South Carolina Press, 2004).

Royle, Nicholas, *The uncanny* (Manchester: Manchester University Press, 2003).

Russo, Mary, *The Female Grotesque: Risk, Excess and Modernity* (London: Routledge, 1995).

Sarup, Madan, *An Introductory Guide to Post Structuralism and Postmodernism* (London: Harvester Wheatsheaf, 1998).

Scruton, Roger, 'Photography and Representation' in "The Aesthetic Understanding," *Essays in the Philosophy of Art and Culture* (London: Methuen, 1983).

Scarry, Elaine, *The Body in Pain* (Oxford: Oxford University Press, 1985).

———. *On Beauty and Being Just* (London: Duckworth, 2006).

Sceats, Sarah, and Gail Cunningham, *Image and Power: Women and Fiction in the Twentieth Century* (Harlowe: Longman, 1996).

Scruton, Roger, 'Photography and Representation' in "The Aesthetic Understanding," *Essays in the Philosophy of Art and Culture* (London: Methuen, 1983).

Shaffi, Sarah, 'Virago plans new Du Maurier editions' in *The Bookseller*, 26 May 2015. Sourced at <http://www.thebookseller.com/news/virago-plans-new-du-maurier-editions> [accessed 26.1.16].

Shakespeare, Tom, 'The Social Model of Disability' in *The Disability Studies Reader*, ed. by Lennard J. Davis, third edn. (New York: Routledge, 2010), p. 266–73.

Shaw, Valerie, *The Short Story: A Critical Introduction* (London: Longman, 1983).

Sidoli, Mara, ed. by Phyllis Blakemore, *When the Body Speaks* (London: Routledge, 2000).

Simmons, Judy, 'The Mask Beneath the Mask: Katherine Mansfield' in *Diaries and Journals of Literary Women* (Hampshire; Macmillan, 1990).

Smith, Andrew, *Gothic Literature* (Edinburgh: Edinburgh University Press, 2007).

Smith, Andrew, and Jeff Wallace, *Gothic Modernisms* (Palgrave: Hampshire, 2001).

Spain, Nancy, 'Nancy Spain Cries—How Improper Daphne!' 7 May 1954. in *The Daily Express,* Sourced at <http://www.ukpressonline.co.uk/ukpressonline/?sf=express> [accessed 5.2.16].

———. 'How The Witch Cult is Growing!' (review of *The Apple Tree*). in the *Daily Express* 7 August 1952. Sourced at <http://www.ukpressonline.co.uk /ukpressonline/?sf=express> [accessed 5.2.16].

Spooner, Catherine, 'Goth Culture,' in David Punter (ed.), *A New Companion to the Gothic* (Chichester: Wiley-Blackwell, 2012), pp. 350–65, p. 165.

Spooner, Catherine, and Emma McEvoy, eds, 'Gothic in the 21st Century' in *The Cambridge Companion to Gothic* (London: Routledge, 2007). pp. 38–43.

Stallybrass, Peter, and Allon White, *The Politics and Poetics of Transgression* (New York: Cornell University Press, 1986).

Stapleton, Michael, and Nicolas Barker, eds. *The Cambridge Guide to English Literature* (Cambridge: Cambridge University Press, 1983).

Szeemann, Harald. Sourced at <monteverita.org> [accessed 29.6.22].

Taylor, Helen (ed.), *The Daphne du Maurier Companion* (London: Virago, 2007).

———. Introduction to Daphne du Maurier, *Myself When Young* (London: Virago, 2004). p. v–xviii.

Thomson, Rosemarie Garland (ed.), Introduction: 'From Wonder to Error: A Genealogy of Freak Discourse in Modernity'in *Freakery: Cultural Spectacles of the Extraordinary Body* (New York: New York University Press, 1996), p. 1–19.

Troup, Freda, British Library, Anti-Apartheid Movement. Correspondence and papers of Freda Troup (Mrs. Leon Levson). Writer and anti-apartheid activist, Add MS 80776 : 1958–1963.

Tsuchiya, Hideo, President of Orient Industries, *Mainichi Daily News*, 11 December 2004. Sourced at <http://mdn.mainichi.co.jp/waiwai/0412/1216doll.html> [accessed 12.4.16].

Uebel, Michael, 'Unthinking the Monster: Twelfth-Century Responses to Saracen Alterity,' in *Monster Theory: Reading Culture* ed. by J. J. Cohen (Minneapolis: University of Minnesota Press, 1996), p. 265–91.

Virago Press, sourced at <virago.co.uk> [accessed 29.6.22].

Vyvyan, Clara, *Down the Rhone on Foot* (London: Peter Owen, 1955).

Wade, Christopher and Diana, *The du Mauriers: A Hampstead Family* ([n. p.]. Matthew Norgate, 1984).

Warner, Marina, *From the Beast to the Blonde: On Fairy Tales and Their Tellers* (London: Vintage, 1995).

Weinstock, Jeffrey A., 'Freaks in Space: "Extraterrestrialism" and "Deep-Space Multiculturalism"' in *Freakery: Cultural Spectacles of the Extraordinary Body*, ed. by Rosemarie Garland Thomson (New York: New York University Press, 1996), p. 327–37.

West, Rebecca, 'The Salt of the Earth' in *The Harsh Voice* (London: Jonathan Cape, 1935), pp. 133–88.

Wheatley, Edward, 'Medieval Constructions of Blindness in France and England,' in *The Disability Studies Reader,* ed. by Lennard J. Davis, 3rd ed. (New York: Routledge, 2010), p. 63–76.

Wilson, Leigh, entry on Elizabeth Bowen, *Encyclopaedia of Women's Writing 1900 –1950*, p. 22–23.

Winterson, Jeanette, *Why Be Happy When You Could Be Normal?* (London: Vintage, 2012).

———. Preface, *Oranges Are Not the Only Fruit* [1985]. (London: Vintage, 1991).

Winther, Per, Eds. Jacob Lothe, Han H. Skei, *The Art of Brevity* (Columbia: University of South Carolina Press, 2004).

Wisker, Gina, 'Dangerous Borders: Daphne du Maurier's *Rebecca*: Shaking the Foundations of the Romance of Privilege, Partying and Place' in *Journal of Gender Studies*, 12:2 (2003), 83–97.

———. '"Don't Look Now"! The Compulsions and Revelations of Daphne du Maurier's Horror Writing,' in *Journal of Gender Studies*, 8:1 (1999), 19–33.

———. 'Starting Your Journey in the Past, Speculating in Time and Place: Daphne du Maurier's *The House on the Strand*, "Split Second," and the Engaged Fiction of Time Travel' in *Journal of the Fantastic in the Arts,* 24:3 (2013), 467–82.

———. 'Undermining the Everyday: Daphne Du Maurier's Gothic Horror,' *Revue LISA/LISA e-journal*, vol. 19:52 (2021), 22.11.2021, URL: http://journals.openedition.org/lisa/13590 ; DOI : https://doi.org/10.4000/lisa.13590 [accessed 22.6.22].

Wolff, Janet, 'The Invisible Flâneuse: Women and the Literature of Modernity,' in *Feminine Sentences: Essays on Women and Culture* (Cambridge: Blackwell Publishers, 1990), pp. 34–51.

Woolf, Virginia, 'Mr Bennett and Mrs Brown,' [1924]. Sourced at <http://www.columbia.edu/~em36/MrBennettAndMrsBrown.pdf> [accessed 29.6.22].

———. *To The Lighthouse* [1927]. (Oxford: Oxford University Press, 2000).

———. *A Room of One's Own and Three Guineas* [1927]. (Oxford: Oxford University Press, 2015).

Wordsworth, William, 'The Solitary Reaper' in *William Wordsworth: The Oxford Series* ed. by Stephen Gill (Oxford: Oxford University Press, 1984), p. 319–20.

———. 'The Solitary Reaper' first published as part of 'Poems Written During a Tour in Scotland,' in *Poems in Two Volumes, and Other Poems* [1807]. ed. by Jared Curtis (New York: Ithaca, 1983), p. 184–85.

———. William Wordsworth, The Complete Poetical Works (London: Macmillan and Co, 1888).

Worthen, Merideth G. F., *Sexual Deviance and Society: A Sociological Examination* (London: Routledge, 2016).

Wosk, Julie, *My Fair Ladies: Female Robots, Androids and Other Artificial Eves* (New Brunswick: Rutgers University Press, 2015).

Žižek, Slavoj, 'Are We Allowed to Enjoy Daphne du Maurier?' sourced at: <http://www.lacan.com/zizdaphmaur.htm> [accessed 29.6.22].

Index

About the Author

Setara Pracha is a senior research fellow and lecturer in the department of English at the University of Buckingham. She has studied at the Universities of Buckingham and Toronto, and was awarded the first Ondaatje Scholarship to Massey College, University of Toronto, where she specialized in postcolonial literature. She is a fellow of the Higher Education Academy, and her research interests lie in the area of difference: the writing of gender; diasporic literature; and otherness and the uncanny in twentieth-century literature. Her critical reassessment of Daphne du Maurier's short stories pulls together these areas of interest.

Ingram Content Group UK Ltd.
Milton Keynes UK
UKHW011835230523
422239UK00003B/10